PEOPLE IN HISTORY

From Caractacus to Alexander Fleming

Also by R. J. Unstead

LOOKING AT HISTORY
1. FROM CAVEMEN TO VIKINGS
2. THE MIDDLE AGES
3. TUDORS AND STUARTS
4. QUEEN ANNE TO QUEEN ELIZABETH II

*

MEN AND WOMEN IN HISTORY
1. HEROES AND SAINTS
2. PRINCES AND REBELS
3. DISCOVERERS AND ADVENTURERS
4. GREAT LEADERS

*

A HISTORY OF BRITAIN
1. THE MEDIEVAL SCENE, 787–1485
2. CROWN AND PARLIAMENT, 1485–1688
3. THE RISE OF GREAT BRITAIN, 1688–1837
4. A CENTURY OF CHANGE, 1837–TODAY
5. BRITAIN IN THE TWENTIETH CENTURY

*

LOOKING AT ANCIENT HISTORY
THE STORY OF BRITAIN
EARLY TIMES

*

BLACK'S JUNIOR REFERENCE BOOKS

A HISTORY OF HOUSES
TRAVEL BY ROAD
MONASTERIES
CASTLES

Mr. Pepys and his friends watch the Great Fire   see page 313

PEOPLE IN HISTORY

From Caractacus
to Alexander Fleming

BY

R. J. UNSTEAD

WITH TWELVE COLOUR PLATES
AND TWO HUNDRED AND THIRTY
ILLUSTRATIONS IN THE TEXT

ADAM AND CHARLES BLACK

FIRST PUBLISHED IN ONE VOLUME 1957
BY A. AND C. BLACK LTD.
4 SOHO SQUARE LONDON W1V 6AD

AVAILABLE ALSO IN FOUR PARTS

SEVENTH IMPRESSION 1970

© 1957 A. AND C. BLACK LTD.
ISBN 0 7136 0786 6

REPRODUCED AND PRINTED IN GREAT BRITAIN BY
REDWOOD PRESS LIMITED, TROWBRIDGE & LONDON

INTRODUCTION

EVERY age has its heroes who stir the imagination and shape the lives of ordinary people. For a child in particular, tales of heroism and adventure, of high courage and achievement, are an important and essential part of his development, as well as his first introduction to history.

In each of the four parts of this book are a dozen or so stories of some of the greatest men and women in our history; in Part One, appear saints and patriots of the early centuries, followed, in Part Two, by some of the colourful figures of the Middle Ages. Then, in Part Three, come people of Tudor and Stuart times whose adventures and struggles added to the brilliance and tragedy of those days, and, finally, Part Four contains a selection from the host of great names in the last 250 years.

These people in history have each made a lasting contribution, through example and achievement, to their age and beyond it, as well as to our understanding of history. Each, it is hoped, also claims inclusion because of his appeal to the imagination of children.

CONTENTS

PART ONE

		PAGE
1.	CARACTACUS, THE BRAVE CHIEF	12
2.	BOADICEA, QUEEN OF THE ICENI	19
3.	AGRICOLA, GOVERNOR OF BRITAIN	25
4.	SAINT ALBAN, THE FIRST BRITISH MARTYR	32
5.	SAINT PATRICK OF IRELAND	40
6.	SAINT COLUMBA, WHO BROUGHT CHRISTIANITY TO SCOTLAND	50
7.	POPE GREGORY AND SAINT AUGUSTINE	58
8.	AIDAN, THE SAINT OF NORTHUMBRIA	67
9.	THE ABBESS HILDA AND CAEDMON THE COWHERD	74
10.	ALFRED OF WESSEX	83
11.	ALFRED THE KING	90
12.	ALFRED THE GREAT	96
	WHEN THEY LIVED	103

PART TWO

13.	WILLIAM THE CONQUEROR, THE FIRST NORMAN KING OF ENGLAND	108
14.	SAINT MARGARET, QUEEN OF SCOTLAND	117
15.	THE KING AND THE ARCHBISHOP	127
16.	RICHARD THE LION-HEART AND THE CRUSADERS	137
17.	THE WELSH PRINCE, LLEWELYN	147
18.	ROBERT THE BRUCE OF SCOTLAND	157
19.	QUEEN PHILIPPA AND THE MEN OF CALAIS	167
20.	WAT TYLER AND THE BOY-KING, RICHARD II	176
21.	GEOFFREY CHAUCER AND " THE CANTERBURY TALES "	185
22.	HENRY V AT AGINCOURT	195
23.	WILLIAM CAXTON, WOOL-MERCHANT AND PRINTER	207
	BACKGROUND TO THE STORIES IN PART TWO	219

CONTENTS—*continued*

PART THREE

	PAGE
24. SIR THOMAS MORE, SCHOLAR AND SAINT	227
25. RICHARD CHANCELLOR, MERCHANT ADVENTURER	235
26. THE PRINCESS ELIZABETH	244
27. DRAKE'S REVENGE	255
28. MASTER WILL SHAKESPEARE	269
29. SIR WALTER RALEIGH	281
30. PRISCILLA MULLINS OF THE " MAYFLOWER "	290
31. MONTROSE, THE GREAT MARQUIS	303
32. MR SAMUEL PEPYS AND THE FIRE OF LONDON	317
33. JOHN AND SARAH CHURCHILL	329
34. LADY NITHSDALE, THE STORY OF A FAMOUS ESCAPE	339
BACKGROUND TO THE STORIES IN PART THREE	348

PART FOUR

35. CHARLES EDWARD STUART	354
36. GENERAL JAMES WOLFE	363
37. THE STORY OF CAPTAIN COOK	376
38. CLIVE OF INDIA	390
39. TWO FAMOUS ENGINEERS	400
40. LORD NELSON	418
41. ELIZABETH FRY	429
42. THE STORY OF DAVID LIVINGSTONE	446
43. FLORENCE NIGHTINGALE	460
44. CAPTAIN SCOTT	471
45. LAWRENCE OF ARABIA	485
46. SIR ALEXANDER FLEMING	493
BACKGROUND TO THE STORIES IN PART FOUR	506
INDEX	510

ILLUSTRATIONS

IN COLOUR

Mr. Pepys and his friends watch the Great Fire	*Frontispiece*
	facing page
Saint Alban is led to his execution	38
Building the monastery on the island of Iona	52
Queen Philippa at the head of her army	168
Richard II and the rebels	177
The Pilgrims at the inn	186
Chancellor presents the King's letter to Ivan	242
The Attack on Nombre de Dios	264
" Welcome ! Me Samoset "	296
Bonnie Prince Charlie and his Highlanders enter Edinburgh	356
Clive at Arcot drives out the attackers	394
Livingstone's canoes on the Zambesi	447

and two hundred and thirty other illustrations in the text

PART ONE

FROM CARACTACUS TO ALFRED

CARACTACUS
The Brave Chief

LONG, long ago, camp fires were twinkling in the darkness of a summer night. An army lay sleeping on the banks of a wide river, which ran softly by, only a few yards away.

The tired soldiers lay on the ground wrapped in their cloaks, with their spears and shields close at hand. But one man did not sleep. Hugging his blue cloak tightly around him, for the night was cold, he walked up and down, up and down by the camp fires.

He was Caradoc, a chief of the Britons, known to the Romans as Caractacus. As he walked up and down, he was thinking of a plan to beat the Roman army. The Romans

The Romans attack across the river

The Roman Army landed in Kent. They marched inland, beating off attacks by the Britons, and crossed the Thames at Brentford. Then they marched east, and captured Colchester, capital of Caractacus' kingdom.

had just come across the sea from Gaul to conquer his country. They were now in camp, somewhere across the other side of the river.

Suddenly, he heard shouts and cries in the darkness, "Awake! Awake! The Romans are here!"

Caractacus drew his sword and quickly roused his men. The enemy, who had swum across the river in the darkness, attacked the sleeping Britons from all sides.

Though they fought bravely, the Britons were taken by surprise. The Romans were splendid soldiers, with better swords and shields, and by daybreak they had forced the Britons to flee to the woods, leaving behind them thousands of dead.

Soon after this battle, the Roman Emperor Claudius came to Britain. He brought a troop of trained elephants and another army. The Britons had never seen soldiers like these. They built forts and straight roads, they marched quickly from place to place, and every soldier did exactly as he was told. They soon defeated the wild Britons.

The Emperor Claudius arrives in Britain

Many chiefs made peace and promised to be friends with the great Roman general.

But Caractacus would not make peace with the Romans. When he had lost his kingdom, he escaped to the mountains of Wales. For eight years, he went on fighting the Romans.

At last, a Roman army tracked him down. He made a stand on the top of a hill called Caer Caradoc—the Fort of Caractacus. He ordered his men to build a wall of stones round the top of the hill, and they waited behind it for the Romans to attack.

" If the Romans defeat us to-day,"

cried Caractacus to his men, " we shall be slaves for ever. It is better to die as free men than to live as slaves."

As the enemy attacked up the slopes of the hill, the Britons threw spears and rocks down on top of them. Then the Romans put their shields close together above their heads like a strong roof. They moved slowly up the hill until they reached the walls of the fort. More soldiers crept up under the shields and pulled away the stones, until there was a hole in the wall. They did this in several places, and then charged through into the camp. A fierce battle was fought inside the walls.

In this battle, all the Britons were killed or captured, and Caractacus was taken prisoner, with his wife and brothers.

The Roman general sent his prisoners in chains to the city of Rome, far across the sea in Italy. They were marched through the streets in a procession on their way to be killed.

The people of Rome came in crowds to stare at the tall, fair-haired chief and his people, who had fought so long against

Caractacus and the Emperor

their mighty legions. But Caractacus was not afraid. He held his head high and looked about him. He was astonished to see the wide, paved streets, and the great buildings and marble temples on every side.

He called out to those who were following him in chains:

" Why did the Romans wish to rob us of our poor huts in Britain, when they have houses like these ? "

At last, he and his family were brought to the high seat of the Emperor Claudius. Some of the Britons fell upon their knees, but Caractacus looked up boldly at the Emperor.

"Do you not know, Briton, that you must shortly die?" asked Claudius.

"I do not fear to die," replied Caractacus. "I did not fear death in battle against you, so why should I fear it here, when you have robbed me of my home and freedom? Put me to death, Emperor, and I shall soon be forgotten. But if you spare my life, your Roman mercy will be remembered for ever!"

The Emperor was amazed at these bold words. He looked at the chief and remained silent for a moment. Then he cried:

"Strike off his chains! Rome knows how to pardon a brave enemy."

At once Caractacus and his family were set free. They were allowed to live in Rome, where, some say, they became Christians.

Another story says that Caractacus was sent home to Britain, where he lived at peace with the Romans. Whichever story is true, Caractacus, the brave chief, has not been forgotten.

BOADICEA
Queen of the Iceni

SOON after the Romans came to rule Britain, Boadicea became Queen of the Iceni tribe. She is the first heroine in our history. The Iceni lived in that part of England we now call Norfolk and Suffolk. They were farming people, famous for their horses and cattle, and they were also fierce, brave fighters.

Boadicea's husband, King of the Iceni, had made friends with the Romans, because he thought them strong and wise. When he was dying, he gave them half his kingdom.

"That will please the Romans," he said, "and they will leave the Queen and my children to rule in peace."

But after he died, the Romans said he owed them a great sum of money. They said that the Iceni must pay heavy taxes.

Boadicea knew this was not true. With her two daughters, she went proudly to see Catus, an important Roman officer. But Catus laughed at her rudely, telling her she must pay the money if she wanted to remain a queen.

"I am Queen of a proud people," she answered, "and my husband was your friend. Take care you do not make me your enemy!"

Catus grew angry at these words and ordered his soldiers to turn the British queen away. They pushed Boadicea and her daughters roughly from the great courtyard. They beat her servants with their spears and laughed loudly as they went away.

Boadicea was very angry. When she told her people of this cruel treatment, they seized their spears and cried:

"Let us drive these Romans out of our land!"

Other tribes and chiefs were growing tired of the powerful Romans, and they

Boadicea captures Verulamium

rushed eagerly to join the Iceni. Soon, the tall handsome queen was at the head of a great army ready to attack the Romans.

At this time, Paulinus, the Roman Governor, was away fighting the Druids in Wales. So the Britons, led by Boadicea in her war-chariot, swept down upon the new Roman towns. They burned them to the ground, and they killed thousands of Roman citizens and Britons who had made friends with them.

Shortly afterwards they beat the Roman Ninth Legion in a battle, and went on to burn down a new town, called London.

When Paulinus heard this news, he hurried back from Wales to fight Boadicea. He chose a place for his army on a slope, with a wood behind for protection. Before the battle, he spoke to his men:

"Soldiers and fellow-Romans! To-day we fight for Rome. We have better spears and sharper swords than these barbarians. They are led by a woman. See! They even have women in their ranks. Stand firm, be brave! Then we shall soon defeat this mob of savages!"

The Britons came to the battle certain of victory. Behind them were waggons full of plunder from the towns, and also their wives and children.

When Boadicea saw Paulinus talking to his men, she stood up in her chariot and cried to her people:

"The Romans treat us like slaves! They call us barbarians! Let us show them we are free men and women. Let us fight them and beat them back into the sea!"

With a great shout, the Britons charged wildly at the Roman ranks. But Paulinus and his men stood firm, making a wall of

"*The Romans treat us like slaves!*"

A British war chariot was larger than the Roman racing-chariot. There was room for the driver and one or two spear-men. Two or four horses were harnessed to the yoke-pole and the charioteer sometimes ran along this pole to attack his foes.

their shields which even the chariots could not break. Then the Roman soldiers, step by step, drove the Britons back towards the waggons. Thousands of men, women and children were killed. Those who were left turned and fled from the battlefield.

Boadicea, her daughters and a few followers, escaped into a wood. But the unhappy queen knew that all was lost. She was certain that the Romans would show her no mercy, so she took her life by drinking poison. Her two daughters died in the same way.

This was the last great battle between the Britons and the Romans, who ruled our land for nearly four hundred years.

AGRICOLA
Governor of Britain

WHEN Queen Boadicea's warriors charged up the slope against the army of Paulinus, there was a young officer named Julius Agricola in the Roman ranks.

He led his men well, and fought so bravely that Paulinus sent for him after the battle.

"You have fought well for Rome," he said. "One day you may be a general, but you will never know a harder battle, and you will never forget this day."

Soon afterwards, Agricola was sent away to serve in other lands. But seventeen years later he came back as a general, and as Governor of Britain.

When some of his chief officers told him

that much of Britain had not been conquered, and that the people were difficult to rule, he said:

"I have not forgotten the Britons, nor the day when I fought against them. They are a brave, proud people, and they fought us because we treated them unfairly. If we rule them with wisdom, we shall bring peace to their land."

Agricola's first task was to make Britain peaceful. From the hills and mountains, wild tribes were still making raids against the Roman settlements. They also attacked Britons who were friendly with the Romans. These wild tribes were often led by their priests, the Druids.

Agricola, who was a splendid soldier, marched to Anglesey, the holy island of the Druids, and killed the priests. He conquered Wales, and afterwards, the north of England. Then he marched his army to Scotland, which was called Caledonia.

He went farther north than any Roman had ever done before. He beat the Caledonians in a great battle, and then attacked the Picts, fiercest of all the northern tribes.

Agricola breaks the power of the Druids

The Druids were leaders of the Britons as well as the priests. In their religion the oak and the mistletoe were sacred, and streams and rivers were considered holy.

But, as Agricola marched on, the Picts burnt their villages and hid in the mountains and forests. The country was so wild that the Romans found it difficult to follow, especially when winter came and deep snow was on the ground. Agricola had to retreat, but he built a line of forts right across Scotland. These forts kept the Picts from attacking the peace-loving peoples in the south.

Now that he had visited Scotland, he wished to know more about it, and how far it reached. So he sent his fleet of ships to sail round the north of Scotland, down into the Irish Sea, and round Land's End into the Channel. By this dangerous voyage, he was the first to discover that Britain is an island.

Agricola was not only a great soldier, he was also a wise ruler, " a gracious, blameless man," said his son-in-law, who was a writer. Agricola now tried to make the Britons content and happy under Roman rule.

The Romans said that people were civilised when they lived in towns. Agricola was sure that if the Britons lived in towns,

Agricola in Scotland

instead of in scattered mud and wattle huts, they would become civilised and peaceable.

He helped them to build towns in the Roman way. The new towns had straight streets, fine buildings, large squares and strong walls to protect them from their enemies. Agricola praised those who followed Roman ways, and spoke sternly to those who wanted to go on living in their rough villages.

A Roman town

Soon, quite large towns were built in almost every part of Britain. They were towns with fine houses of stone or red brick, with floors made of beautiful tiles and rooms with gaily painted walls. These towns were joined by straight roads, which the Romans made so well, that some have lasted to this day.

The Britons began to enjoy living like Romans. Many of them dressed in Roman clothes, and went to the public baths and the temples, which stood in every town. Some learnt to speak Latin, and Agricola started schools for their sons. The ladies curled their hair in the latest style, and went shopping in the main street to buy new things for their homes—fine red plates, glass bottles, silver ornaments and beautiful cloth.

Agricola did not tax the Britons too heavily. He told them that these fine towns must be paid for, but he gave them time to pay their taxes. He ruled them in a kindly way and well, and the land became richer and more settled than it had ever been before.

After several years, Agricola was called back to Rome by the Emperor, who, some men said, was growing jealous of his fame. But the people gave him a great welcome and cheered him through the streets of Rome.

For the rest of his life, he lived in a beautiful villa with his family. On fine days, he loved to sit in the sunny courtyard where a fountain played. There he talked to his son-in-law, Tacitus, the writer, telling him how he changed the life of the people in that far-away island called Britain.

SAINT ALBAN
The First British Martyr

ONE of the finest towns in Roman Britain was Verulamium. It stood on the important road called Watling Street, and had splendid houses, a square or forum, and an open-air theatre. Outside its thick walls, the little river Ver flowed between green banks, which rose to a steep hill on one side and grassy slopes on the other.

In one of the finest houses in Verulamium lived a young man named Alban. He was rich, handsome, and generous to the poor. When he was a little boy, his father had sent him to school in Rome, and afterwards he had served in the Roman army. But he had come back to live in his own town in Britain, where he was born.

Alban often heard stories of the new religion of some people who called themselves Christians. No one knows who first brought the story of Jesus Christ to Britain ; perhaps it was a soldier who had heard Saint Paul preach in Rome. For a time the Romans allowed the Christians to preach and to build churches. Many Romans became Christians but most of them, like Alban, remained true to the old Roman gods—Jupiter, Mars, Diana and many others.

The Romans also had the habit of calling their Emperor a god. The Christians said that there was only one God, who was far, far greater than any man, even the most powerful Roman Emperor. This made the Emperor angry, and he ordered that all Christians, in every part of the empire, must be put to death.

One day, Alban arrived home after a visit to some friends, and found a feeble old man resting in his porch. Seeing he was faint with weariness and hunger, he helped him into the house. He asked him who he was.

Alban carries the old priest into his house

"I am Amphibalus, a priest of Christ," said the old man. "The Roman soldiers seek my life."

"Then why have you come to me?" asked Alban. "You know I am a Roman."

"I also know you are a man of good and noble heart," replied the priest. "My brother Christians have been killed or have fled, so I ask you for shelter, until I am strong enough to go away."

Full of pity, Alban took the old priest into his own room. He gave him food and drink, and his own bed to rest upon.

For many days the Christian priest remained hidden. Alban often asked him questions about the invisible God to whom he prayed. Amphibalus told him the story of Jesus, His teachings, His life and His death upon the Cross.

Alban began to think that this religion of love and gentleness was far better than his own, but Amphibalus warned him of the dangers he must face if he too became a Christian.

"You must expect suffering and even death, if you follow Christ, Who died for us," said the old man.

Without another word, Alban went to him and knelt down, asking him to bless him and to teach him how he might serve his new Master.

As they were speaking, there came a loud knocking at the outer gate. A servant rushed in to tell Alban that soldiers had arrived to search for a Christian who, it was rumoured, was hiding in the house.

"Quick!" cried Alban, "give me your robe and hood, and take my cloak. Wrap it about you. Here is a purse of gold. Go

The escape of Amphibalus

quickly by the rear gate ; my servant will show you the way."

" No," said Amphibalus, " I cannot let you be taken in my place, for it will mean your death."

" Go ! Go quickly ! " cried Alban. " You are a priest of Christ and can teach others as you have taught me. Leave me to serve my Master as best I can."

The old priest blessed him with the sign of the Cross, and then hurried away to safety.

A moment later, the soldiers burst into the room. Seeing a man kneeling in the

The soldiers arrest Alban, disguised as a Christian priest

robes and hood of a Christian priest, they seized him and led him away.

He was taken before the Roman governor. The hood was thrown back, and everyone saw, to their astonishment, that it was Alban, a well-known citizen of Verulamium. The Governor was very angry at losing the priest and at Alban's action in helping his escape.

"Because you are a Roman citizen and of noble birth," he said, " I will spare you, but first you must offer sacrifice to the Roman gods of your fathers."

"I cannot do that," replied Alban, " I am now a Christian and there is only one God, the God of Love."

"Take him away," cried the Governor, "and put him to death, by the order of the Emperor."

The news of Alban's arrest spread quickly through the town, and people gathered to watch the well-loved young man as he was led out of the town gates. They followed him over the river and up the steep hill to the place of execution.

At the top of the hill, Alban asked for a drink of water, and, it is said, a clear spring of water bubbled suddenly from the ground. Then he knelt down and prayed God to forgive those who were about to kill him.

The officer of the guard gave an order, but the soldier whose duty it was to cut off Alban's head, threw down his sword, saying, "I cannot do it. This is a holy man."

The officer angrily drew his own sword,

Saint Alban is led to his execution

and, with one blow, beheaded Alban. Then, with another, he killed the soldier.

Although it is many years since Alban died, he has never been forgotten. Some time later, when Christians were again allowed to follow their religion, a little church was built on the spot where he was put to death. Later, a great church was built, and it still stands there to-day. The town which grew up around the church is called St. Albans. The Roman city of Verulamium lies buried beneath the woods and fields on the other side of the river.

The Abbey of St. Albans to-day

SAINT PATRICK
of Ireland

LONG, long ago, when the Romans were still ruling Britain, a boy named Patrick lived on a farm near the sea. His home was somewhere in the west of our country, perhaps in Glamorganshire, South Wales.

Patrick's father and mother were Christians, and his grandfather had been a priest. When he was quite a small boy, his mother taught Patrick and his brothers and sisters about Jesus, and how to say their prayers.

Irish pirates capture Patrick

One day Patrick and some of his friends went down to the seashore near his home. While they were playing, they did not notice a long boat sailing towards the beach. Suddenly, a band of fierce men leapt ashore and, before the boys could run away, they seized them and carried them off to the boat. The square sail was quickly hoisted and the ship put out to sea, leaving the land farther and farther behind.

The boys had been captured by Irish pirates, who came across the sea to Britain to trade and, sometimes, to capture slaves.

Patrick was taken to Northern Ireland, where the pirates sold him to an Ulster chief, called Milcho, who sent him to look after his cows and pigs.

Patrick was lonely and sad among these strange, fierce people. They had never heard of Jesus Christ, and they believed in magic and spells worked by their priests, called Druids. Every morning, when he had led his master's herd to the hillside, Patrick would kneel down on the grassy slope and ask God to help him to be brave and good. He had not forgotten the prayers which his gentle mother had taught him, and he prayed that God would help him to reach his home again.

When he had been a slave for six years, Patrick made up his mind to run away. In his dreams he kept hearing a voice telling him that a ship would carry him home. So, one night, he slipped away, and after days of walking and hiding, he at last reached the sea coast. Presently he came upon some sailors who were leading a number of fierce-looking dogs towards a ship, which was drawn up on the shore.

Patrick takes the wolf-hounds aboard

"Sailor," cried Patrick to one of the men, "Where are you going, and when do you leave?"

"We sail in an hour," answered the tall seaman. "We are bound for Britain, to sell these wolf-hounds for hunting."

"Can I go with you?" asked Patrick eagerly.

"If you can mind these dogs in a rough sea, you can come," said the sailor. "Here, take this pair aboard."

Patrick joyfully agreed, and the men were astonished at the way the great dogs at once obeyed him.

After they had set sail, a storm arose and blew the little ship to the coast of France instead of to Britain. Patrick left the Irish sailors and set out on foot to find his way home from this strange land. For many months he wandered about, until at last he reached Britain and his own home, to the great joy of his family.

Although he was very happy at home, and everyone loved him because he was good and kind, Patrick could not settle down. He felt sure that God had some special work for him to do. He could not forget the people in Ireland, and he longed to go and teach them about Jesus. But he knew he must first make himself ready for this great and difficult work.

So Patrick made up his mind to become a priest. He said goodbye to his family, and made his way back to France. There he became a priest, and for seventeen years he lived in a monastery. He read the Bible and learned how to teach the Gospel of Jesus Christ.

At last a great day came. Patrick was made a bishop, and given permission to go

Patrick says goodbye to his family

to Ireland to convert its people to Christianity. Once more, Patrick crossed the stormy sea to the land where he had been a slave, but this time he had with him a band of brave monks. After they had landed and prayed for God's blessing, they made their way inland to the home of Milcho, Patrick's old master. They found that Milcho had been killed in a battle against a neighbouring tribe, and his home was blackened by fire and in ruins.

Some of the wild Irish threw stones at the monks and tried to drive them away, but Patrick made peace with them and led them to the Hall of the greatest chief in those parts. This chief was feasting with his warriors and Druids, when a messenger rushed in to say that strangers had arrived. In the long, smoky hall the noise and singing ceased as the little party of quiet, calm men entered. One of them was carrying a tall cross. The chief stared curiously at them, for visitors were rarely seen in this distant land, and he asked who they were and where they had come from.

Lifting his hand, Patrick began to speak to them in their own language:

" We are men of God," he said. " We have come to bring you good news—the news of Jesus, the Son of God, and of his love and goodness to us all."

As he spoke to them, the fierce warriors saw that here was a man who was not only filled with love for all men, but who was without fear. So they let him speak, and they listened to his message.

The Druids were angry and alarmed at this new religion, but the chief became Patrick's friend. He was baptised a

In the Hall of the Irish chief

Christian, and he gave the monks a piece of land on which they built their first wooden church.

Patrick himself set out on journeys all over Ireland. He preached the Gospel to the people, telling them about Jesus and the Christian way of life. Wherever he went, he left monks and priests to build a church and start a monastery. He also wrote

Patrick baptising the Druids

prayers and books in Latin, the language of the Church.

In time, even the Druids, who were the poets and musicians of their people, came to be baptised. They brought with them their harps, on which they played so beautifully that people said the angels in heaven bent down to listen. Ever since those days the harp has been the badge of Ireland.

Patrick lived in Ireland for many years, and he was known and loved all over the country. He died near his first wooden church, and he was buried in the green country, which he had made into a Christian land.

Soon afterwards Patrick was made a Saint. He has always been the special, or patron, saint of Ireland and of Irish folk everywhere, and the 17th of March is kept as Saint Patrick's Day.

SAINT COLUMBA
who brought Christianity to Scotland

ABOUT sixty years after Saint Patrick died, a small boy named Columba went to school at the monastery near his home in Ireland. His father was a chief and he wanted his son to be able to read, which was something that very few people could do.

On his first day at school, Columba saw an old monk sitting at a desk in the porch of the monastery church. He went and stood on tiptoe to see what the monk was doing. He was writing very slowly on parchment and he was using a quill pen. At the top of the page was a big capital letter, painted in beautiful colours.

Columba watches an old monk seated at a desk

" What are you doing, Father ? " asked the little boy.

" I am writing, my son," replied the old monk. " This is a Psalm of David, and I am making a copy."

" Can I do writing ? " said Columba.

" No, my son, not until you have learned to read. Then we shall teach you to write. But it is slow work, which you must do with care, for it is God's work."

Columba was quick at his lessons, and soon he was helping the old monk to copy out prayers and stories. He loved books and made up his mind to be a monk, instead of being a chief or a warrior, like his brothers.

When he grew up, Columba built a little church near the sea. Later, he was made Abbot of a monastery at Derry.

Then he did a foolish thing. He borrowed a book from another monastery and it was so beautiful that he copied it without asking permission. The monks who owned this famous book were very angry with him and they told their king. This king was waiting to pick a quarrel with Columba's family. Although Columba gave back his copy of the book, there was a battle and many men were killed.

Columba was very sad when this happened, and he said to his monks, " My brothers, I have done wrong and I must go away from here."

The monks cried out, " But, Father, where will you go ? The world is full of dangers."

" I must go," said Columba, " to win more souls for God than were lost in that battle."

So Columba left Derry. He set out

Building the monastery on the island of Iona

Columba landing on the island of Iona

across the sea to Scotland, where he hoped to teach the heathen Picts about Jesus. Twelve faithful monks went with him.

The little boat brought them to a small, windy island called Iona. This island belonged to a friend of Columba's father. who allowed the monks to stay there. They built little huts, or cells, to live in, and they cut down trees to build a church. They ploughed the land and planted seed. In this way a new monastery was built. After a time, more monks came from Ireland. and Columba was made Abbot of the monastery.

When the work was nearly done, Columba said to the monks, " I am going on a journey to take the word of God to the Picts of the north. Pray for me when I leave you."

He rowed across to the mainland in his coracle, and then he travelled for many days across the hills. At last he came to the kingdom of the Picts.

The Picts were a fierce, heathen people and they bolted the gates of their town against the tall stranger, for they had heard he could work magic. Columba knocked on the gates and cried :

" Open in Christ's name ! "

At once the bolts fell open and he walked unharmed into the town.

Buda, King of the Picts, was now ready to welcome the stranger, and he asked him to stay awhile. Columba stayed many weeks with the pagan king and his warriors. Every day he would tell them about Jesus and His love for all men. One day Buda himself became a Christian, and he sent an order to all the tribes that they must give up their old gods and be baptised.

Columba tells King Buda about Jesus

Full of joy, Columba returned to Iona. Now he could send his monks to all parts of Scotland to build churches and monasteries. But wherever they went, the monks looked back to Iona as their holy island, and to Columba as their Abbot.

Columba was tall, with twinkling eyes and a gentle voice. He lived and dressed like the rest of his " family," as he called the monks. He wore a rough cassock and hood, with sandals on his bare feet. At night, he slept on the hard flagstones of his tiny cell, with a stone for his pillow.

He was kind, not only to men, but to animals, for, as he taught his monks, they all had the same Heavenly Father. At one time the seals, which often swam near Iona, made so much noise barking on the shore during prayers, that the monks decided to kill some for food. But Columba went out and spoke softly to the seals, who leapt into the sea and never troubled them again.

Sometimes, sea-birds, on their long journey north, fell exhausted on the island, and Columba would care for them until they were strong.

His special friend was an old white horse. One day, when Columba was very old, he went round the island, blessing its fields and barns. The white horse ran to him and laid its head in his lap, whinnying sadly.

"See," said Columba to the monks, "he knows his master is about to leave him."

That same evening, the monks, carrying lighted candles, came into the dark church for service. They found Columba lying dead by the altar.

He was buried on the holy island of

Iona, and one of his monks wrote, long ago :

"He had the face of an angel : he was holy in work, great in wisdom. And, with it, he was loving to all."

Columba says farewell to the old horse

POPE GREGORY

and

SAINT AUGUSTINE

AFTER about four hundred years in Britain, the Romans returned home. Barbarians were attacking Rome, and the soldiers were needed to defend the city. In many ways the Britons were sad to see the Romans go, for they no longer had soldiers to protect them. Already fierce tribes of Angles, Saxons and Jutes, were attacking the shores of Britain.

These fair-haired heathens came across the North Sea in their long ships. They would sail up a river, leap ashore and attack the nearest town or village. They killed the Britons, and stole their gold, cattle and goods. Then they would set fire to the houses and sail away.

Soon, the raiders, with their battle-axes and round shields, stayed to make their homes in Britain. They drove the Britons

Angles attack a British village

The Angles and Saxons crossed the North Sea in their long war-galleys, and sailed up the rivers of Eastern Britain to attack villages and towns. Often, they captured horses and rode across country, robbing and plundering the farms.

away from the rich lands of the south and east, into the hills of Cornwall and Wales.

The Angles, Saxons and Jutes were pagans, worshipping such gods as Woden and Thor. Most of Britain again became a heathen land. The monks still preached Christianity in Ireland, Iona and the west.

Now it happened at this time, that a Christian monk, far away in Rome, was walking one day through the busy market-place. His name was Gregory and, looking around him, he noticed that there were many slaves for sale. This was a common sight, but among these slaves there was a group of very beautiful children with fair hair and blue eyes, such as were not often seen in Rome.

" Where do these children come from ? " asked Gregory.

" They are Angles, from the island of Britain," said the slavemaster, thinking that the monk might buy one, to give him his freedom.

" Angles ? " replied Gregory, in surprise. " They look more like angels from Heaven to me."

Gregory in the slave-market of Rome

The fair-haired children were Angles whose parents had settled in Britain (soon to be called Angle-land). They were captured in a raid by pirates, who brought them to Rome, where slaves fetched a good price.

"So they do, good father," the slave-dealer laughed, "but for all their looks, their people are fierce heathens."

Gregory went to the Pope and begged to be allowed to go to Britain. He wanted to take the word of Jesus to people whose children were so beautiful. But the Pope needed Gregory and would not allow him to go.

Years later, Gregory became Pope and he remembered the Angles. He could not go to Britain himself, but he chose a prior named Augustine to lead the way.

Augustine and forty monks set out on foot on the long dangerous journey to Britain. After many weeks, they stopped to rest at a monastery in France, where they heard tales of the fierce heathens in Britain. The monks were afraid to go on, so they begged Augustine to return to Rome and tell Gregory that the dangers were too great.

Pope Gregory listened sadly to Augustine.

"No, my son," he said, "you must go back and finish your journey, no matter what the dangers. God has called you to this work and He will help you."

Saint Augustine lands in Kent

Augustine felt ashamed and made up his mind to obey Gregory. He hurried back to the monks and told them to take courage. He had heard that Ethelbert, King of Kent, had married a Christian lady, called Bertha, daughter of the King of Paris.

Cheered by this news, the monks took ship for Britain and landed at Ebbsfleet, in Kent, in the year A.D. 597.

Augustine at once sent a message to Queen Bertha telling her that they had come from Rome with a joyful message. The queen asked her husband, who loved her dearly, if the monks might come to speak to him of Jesus Christ.

To please his wife, Ethelbert summoned his nobles and followers to a meeting-place in the Isle of Thanet. He was careful to have his chair placed out-of-doors under an oak-tree, since he feared that these priests might work magic indoors.

Augustine and his monks, led by a monk carrying a silver cross and another with a picture of Jesus, drew near to the king.

" Tell me your message," said Ethelbert.

Augustine spoke for a long time, telling the king about the life and teaching of Jesus. The king listened carefully, and then he said, " You speak fair words, but the meaning is not clear to me. I cannot give up my own gods, not even for the sake of my dear Queen.

" But you have travelled far and seem good men. We shall not hurt you, and you are free to preach to my people and to win as many as you can for your religion."

The king had already given Bertha the ruined Roman church of St. Martin, outside Canterbury. Full of joy, the monks now went with the queen, to pray in the little church.

King Ethelbert and Queen Bertha listen to Augustine

The people took a great interest in these strangers. When they saw that they were good and holy men, who helped the poor and the sick, many Kentish men and women were baptised. Queen Bertha spoke every day to her husband about Jesus. She knew that many of the nobles wished to become Christians, but were waiting to see if the king would change his religion. With Augustine's help, it was not long before she had persuaded Ethelbert to be baptised. Many others were baptised and Kent became a Christian kingdom.

Augustine and the monks now built a church inside the walls of Canterbury. They chose the same spot where a Roman church had once stood. Many other ruined churches were rebuilt and a monastery was founded, which to-day is called St. Augustine's.

Pope Gregory was overjoyed when this good news reached him in Rome. He sent more monks to spread the Gospel to the Saxons who lived north of the Thames.

Augustine became a bishop, and he made a long journey to meet the Welsh Christians at a place called Augustine's Oak, by the river Severn.

Canterbury became the chief city of the Christian Church in Britain. It has remained so until this day, nearly fourteen hundred years after Augustine and the forty monks landed on the beach at Ebbsfleet.

AIDAN

The Saint of Northumbria

IN the north of Britain, many days journey from the kingdom of Kent, was the kingdom of Northumbria. Edwin, and his beautiful queen, Ethelberga, had made its people Christians. But soon afterwards Penda, the heathen King of Mercia, killed Edwin in battle, and drove Ethelberga and her priests back to Kent.

Just when it seemed as if all Northumbria was lost, a young prince, named Oswald, arrived. He rallied the Northumbrians and drove Penda away.

For several years Oswald had lived in hiding on Iona, where the friendly monks had taught him to be a Christian. Now that he was King, Oswald sent to Iona for a monk to come and teach his people about Christ.

The monk who came was a good man, but very stern. He did not explain things in such a way that the Northumbrians could understand them. After a time, he went sadly back to Iona and told the abbot and monks that he could not convert these wild, stupid people.

One of the monks, who heard him talk about the stupid Northumbrians, was named Aidan.

" It seems, brother," he said, " that you have been too severe. Perhaps you were too stern with these heathen folk.

" Did you not try to give them meat instead of milk ? They are like little children, and must be led gently to God."

The abbot and the monks cried out together :

" Here is the man to go to Northumbria ! Aidan must go ! "

So Aidan went from Iona to North-

Aidan preaching to the peasants

umbria, and he soon became a close friend of King Oswald. At first Aidan could not speak the Northumbrian language, and Oswald would explain his teaching to the thegns, or nobles of the Court, and together they spread the Gospel of Christ.

Aidan wanted to build a monastery, and he chose the island of Lindisfarne, which, like Iona, lies just off the coast. Oswald gladly gave him the island and here he built a monastery, where monks from Iona came to join him.

Aidan always spoke gently and kindly to the people, and soon folk from all parts flocked to hear the new teaching of love

King Oswald gives his silver dish to the beggars

and kindness. Aidan travelled about on foot, preaching wherever he went. By his own example, he showed the people how to live a good life.

He asked nothing for himself, and he gave away to the poor all the rich gifts that the king and nobles had given him.

One Easter, Aidan was having dinner

with King Oswald. The royal servant, who was giving alms to the poor, came in to say that he had no food or money left for those who were still waiting outside. Then the king, who loved Aidan, ordered his great silver dish to be broken up and the pieces given away.

Aidan seized his friend's hand and cried, " May this hand never perish ! "

Only a short while afterwards, Oswald was killed in battle against his enemy, Penda of Mercia. When his body was found, the right arm and hand were missing. For many years the bones were kept as holy relics in the Church of York.

Helped by Aidan's prayers, the Northumbrians at last drove Penda back. Their new king, Oswini, also became a close friend of Aidan.

Oswini gave Aidan a beautiful and valuable horse, so that he could ride about the country instead of travelling on foot. Soon afterwards, the King heard that Aidan had given the horse to a poor man. He was angry that his rich gift should be treated so lightly.

"It is true that I gave away the horse," said Aidan gently, "and it is also true that Jesus Christ gave his life for us. Is a horse worth more than the Son of God?"

Oswini knelt at Aidan's feet and begged for pardon.

Aidan raised him up and then sat in thoughtful silence.

"What ails you, my father?" asked the King.

"I know that so humble a king cannot live long upon this earth," answered Aidan.

A few days later, Oswini was murdered and a new king gained his throne.

Aidan went back to his island of Lindisfarne, but he did not live long after his friend. He died one evening in his little hut, next to the church.

The same evening, Cuthbert, a shepherd lad, was guarding his sheep on a hillside. Looking up he saw stars falling from the sky, and angels bearing Aidan's soul towards heaven.

Cuthbert became a monk and, with his brother monks, he helped to spread the Gospel throughout Northumbria and in the kingdoms beyond. All the north and east of England became Christian, and the Christian people looked to Lindisfarne as their holy isle, and looked upon Aidan as their own Saint.

Cuthbert, the shepherd-boy

Hilda is baptised by the monk Paulinus

The Abbess HILDA
and CAEDMON the Cowherd

IN Saint Aidan's time, there lived at the royal court of Northumbria, a princess named Hilda. When she was a little girl, she had been baptised by the monk Paulinus. She was filled with joy when Aidan came from Iona to spread God's Word among her people.

Hilda loved the teaching of Jesus so much that she became a nun. She put away her brightly-coloured gowns and wore a long black robe, and her hair was hidden under a hood.

One day she went to Aidan and said, " I have come to say farewell, Father Aidan. I am going to France to be with my sister in a nunnery."

Aidan looked at her and answered: "Do not go, Sister. We need you here in Northumbria."

" But, Father," said Hilda, " I want to give all my life to God, and there is no nunnery here."

" You can do God's work here," said Aidan. " We are building a new monastery across the river at Hartlepool. I want you to be its first abbess."

So Hilda did not go to France. She became abbess of a monastery for both monks and nuns. They spent their days working, praying and praising God. Some looked after the sick and poor people, while others helped to teach boys and girls to read the scriptures.

Hilda was loved by all the people for miles around and they called her " Mother." She was gentle, and so wise that kings and princes, as well as ordinary people, came to her for help and advice.

One day, Oswy, the new King of Northumbria, came to visit her with his wife and baby daughter, Elfleda. Oswy had just won a great battle against the heathen King Penda. To show his thankfulness to God, he had promised that he would take little Elfleda to Hilda to be brought up as a nun.

The Abbess Hilda decided to build a new monastery for her home. She chose a place at Whitby on a high, windy cliff, looking out across the stormy waters of the North Sea.

The monastery at Whitby became famous, and there little Elfleda grew up. Mother Hilda loved the child. She taught her carefully, and in time, Elfleda, too, became a nun. Many years later, she was chosen to be abbess of the same monastery.

Around the monastery at Whitby were fields, where the monks grew wheat, barley and rye. On the grassy hillsides grazed cattle which gave them milk, cheese and meat; and they kept sheep from whose

King Oswy brings his baby daughter to the Abbess Hilda

wool they made their long gowns. The monks worked hard, but they also needed time for prayers, for their books and for helping the poor. So they had other people to help them with the farmwork.

These ordinary workers lived in small huts near the walls of the monastery. Every evening, when their work was done, they would gather in a big hall which was part of the monastery. Here they sat down to supper. Afterwards, on winter nights, they would sit on benches round the fire, which was made on a stone hearth in the middle of the dim, smoky hall. None of them could read or write, but they enjoyed themselves by singing.

"Pass the harp," one of the shepherds would say. Then the harp was taken down from the wall, and each man in turn would sing a verse of a song which told of the great deeds of some hero of long ago. Everyone praised a good singer, especially if he could make up some verses of his own to add to the song.

But there was one man among the shepherds, ploughmen and cowherds who could not sing. His name was Caedmon. As the harp was passed round and his turn drew near, he would get up and slip away from the fire.

"There goes old Caedmon," someone would say. "He can't sing a note." The others would burst out laughing as he hurried out into the darkness.

One night Caedmon slipped out to tend the cattle. He was tired and he soon fell asleep in the cowshed. Suddenly he seemed to hear a voice saying, "Caedmon, sing something to me."

Caedmon hears the voice

"Alas," he replied, "I cannot sing; that is why I have left the fireside."

"Caedmon, you shall sing to me."

"But what shall I sing?" he stammered.

"Sing," said the voice, "sing about the beginning of the world, sing of the beginning of created things."

In a trembling voice, Caedmon began to sing the story of how God created the world, a story which he had heard from the monks. The words seemed to come easily to him, and he found himself singing as he had never done before.

In the morning Caedmon awoke and remembered his dream. He tried to sing again, and, to his great wonder, the words came as easily and beautifully as before.

Hurrying outside, he saw the head steward of the abbey farm.

" Good bailiff," he cried, " the voice of an angel spoke to me in a dream telling me to sing. Thou knowest I never could sing, but, wonder of wonders, the words poured out like a running stream, and they are still with me."

The steward at once took him into the monastery, and led him to where Abbess Hilda was seated with some of her wisest monks and nuns. She spoke to him gently and asked him to tell her his dream. Caedmon felt very shy at first, but her kind voice helped him to tell all that had happened in the dream.

" Can you sing the Creation to me ? " asked Hilda.

"I will try, good Mother," said the cowherd.

He stood before her and sang of how God made the world and how He founded

Caedmon sings to the Abbess

His Heavenly Kingdom. Verse after verse he sang, in a pure, lovely voice. At the end, the monks and nuns were speechless with wonder.

"It is a gift of God," said Hilda quietly. "Caedmon has been given the power to sing God's praise, and we must use His gift."

Then she turned to one of the older monks.

"Brother Edwin," she said, "Caedmon shall not mind cattle any more. You must teach him the Bible stories, so that he may turn them into verses as wonderful as these we have heard."

So Caedmon changed his short tunic for a long brown robe. The monks would tell him a story from the Bible, and he would go away and think awhile. Then he would come back with the story turned into the most beautiful poetry, which was copied down by one of the monks.

Caedmon lived at the monastery for many years, making music and poems for the glory of God. He was, perhaps, the first great English poet.

ALFRED OF WESSEX

AFTER the Angles and Saxons had settled down as one Christian people, a great trouble came upon them.

Fierce raiders began to attack the east coast. These Danes, also known as Vikings or Northmen, came in long dragon-ships to steal and burn. But after a time, they stayed to make homes. They drove out the English and took their farms and villages for themselves.

For many years there was fighting between the Danes and the English, who still called themselves Saxons. It was in these troubled times, in the year 849, that Alfred was born. He was the fourth son of

Ethelwulf, King of the West Saxons. His mother was Osberga, daughter of a noble thegn who was the King's Cupbearer.

In those days very few people, except the monks, could read. Books were copied out slowly by hand on to thin sheets of parchment. Even the sons of a king did not go to school regularly. Alfred and his three older brothers went to an abbey nearby to learn parts of the Bible by heart, to learn prayers, and songs of the minstrels.

One day, the Queen was sitting on a window-seat in the Great Hall, and she called her four sons to her:

" What is this I am holding, my sons? "

" It is a book, Mother," answered the eldest, Ethelbald.

" Yes, it is a book of Saxon poetry. Which of you can read it to me? "

" Reading is for monks. We learn to hunt and to fight the Northmen. Letters take too long to learn."

" But, my son," said the Queen, " I want you to learn your letters. A prince who cannot read will make a sorry king.

Queen Osberga shows her four sons a book of Saxon poetry. None of them can read, but Alfred immediately longs to have the book for his own

"I will give this book to the one who first learns to read it."

Alfred pushed between his brothers and looked at the beautiful writing, copied by monks, and at the great letter which stood at the top of each page, painted in glowing colours. He longed to have the book for his own.

"Will you really give me this book, Mother, if I can read it to you?" he asked.

"Yes, Alfred," answered the Queen. "If you can read it before your brothers, it shall be yours to keep."

The four princes began to learn their letters, in the hope of winning the beautiful book. They found it dull work, and soon three of them went off to practise shooting with a bow, and fighting with battle-axes. But Alfred went to the abbey and asked the monk who had taught him parts of the Bible if he would also teach him to read. He worked every day at his reading lessons, until at last he was able to read the book of Saxon poetry, and to claim it from his mother.

Alfred learns to read

Yet, as he grew up, Alfred seemed to have little time for reading. All his life was spent in fighting the Danes or planning how to defeat their next attack.

His father died, and, in turn, each of his brothers became king. Alfred's first two brothers did not live very long. By the time Alfred was nineteen, his third brother, Ethelred, was King of Wessex.

The Danes had now conquered nearly all England and they began to attack Wessex. They sailed up the Thames in their long boats and made a strong camp on the bank of the river. This gave them a fort to retreat to, if they were defeated in battle.

Ethelred and Alfred led the Saxons against the Northmen and won a victory at the great battle of Ashdune. But the Danes soon came again, some landing on the shores and others sailing up the river. Alfred fought them in nine battles in the year 871. Then his brother died and Alfred became King of Wessex.

At the end of the year, Alfred made peace with the Danes. They promised on the holy bracelet, their most solemn oath, that they would leave Wessex in peace.

But although they went away to fight and plunder in another part of England, the Danes meant to come back. Alfred knew this, and he made ready a plan of attack. He sent for shipbuilders and had a fleet of ships built. He meant to fight the

Alfred rides to meet the Danes

Danes at sea, before ever they reached the coast.

This is why Alfred is sometimes called " Father of the Navy."

Time after time, the Saxons beat the Danes, yet they always returned. In winter, the fighting often stopped while both sides had a rest, and the Saxons went back to their farms and homes. But one winter, the Danes planned a new attack. They gathered their warriors into camps in Mercia, and in January, when the Saxons were not expecting trouble, they suddenly attacked. They poured into Wessex, burning, killing and plundering.

The whole kingdom fell into their hands. Wessex was conquered. King Alfred disappeared and no man could say whether he was alive or dead. Without their leader, the Saxons were helpless.

ALFRED THE KING

WESSEX had been conquered. The Danes ruled over the kingdom and the King had

The capture of the Raven Banner

vanished. But Alfred was not dead. He had escaped with his wife and a few nobles to the lonely swamps of Somerset.

There, among the reeds and willow-trees, a patch of land rose like an island in the marsh. Only the rough half-savage marsh people could find the way through the swamp to this island. A trusted cow-herd led Alfred to his hiding-place.

Soon, the King and his few nobles began

to build a strong fence round the little island, until it was like a fort. They called it Athelney, which means the "Isle of Nobles." Even if the Danes learned of the hiding-place, it would not be easy to capture.

Secret messages were sent out that Alfred was gathering an army again. In twos and threes, Saxons came to Athelney to join him.

Presently they were strong enough to sally out and attack small parties of Danes. News of this soon spread among the Saxons, and gave them new hope.

One day a band of Saxons took the Danes by surprise, and captured their famous standard, "The Raven." This flag had been woven in one day by three princesses. The Danes believed that when it went in front of them to battle, a live raven was flying in the middle of the flag to give them victory. The loss of their magic banner made them feel that the Saxon God was more powerful than Odin and Thor.

At last Alfred was almost ready to make a big attack upon the foe. But before doing

Alfred in the Danish camp

so, as the old story-teller says, he disguised himself as a wandering minstrel and went boldly into the Danish camp. The Northmen loved music and they welcomed this merry fellow who sang so well to his harp. He pleased them so much that they took him to play before their leader, King Guthrum himself.

Alfred spent two or three days in the camp, keeping his ears and eyes open. He noticed that the Danes had no great stores of food. They thought the Saxons were defeated, and they spent their time feasting and merry-making. Then he slipped away, back to Athelney to tell his men of the Danes' plans.

Next day, the Saxons set out from Athelney. Messengers rode in every direction to tell the people that Alfred was ready for war. As the news spread, Saxon fighting-men came hurrying to meet him at the Stone of Egbert. They shouted for joy to see their king alive.

When the Danes learned that the Saxons had raised an army, they marched out to meet them, and a great battle was fought at Ethandune. The Danes were utterly defeated, and those who were left alive retreated to their fortified camp.

Alfred quickly followed and surrounded the fort, so that no one was able to escape. He knew that they had little food. After fourteen days, the Danes were so cold and hungry that they had to ask for peace.

What was Alfred to do? He had Guthrum and all the Danes in his power. Should he put them to the sword and leave not one alive?

Now Alfred showed how wise and merciful he was. He said to the Danes, "If you

Guthrum swears never to attack Wessex

promise to leave Wessex for ever, I will spare you."

Then the Danes swore on the holy bracelet, and by their gods Odin and Thor, that they would never again attack Wessex.

" But how can I trust you," asked Alfred, " when you have so often broken your promises ? "

" I will promise by a greater God than these," cried Guthrum. " I will swear by your God, who is much stronger than mine."

To Alfred's joy, Guthrum kept his word. He and thirty of his nobles became Christians and were baptized near Athelney.

A great peace was made. The Danes were allowed to keep the eastern part of England, which was called the Danelaw, but Wessex remained Saxon. Alfred had won back his kingdom.

ALFRED THE GREAT

ALFRED reigned for a number of years after the peace with Guthrum, and he ruled his people wisely and well.

First he had to make Wessex safe. Guthrum would keep his promise, but there were many other Danes who might come to attack the kingdom. So Alfred decided that he must always have an army ready.

Alfred's army was made up of men who served as soldiers for only two months. The men then returned to their homes. This meant that sometimes he had a very large army and at other times a very small one. Alfred worked out a plan so that his army was always strong enough to meet a sudden attack by the Northmen. He ordered that some men must serve as soldiers, while

Rebuilding the walls of London

others stayed at home to look after the farms. Then, when one party had finished their two months' service, others must come and take their places in the army. Alfred's plan worked very well.

He taught his fighting-men to make forts like the Danes. He made townsfolk dig a ditch and build a wall round their towns, making the towns difficult to capture.

The capital of Wessex was now Winchester. London had been in ruins for many, many years. Alfred rebuilt London and stationed soldiers there to stop the Danes from sailing up the river Thames. More ships were added to the fleet until there were a hundred in all. An old writer said :

"They were full-nigh twice as long as the others; some had sixty oars and some had more; they were both swifter and steadier and also higher than the others."

While he was making his kingdom safe by these wise plans, Alfred worked very hard to make it a good and Christian land for his people. He himself was good and pious, and a monk said of him :

"The King attends daily services of religion; he is often at prayer and psalm singing. He goes to the church at night-time, to pray secretly, unknown to his nobles."

Alfred had churches and monasteries built, one of them at his old island hiding-place, Athelney. He gave one half of all his money for the building of churches, and went himself to see that the work was well done.

He built again the monasteries burned down by the Danes. Very few people could read, as many monks had been killed

The candle-clock

by the Danes and there was no one to teach them. Even the stories of the Bible were being forgotten.

Alfred worked very hard. He planned out every part of his day, giving eight hours for work, eight hours for study and religion, and eight hours for rest. Since there were no clocks in those days, he invented one for himself. It was a candle-clock.

He ordered some big candles to be made, all of exactly the same size. He found that a candle took four hours to burn out, so he had each candle marked into parts which took an hour to burn.

Since even the King's palace was

draughty, each candle was placed in a lantern made of wood, with windows of thin horn. It was the duty of one servant to watch the candle. When he could see that the flame had reached an hour-mark, he would go to the King and say, " O King, another hour has passed away."

Alfred had never forgotten the beautiful book that his mother gave him for learning to read. He wanted every boy in the land to be able to read. But this was far from easy. Although Alfred had some schools built, and sent for teachers to come from across the seas, the books of those days were written in Latin, a language which few people in Wessex could understand.

" There are few monks to teach my people Latin," said Alfred, " so I will learn Latin myself and translate the books into English."

A monk named Asser taught him Latin. The King soon set to work to translate some old stories and the writings of the great Pope Gregory, as well as Bede's " History."

Asser, the monk, became his great friend

Alfred and Asser, the monk

and they sat together every day, copying out the stories and making new books which were then sent to monasteries in all parts of the land.

The people loved their wise and kindly king. He made their country safe from the Danes. He gave them churches, monasteries and books. He also gave them good laws, which were called Alfred's Dooms. People said he made the land so peaceful, that a man might hang a gold bracelet on a tree by the side of the road and find it still there a year later. There are many stories told about

Alfred which show the people's love for him. They said that he was the only man in the kingdom to whom the poor could look for help.

Alfred did not live to be an old man. All his life he had had a strange illness which no one could cure. When he lay dying in his own city of Winchester, he called his son Edward to him, and said, " I pray thee, my good son, to be a father to my people. Comfort the poor, protect and shelter the weak, and put right the things that are wrong."

He was buried in Winchester Cathedral. He was a wonderful man, wise and good and kind. He did more for his people than any other king in English history, and Alfred is the only king we have ever called " The Great."

WHEN THEY LIVED

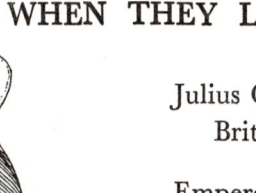

B.C.

Julius Caesar visited Britain   54 & 55 B.C.

Emperor Claudius invaded Britain   A.D. 43

CARACTACUS fought the Romans   48–51

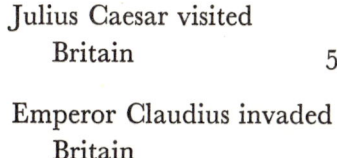

CARACTACUS

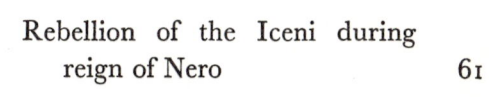

Rebellion of the Iceni during reign of Nero   61

BOADICEA (or Boudicca)

BOADICEA

Conquest of Britain   75–85

Julius **AGRICOLA**, Governor   78–84

Christian religion forbidden about 304

SAINT ALBAN

Emperor Constantine adopted Christianity   313

AGRICOLA   SAINT ALBAN

The Romans left Britain   410

SAINT PATRICK   about 385–461

Heathen Angles and Saxons raided our shores. Gradually they took the land for themselves, driving the Britons into the west.

SAINT PATRICK

	A.D.
SAINT COLUMBA	521-597
sailed to Iona	563

SAINT COLUMBA

Pope Gregory	590-604
SAINT AUGUSTINE	
landed in Kent	597
Northumberland ruled by Oswald and Oswy	
SAINT AIDAN	about 635

SAINT AUGUSTINE   SAINT AIDAN

ABBESS HILDA at Whitby and CAEDMON, who died in   680

England was divided into several kingdoms—Northumbria, Mercia, East Anglia, Kent, Wessex—for about 300 years

THE ABBESS HILDA   CAEDMON

The Danes came	800
ALFRED THE GREAT	
	about 849-900
Peace of Wedmore	878
The Danes settled in Eastern England and became Christians	

ALFRED THE GREAT

104

PART TWO

PART TWO

FROM WILLIAM THE CONQUEROR TO WILLIAM CAXTON

WILLIAM THE CONQUEROR
The First Norman King of England

DUKE William of Normandy was dining with his nobles at the high table in the Great Hall of his castle. His knights and men-at-arms, the best fighting men in Europe, were seated at long trestle tables farther down the hall. The Duke was a short, thick-set man with a sharp tongue, and an air of authority. His friends and his enemies feared his anger, but they admired his skill in war.

A man in a short cloak came quickly through the hall and knelt on one knee before the Duke's high table. Duke William looked at him.

" What news, messenger ? " he asked.
" I bring news from England, my lord,"

Duke William hears news from England

the messenger said. " Edward, whom men called The Confessor, is dead. Harold, son of Godwin, is crowned King of England."

There was a silence in the Great Hall. The Duke's face grew dark with anger. He leaned forward, twisting and untwisting the gold clasp of his cloak.

" The Saxon dog has broken his oath ! " he cried. " Did he not swear in this Hall to help me gain my uncle's crown ? "

" Aye, he swore on the bones of a saint," murmured the knights.

" Then, by Heaven, and by those holy bones," cried William, " he shall lose in war what he will not yield in peace ! "

A fleet is built on the beaches of Normandy

Without delay, he sent out word to all his knights and barons.

"If you follow me to England with arms and men, I will reward you with fair lands and riches, such as you have never seen."

From all parts of Normandy and France, knights, archers, and men-at-arms flocked to join the Duke. Blacksmiths and metal workers were ordered to work day and night making shields and armour. Trees were cut down in the forests to build a great fleet of ships on the beaches of Normandy.

The work went on quickly and by the end of the summer all was ready. The great fleet sailed towards England with the flag of Normandy at the mast of William's ships.

When the Normans reached the Sussex coast, there was no Saxon army to meet them, for Harold was far away in the North of England. There he won a great battle against his brother, Tostig, and the King of Norway, who had also invaded his kingdom.

As the first Norman ship touched the land, William sprang ashore, but he stumbled and fell upon his face. A groan went up from the knights.

" Look, he falls," they whispered, " 'tis a sign of ill-fortune."

But William stood up, laughing, and, turning round, he held up both his fists full of sand.

" See," he cried, " I have England already in my hands ! "

With a cheer, the Normans leapt down from the ships and they began to unload the stores and horses. When this was done, William ordered them to sink or burn all the ships.

" We must win England or die," he said. " We cannot go back to Normandy in disgrace."

On the morning of the 14th of October, 1066, Duke William led his army towards Senlac Hill near Hastings. King Harold had made his camp on Senlac Hill after a long and weary march from the north, and his men were tired. Harold's brother, Gurth, urged him to burn all the farms so that the Normans would be short of food.

"How can I hurt my own people?" Harold said. "We have beaten one foe, let us now drive out these Norman wolves."

When the trumpets blared for the battle to begin, the Norman knights charged up the hill. In the lead rode the Duke's minstrel, singing, and whirling his sword in the air like a juggler. But he was one of the first to die, as the Normans crashed against the wall of shields. The Saxon house-carls fought their enemies on foot with shield, spear and battle-axe.

All day the battle went on. The Norman archers fired their arrows and the knights charged, but the Saxons stood firm and smashed them back. William's horse was killed under him, and a cry went up that he was dead. Then the Normans,

" See, I am alive ! Back into the fight "

feeling all was lost without their leader, began to turn tail. But William snatched off his helmet so that all could see his face, mounted another horse and shouted:

" See, I am alive ! Back into the fight. Victory is ours ! "

He ordered his knights to charge once more, and then to pretend to run away. Some of the Saxons forgot Harold's order to stand firm. They thought the battle was won and began to chase the enemy downhill. The Normans wheeled round and cut them to pieces. Fresh horsemen poured into the gaps between the Saxon shields, as William's archers fired high into the air.

An arrow struck Harold in the eye. He tore it out, and continued to fight under the great yellow banner of Wessex, but he was mortally wounded. His peasants and farmer soldiers began to retreat into the woods.

Around the dying King, his bodyguards fought on. They would not yield or fly. Even the Normans were amazed by their courage, as, one by one, they died fighting for their king. When twilight came, Harold and the last of his house-carls lay dead on Senlac Hill.

After the battle, William did not delay. He marched towards London, burning and killing as he went. There was no one left to lead the English, and, on Christmas Day, 1066, the Duke was crowned William I of England, in his uncle's Abbey at Westminster.

Once he had won his kingdom, William made sure that no man would take it from him. He gave English land to his followers, keeping a great part for himself and the Church. Then he made every knight and baron kneel before him and swear:

" I promise to be your man for the land

Harold meets his death on Senlac Hill

I hold; to serve you faithfully and to give you help against all folk."

Though he built abbeys and churches for God, William also built castles to hold down the English. He found out the value of every piece of land, and he taxed the people without mercy.

But though he was stern and cruel, William was also a great man. He gave the people good laws, and made everyone obey them, including the barons. He was fair to those who obeyed him, and he never stopped working to make the country strong.

At the end of his life, when he lay dying, in Normandy, he was sorry for his cruel deeds. His son, William the Red, snatched the great ring from his father's finger, and hurried off to England to be crowned. William the Conqueror was alone with a priest.

" I am sorry for my sins," he whispered ; " I have killed thousands of those fine people in England, both young and old, and many have died of hunger or by the sword. May God forgive me."

Then the great Conqueror died, and his son, William Rufus, became King of England.

SAINT MARGARET
Queen of Scotland

AFTER Harold was killed at the Battle of Hastings, the Saxons chose a new King. They chose a boy named Edgar Atheling, because he was a relative of Edward the Confessor. But William of Normandy was too strong for a boy without friends or an army. So Edgar took flight in a ship with his mother, Agatha, and his sisters, Margaret and Christina.

Their ship was blown by gales towards the coast of Scotland, and the captain steered into the Firth of Forth. He dropped anchor in a bay which is still called Saint Margaret's Hope.

The king of Scotland at this time was Malcolm Canmore. When he heard of the arrival of some English visitors, he rode down from Dunfermline to the shore. A crowd of Scots had gathered, staring with astonishment at the richly dressed strangers.

Edgar's mother, the Lady Agatha, spoke to the king :

" Greetings, Malcolm Canmore," she said. " We have been driven from our home to your shore, and we ask shelter of Scotland's noble king."

" You are welcome, gracious lady," Malcolm replied. " When I was only a boy, my father, Duncan, was foully murdered by Macbeth. Edward the Confessor gave me shelter at the English court. Now I am glad to welcome his kinsfolk. Come with me to Dunfermline as my guests."

With these kind words, Malcolm led them to the royal castle, and the English family settled down at the Scottish court.

Margaret, the eldest of the three

Margaret choosing materials and ornaments in Dunfermline

children, was a beautiful girl of twenty. She was already known for her learning and goodness, and she longed to become a nun. As soon as he saw her, Malcolm was so struck by her beauty and gentleness that he wished to marry her, and make her Queen of Scotland.

Malcolm was a great warrior who had known fighting and bloodshed all his life, but in spite of his rough ways, he won the love of Margaret, and she married him. The wedding was the most splendid that Scotland had ever seen.

At first, life at Dunfermline seemed very

rough to Margaret. The royal palace was no more than a strong fort. Its Great Hall was dark and gloomy, since the only light came from slits in the walls and from the fire in the centre. There were reeds on the floor and little furniture, apart from some rough-hewn tables and benches.

Margaret soon began to make Dunfermline more like a king's dwelling. She invited traders to Scotland, and they brought fine cloth, ornaments, and gold and silver dishes for the royal table. She was clever with her needle, and she taught the ladies fine needlework and embroidery. Soon the Court became better dressed and the king was surrounded by splendour and dignity.

The Scots were a warlike, hardy people, and at first they did not much care for these fine clothes and manners. Margaret noticed that it was the custom of the nobles to rush away from the table as soon as they had finished eating. They never waited for Grace to be said. One day, she called a servant and said :

" Bring, I pray you, my new silver cup

Margaret offers the Grace Cup to the King

filled with our choicest wine. When I have eaten, I shall pass my cup with a blessing to those knights who sit at table. When we have drunk, we shall give thanks to God."

This special cup was called the Grace Cup, for, after it had been passed round, Grace was said. This custom, kept for hundreds of years at Scottish feasts, was known as Saint Margaret's Blessing.

Queen Margaret was deeply religious, living her life for God and spending much of her day in prayer. Every day she fed nine orphans with her own spoon. Often as many as 300 poor people gathered in the Great Hall, and the gentle Queen gave them food and waited on them herself, with only a few servants to help her.

She loved to help travellers, especially pilgrims on their way to the shrine of St Andrew. She provided a ship to carry them across the wide Firth of Forth, and she built rest-houses for them on each side, at the places now called North and South Queensferry.

All these good deeds filled Malcolm with even greater love for his Queen. Above all, he loved to hear her read aloud, for, although he was King of Scotland, he could neither read nor write. Whenever he saw that Margaret specially loved a book, he would send for a goldsmith.

" Ornament this book with gold and jewels upon its covers," he would command the man. " Use your best skill. Then bring it secretly, and lay it here on this window-seat, where the Queen may find it. So it may please her."

Margaret's favourite book was her

The feeding of the nine orphans

Gospel, which contained beautiful pictures of the Saints. One day, when the royal party was crossing a little river, a servant was carrying the book in a wrapper. It slipped unnoticed from his hand and fell into the water. There was a great search for the precious book and the Queen was very unhappy, but no one could find it. After several days it was seen lying on the river bed, with ripples turning its beautiful pages. A servant jumped into the clear water and brought it safely to the bank. Strange to tell, it was not damaged except for a few marks of damp. This same book can now be seen in the great library at Oxford.

England and Scotland were often at war in Malcolm's time. The Scots fought fierce battles against William I and, later, against his son Rufus. The good Queen hated war and she tried to stop Malcolm from making raids on Northumbria. When he brought back English prisoners as slaves she would pay ransoms to set them free. She gave away vast sums of her own money, and even borrowed from the King's treasury.

Margaret begged Malcolm not to go on his last raid, but he wanted revenge for being treated rudely when on a visit to England. He set off to war with two of his sons.

Lying ill in the castle at Edinburgh, where Saint Margaret's Chapel still stands, the Queen prayed for them. Then she turned to a priest and said:

Edgar brings terrible news

" I fear that on this very day, a terrible disaster will fall upon Scotland."

A few days later, her son Edgar entered the Queen's room. He was heavy with sorrow, for his father Malcolm and his brother had been killed in battle against the English.

" How is it with the King and thy brother, my son ? " whispered the Queen.

Edgar was afraid to tell her the truth.

"All is well with them, dear Mother," he said.

She cried out in despair.

"I know it is not so. By this Holy Cross, tell me the truth."

Edgar knelt beside her and stammered out the terrible news.

With a last prayer for those she loved, Queen Margaret closed her eyes and died.

Sadly, her people carried her to Dunfermline. There she was buried, and the body of Malcolm Canmore was brought from the battlefield to lie by her side.

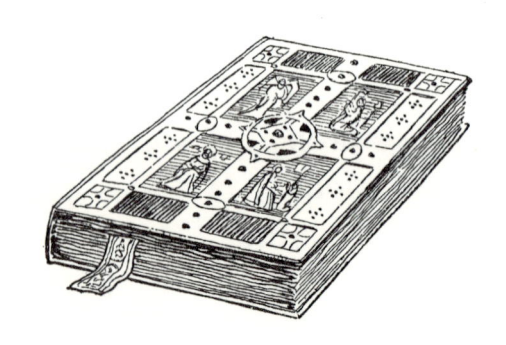

THE KING
and
THE ARCHBISHOP

"LONG live the King! Long live Henry of Anjou!" cried the people of London, as their new King rode by on his way to Westminster Abbey. The bells rang out to welcome him and everyone hoped that Henry II would be a strong ruler. For many years there had been cruel wars between the barons, and the people knew that only a good king could bring peace.

Henry was twenty-two years old. He was handsome, tough, and as full of energy as his great-grandfather, William the Conqueror. He had the same furious temper that all men feared, but he made up his mind to rule well.

He set to work at once to break the power of the barons.

"You must pull down your castles and live in houses," he ordered them. "All foreign soldiers must go home. You shall not keep private armies, nor shall you torture and kill my people."

The barons did not like these orders, but Henry forced them to obey. They called him "The Lawgiver," and they said that he worked so hard that he never sat down, except to eat.

To help him in his work, he chose a clever young churchman, who was not a noble but the son of a rich merchant. His name was Thomas Becket. Henry liked him very much, and they went everywhere together. The two friends worked hard to rule the country but they also enjoyed hunting and hawking.

Though the nobles hated Becket, Henry made him his Chancellor, the greatest man in the Kingdom. He gave him splendid presents of land, houses, and money. Becket lived like a prince, and at his great banquets, the guests were served from plates of silver and gold. Even the serving-men were dressed in magnificent uniforms.

Once Becket went to visit the King of France, and the people came out of their

*King Henry and Thomas Becket
hawking together*

houses to watch the glittering procession of soldiers, horses and laden wagons.

"Who is this great person?" they asked.

"The Chancellor of England," said a passing soldier.

"What can the King be like, if his Chancellor is so splendid?" the astonished bystanders asked.

When Henry had broken the power of the barons, he made up his mind that he would control the clergy as well. At this time, everyone in Europe belonged to the

Catholic Church. The Pope, in Rome, who was Head of the Church, was obeyed by all Christians, even by kings and princes.

In England, the bishops and abbots were very powerful. They said that priests and clergymen should have different laws from the rest of the people. If a priest did wrong, he was tried by the Bishop's Court, and his punishment was not very heavy. He might have a whipping, or he might be sent on a pilgrimage to a holy place.

Henry wanted good laws for all his people, and he knew that many wicked men called themselves clergy to escape punishment. Any rogue who worked on an abbot's land or anyone who could mumble a Latin prayer, could not be tried in the King's Court for a crime.

One day, Henry strode joyfully into Becket's rich London house.

"Thomas," he cried, "good news! The old Archbishop of Canterbury is dead, and I shall ask the Pope to put you in his place."

"No, my Lord King," replied Becket quietly, "not that, I beg you."

The Archbishop of Canterbury blesses the poor

"You shall not say 'No' to me, my Thomas," said Henry; "why should you not be Archbishop of Canterbury?"

"Because," said Becket, "I serve you as my lord and master, but if you make me head of the Church, I must serve the Church as my master. If that should happen, we should no longer be friends."

Henry would not listen. He made Becket Archbishop of Canterbury because he needed help. He thought the new archbishop would order the priests to obey the king.

But a strange and wonderful thing

happened. Thomas Becket, the richest, proudest man in England, put away his gorgeous clothes and put on the dark robe of a Canterbury monk. He gave up his lands and rich houses, the hunting and the banquets he had loved. He even gave up being Chancellor. Instead, he tried to serve God and the Church with all his heart. He went to mass at midnight, and daily prayers in the cathedral. Every day he blessed the poor and washed the feet of beggars and pilgrims.

Henry's anger was terrible. Becket refused everything the King commanded. The quarrel between them grew so fierce that the Archbishop had to flee to France in fear for his life, and Henry ruled alone.

After six years, Henry realised that he must not anger the Pope any longer. He went to France to ask Becket to come back. It seemed as if they were friends again, but men noticed that they did not give each other the kiss of peace when they met.

As soon as he landed at Sandwich, Becket said that he would punish the bishops who had obeyed Henry while he

King Henry flies into a terrible rage

was away. Then he set out for Canterbury. All along the way, people knelt at the roadside to ask his blessing. In the city, he was met by crowds singing psalms of praise, and as he entered the great cathedral, his pale face shone with happiness.

"Lord Archbishop," cried the joyful monks, "Christ has brought you back. Christ is King today!"

But in Normandy, a messenger brought Henry news that Becket was about to punish the bishops who had obeyed the King. He flew into one of his terrible rages. For a while he could not speak, but hurled himself up and down the Hall in fury. At last, he burst out:

"What idle coward knaves sit at my table, that they let their lord and king be mocked by a low-born priest!"

Without a word, four knights, Richard, William, Reginald, and Hugh, left the Hall and took ship for England. They went to the home of Sir Ranulf de Broc, a bitter enemy of Becket, where they collected some men-at-arms. They reached Canterbury just as the Archbishop was sitting down to his dinner. They burst into his room with curses, telling him to swear to obey the King in all things or to leave the kingdom.

"I have not come back to flee again," said Becket calmly. "Ye need not curse. Go, for here I stay, and here ye may find me."

The four knights went away, but they came back to the cathedral at night. They were dressed in armour and they carried drawn swords. The trembling monks hurried Becket towards the altar for safety. Then they tried to bolt the great door of the church.

"No," said the Archbishop, "do not make the house of God into a fortress."

Suddenly, into the dark cathedral clattered the knights, shouting:

"Where is Becket, traitor to the King?"

The answer came:

"Lo, I am here, no traitor but a priest of God."

The four knights rushed towards him. They wounded the crossbearer and tried to drag the archbishop outside. He clung to a pillar, until they struck him down to the stone floor of the cathedral. Then they rushed away into the darkness, to escape from the city before daybreak.

When the news became known, all Europe was filled with horror at the murder of an archbishop on holy ground. Henry shut himself away in his room for three days, weeping and praying aloud for forgiveness for his angry words. At last he obtained pardon from the Pope. He showed his sorrow by walking barefoot into Canterbury to pray at the Saint's tomb, while monks lashed his bare back with knotted ropes.

So the name of Thomas Becket, the proud, obstinate priest, became the most famous and best loved in England. Miracles were worked at his jewelled and gleaming shrine. For hundreds of years, pilgrims from all over Europe made their way to pray at the tomb of the " holy, blissful martyr," Saint Thomas of Canterbury.

RICHARD THE LION-HEART
and the Crusaders

IN the year 1187, all Europe was shocked by the news that Jerusalem had been captured by the Saracens, led by Saladin.

Kings, princes and dukes began to gather their armies for a Crusade to win back the Holy Land.

Richard I, newly-crowned King of England, sold castles, lands, and farms to raise money for the great adventure. He was not only strong and brave, but he was generous of heart and quick to ask pardon for his fierce temper. Already his people and his soldiers regarded him as a hero.

When his splendid army was ready, Richard sent for his old friend, William Longchamp.

"I leave England in your keeping, William," he said, "but set a careful watch on that fox, my brother John, lest he try to steal my kingdom."

Wearing the Cross on their surcoats and on their shields, the Crusaders set sail for the Holy Land. After many adventures, they reached the important town of Acre.

For two years, Philip, King of France, and Duke Leopold of Austria had been trying to capture the town, but all their efforts had been in vain. The Crusaders began to think that Richard would never come.

When Richard landed, he was greeted with joy, and he soon put new heart into the tired soldiers. Siege-towers and battering-rams were brought up, and fresh attacks were made. Richard offered a reward for every stone pulled from the walls. He himself was always in the thick of the fighting.

Then Richard fell ill, but he ordered his pages to carry him from his tent and set him down near the walls. Propped up on silken pillows, he directed the attacks and fired at the enemy with a cross-bow.

At last, Acre was captured, and Richard led the way into the town. His deeds had won him the name of " Lion-heart."

Now the Crusaders could make ready

Richard, who is ill, fights on

for the march to Jerusalem. But quarrels broke out between the leaders. Philip of France, a cold and crafty man, was jealous of Richard's fame, and also of his fine army.

"The kitchen-boys in Richard's army eat better food than Philip's own cup-bearer," the soldiers jeered.

Philip decided to go home. He was secretly plotting with Prince John to share Richard's lands in England and France.

Some English soldiers pulled down the flag of Austria from the walls, and trampled it in the mud. Vowing to have his revenge one day, Duke Leopold also returned to his own country.

Richard set out at the head of the Crusaders on the long, difficult march to Jerusalem. The knights in heavy armour advanced slowly in the burning heat, yet at night the desert was bitterly cold. Many fell ill from fever. All were tortured by thirst, for the enemy destroyed many of the wells along the way.

As the Crusaders struggled forward, Saracens and Bedouins attacked them again and again, darting from the hills on swift ponies. In these constant battles, even the Saracens marvelled at Richard's strength and courage.

Each night, when the army rested, the King went through the camp to cheer and comfort his weary, fever-stricken men. The Royal Herald sounded his trumpet and cried out:

"Help us! Help us! Holy Sepulchre!"

Stretching out their arms towards the Holy City, the knights repeated the cry.

But as they drew near Jerusalem, they became still weaker from their wounds and suffering. Richard knew that his army

The Crusaders struggle on to Jerusalem

was no longer strong enough to besiege and capture the city.

Suddenly an outrider dashed back to tell the King that he had seen the domes and towers of Jerusalem gleaming in the distance. But Richard groaned, for he knew that it was too late.

"Oh, let me not see that sight," he cried. "Lord, since I cannot reach Thy city, my eyes shall not look upon it."

"But, my lord King," said the rider, "we are almost there."

"Nay," replied Richard sadly, "we are too faint, too weak to go forward another step. Saladin lies in wait for us. I will go on as a common soldier, but I will not lead my army to certain destruction."

With heavy hearts, the Crusaders turned back towards Acre. Richard learned that his brother John had taken his kingdom, and he knew that he must return to England.

He vowed to come again to capture Jerusalem. Before leaving, he made a truce with Saladin, who promised to allow Christian pilgrims to visit the Holy Places without harm. Saladin sent him a message, saying,

"If ever I must surrender Jerusalem, it shall be only to you, prince of enemies."

Richard wept as his ship set sail for England, but further troubles lay in wait for him. The ship was wrecked, and he was forced ashore. Soon, he found that he was in the land of his enemy, Duke Leopold of Austria.

The Lion-heart disguised himself as a

Saladin sends a message to Richard

merchant and started on foot towards England, with only one knight and a page for company.

They travelled for some miles and then they came to a town. Richard sent the

The King disguised as a merchant

page into the market to buy food, while he and the knight waited at a small inn.

In the market, the page bought some bread, and offered the baker a gold piece. The man looked at him closely.

"Who are you, boy?" he asked. "Where do you come from?"

"I am a scullion boy, good sir," answered the page.

"Scullions don't pay in gold, and here, what is this?" he cried, snatching a pair of gloves which the page had stuck carelessly in his belt. "Gloves, eh? Only the great ones of the world wear gloves."

"They belong to my master, Hugh, a rich merchant," cried the luckless boy.

"Rich merchant, bah! these are jewelled gloves, fit for a duke or even a king. Here, fetch the Mayor! Arrest this knave!"

The page was taken before the Mayor. He was beaten, but he would not tell the real name of his master. So they dragged him before Duke Leopold and tortured him until he confessed. Soldiers surrounded the inn and after a struggle, they captured Richard. In triumph, Leopold threw his enemy into prison.

Presently the Duke sold his royal prisoner to the Emperor of Germany, who, to please Philip of France, shut him up in a castle.

When the people of England learned that their King was held prisoner, they collected a vast sum of money for his ransom. Even though he had spent little time at home, they loved their warrior-king and hated his brother John.

At last Richard was ransomed and set free. He set out for England. Philip of France sent a message to John:

"Look to yourself! The great Devil himself is unchained."

John fled to France, but Richard, always generous, forgave his wicked brother.

"I forgive him," he said, "and I hope I shall soon forget his deeds. I know he will soon forget my pardon."

Richard did not stay long in England. He quickly collected an army and went off to fight Philip for the lands he had taken. He was killed by an arrow when besieging a castle, and John, the worst of men, became King of England.

The Welsh Prince,
LLEWELYN

HUGH, the shepherd boy, came running into his village, just as the people were leaving church.

"The Welsh are coming!" he cried, pointing towards the hills.

As they looked, the startled villagers could see smoke rising in the distance. That meant that a farmstead was already in flames.

The church bell rang out, warning the village people, who rounded up their cattle and sheep and drove them towards a nearby castle. This castle was one of many which the Normans had built to protect their English lands from the Welsh tribesmen. The soldiers of the castle were fighting some miles away, but the frightened villagers knew that the thick walls and heavy gates would shelter them.

Within an hour, the Welsh raiders were in the village, carrying off everything of value, and setting fire to the wooden huts. They were dark, wild-looking men, armed with swords and round shields. Most were on foot, but a few rode shaggy ponies.

Presently they went away, shaking their fists at the castle and shouting threats in their own Celtic language. The village was a smoking ruin.

All along the border between England and Wales, fighting, killing and burning were taking place. Llewelyn, prince of North Wales, was laying waste the countryside.

In Henry III's reign, Llewelyn was the greatest of the Welsh chieftains. He was a dark, sturdy man of enormous strength. He was so skilled in mountain-fighting that the English never knew where he would appear next.

After he had become master of North Wales, Llewelyn marched into South Wales.

The bards sing on the banks of the Wye

He made all the Welsh barons kneel to him in homage.

Then he called a meeting of chiefs on the banks of the river Wye. First, the bards played their harps and sang songs about Welsh heroes of ancient times. Then a bard sang of the great deeds of Llewelyn, son of Griffith. He told how, one day, a Welsh prince would be crowned King in London.

Llewelyn stood up and began to speak.

" My brothers," he said, " some of you do not wish to have me for your overlord. But if we all join together, we can win freedom for Wales.

" Now is the time to strike at the English. Too long have they called themselves our overlords. Too long have they driven us back into the mountains, and too long have they ruled our lands.

" Now they are weak. King Henry is at war with his barons. Let us take our chance ! Let us drive the English out of Wales, and take back the land of our fathers ! "

Soon, Llewelyn became prince of all Wales. The English king was too busy fighting his own barons to heed the troubles on his borders. Llewelyn was generous to his friends and fearless of his enemies. He laughed when the Archbishop of Canterbury threatened to excommunicate him for his conquests. He pushed on to the gates of Chester. Then, the Pope himself ordered him to stop seizing the English lands.

Welsh raiders on the English border

When Henry III died, his warrior son became Edward I. Llewelyn was ordered to go to the coronation of the English king. He refused scornfully.

" Shall I," he asked, " prince of all Wales, lord of twelve castles and a score of barons, kneel to an English king ? "

But Edward I was a great soldier. He made up his mind to stamp out this trouble along his borders by making Wales part of his kingdom. He began to make careful plans.

First, he invaded Wales with three armies, striking at the south, the centre,

Edward's army marching down the forest road

and the north, which was the hardest part of Wales to conquer.

Next, Edward ordered his ships from the Cinque Ports to sail up and down the coast, to cut off Anglesey from the mainland. Anglesey was the island which supplied Llewelyn with corn for his army.

Then Edward himself advanced into North Wales from Chester. When the Welsh kept attacking him from a great forest, he cut a wide road straight through it, so that his soldiers could march quickly. Llewelyn retreated to the mountains

Llewelyn does homage to Edward before Parliament

round Snowdon, knowing that the English could not follow him through that wild country. But Edward did not try. He placed strong forces of soldiers at the ends of the narrow valleys, so that no one could escape.

When the winter came, cold and hunger forced Llewelyn to come down from the mountains and surrender.

Edward said to his prisoner:

" Llewelyn, son of Griffith, I shall treat you well. You shall hand over all your prisoners and all the land you have taken from my subjects. I will leave you to be

Prince of North Wales, and five barons will do you homage.

"But first you shall do homage to me as your overlord."

Llewelyn agreed that he would do all these things. Edward took him to London and made him do homage before Parliament, so that all men should know that the English King was his overlord.

When he went back to Wales, Llewelyn soon grew tired of the bullying ways of the English barons, who were not as wise as their royal master. With his brother David he planned to revolt and secretly they gathered an army together.

At Easter they suddenly attacked and captured three castles in North Wales. Llewelyn was welcomed joyfully everywhere, and South Wales joined in the revolt.

Edward was furious.

"Is this how that princeling repays my kindness?" he stormed. "I will break him once and for all time. He and his turncoat brother shall have no rest until their heads stand on London Bridge."

Once more he entered Wales with an

Llewelyn is killed in a forest clearing

army. Once more Llewelyn retreated to the mountains of Snowdon. Then, as winter came on, he vowed not to be trapped again by hunger. With a small band of followers, he slipped through the English lines at night, and escaped into Central Wales.

Next day, as he was travelling south to join his friends, he heard the clash of swords through the woods. He hurried towards this skirmish between English and Welsh soldiers. As he entered a clearing, he ran full tilt into a man-at-arms, who killed him instantly.

At the death of their great leader, the

Welsh lost heart. David was captured and executed; and Edward speedily conquered the whole country.

After the fighting, Edward's first son was born at Carnarvon Castle. The wise English king summoned all the Welsh chieftains to a meeting at the castle. There he said to them:

"I will give you a prince of your own, one born in Wales, who cannot speak a word of English and who has never done harm to man, woman or child."

Then the royal nurse brought in the baby prince and held him up for all to see. The jest pleased the Welsh people, for they knew that Edward was promising peace between the two countries. Later, the King made his son Prince of Wales, and ever since it has been the custom for the eldest son of the King of England to take the title of Prince of Wales.

ROBERT THE BRUCE of Scotland

AFTER he had subdued Wales, Edward I made himself master of Scotland. At this time there was living at his Court a young Scottish noble named Robert Bruce who had taken no part in the fighting against the English.

But when Bruce saw William Wallace, heroic leader of the Scots, put to death in London, he was filled with angry determination to free his country from the English overlords.

He knew that it would not be easy to leave the Court, but he managed to send a message to Red Comyn, one of the Scottish leaders, to make a secret arrangement that they should work together for Scotland's freedom.

However, Red Comyn, jealous perhaps that Bruce had a claim to the throne of Scotland, informed Edward of the secret plan.

The English king at once ordered the arrest of Bruce. Fortunately a good friend overheard this order. He dared not write a letter, so as a warning he sent Bruce a gift of a pair of spurs and twelve silver pennies.

Bruce was at supper when the gift arrived. He looked at it for a while, then called his trusty servant, and said:

"Saddle three good horses. We ride to Scotland tonight, with your brother Will."

"Tonight, my lord?"

"Tonight. These spurs must mean that I should ride with speed. The pennies mean there is no time to collect money. Let us away."

With his faithful servants, Bruce left London, riding hard for the north. As they came near to the Border, they met a servant wearing the badge of Red Comyn.

"What business takes you on this road?" asked Bruce.

"I bear letters from my master to the King of England," replied the servant.

Bruce forced him to hand over the letters. He broke the seals and read Comyn's message to King Edward. "Robert Bruce

Bruce rides hard for the north

should be put to death," he read in the letter.

Mad with rage, Bruce rode to Dumfries, where he found Comyn in church. Striding up to him, he called him villain and traitor. A furious quarrel broke out, and Bruce, forgetting he was in church, stabbed Red Comyn with his dagger.

Though he was horrified at his deed,

Bruce acted boldly. He gathered his friends around him and had himself crowned King of Scotland at Scone Abbey. But there was no stone of Destiny, no crown, no robes, for Edward had carried them all away. Even the Earl of Fife, who alone of the Scottish nobles had the right to crown the King, was a prisoner.

Bruce had a plain gold crown made, and the Earl of Fife's sister, the brave Countess of Buchan, placed it on his head.

Once more there was a King of Scotland, but a long struggle lay ahead before he won his kingdom. Edward vowed that he would not rest until Bruce was taken. An English army scattered the Scots and Bruce fled to the hills.

His Queen, with the Countess of Buchan and a few nobles, followed him. For months they lived in wild, lonely places, hiding in caves and little huts. They fished and hunted, but they were often cold and hungry.

When winter came on, Bruce sent his ladies for safety to his brother Nigel at Kildrummie Castle. But they were captured and Nigel was put to death. The

Bruce and his Queen and his nobles in a mountain cave

gallant, beautiful Countess of Buchan was kept in a cage at Berwick Castle.

Further troubles befell Bruce. Two of his brothers were captured and executed, and he himself had many narrow escapes.

At last he had no more than sixty men left. They were hunted from place to place in the mountains, and tracked by enemies and bloodhounds. But Bruce never lost heart or gave up the struggle. Slowly, his brave deeds brought him fresh followers and he began to make attacks on the English.

Then King Edward decided he himself must go to Scotland, to put an end to the trouble. He was old now, and so ill that he could neither march nor ride. But the tough old warrior was carried in a litter at the head of his army. When he drew near to Scotland, he knew that he was dying. He called for his son, Prince Edward, who came to his tent.

"My son," said the old king, "I leave my task to you. Swear to me that you will never cease this war until Scotland is conquered. Carry my bones in front of the army until the task is done."

The prince swore by the holy saints that he would do as his father wished. But as soon as his father died, Edward broke his promise. He sent the body of the old king to be buried at Westminster. Soon afterwards, he himself returned to London to be crowned Edward II.

Edward was weak and idle, so Bruce took his chance. He and his men captured castle after castle. Soon, only Stirling Castle was left to the English. The Governor of the Castle was so hard pressed that he promised to surrender unless help came by Midsummer Day. This made

Bruce and his army arrive at Stirling Castle

even Edward II stir himself. He raised a huge army and marched to Stirling.

Bruce drew up his army in a strong position near the castle. There was a steep slope on one side and a stream or burn, called the Bannock, on the other. In front of his army, he made his men dig holes. Twigs and turf were laid over the holes, to make it look as if the ground was flat and solid. Sharp spikes were stuck into the ground to hinder the horses.

The great English host, with its archers, banners, and knights in gleaming armour, drew near and halted. Bruce went along the front rank of his army to see that all was well. He was riding a brown pony, and armed only with a battle-axe.

Suddenly a knight dashed from the English ranks. He was Sir Henry de Bohun, who hoped to win glory by killing the Scottish king. In full armour, and with levelled spear, he thundered towards Bruce, as both armies watched breathlessly. When Bohun's spear was almost upon him, Bruce suddenly wheeled his pony aside. He rose in his stirrups and, as Bohun charged past, brought his axe crashing down upon the knight's head. The steel helmet was split in two by the mighty blow, and Bohun fell dead. Cheer upon cheer burst from the Scottish ranks, but Bruce only said to his nobles, as he rode away:

"I have broken my good axe."

Early next morning the English attacked. At first, the archers did great damage to the Scottish spearmen, until horsemen rode down the archers from one side. Then the terrible English cavalry, on great warhorses, rode to the charge. But Bruce's position did not allow them to spread out. The English were crowded in

The death of De Bohun

thick masses, with hardly room to swing their swords.

As the first horses stumbled into the hidden holes, others, following, crashed into them in wild confusion. Knights in heavy armour could not rise from the ground. Terrified horses were rearing and plunging, while fresh waves of cavalry rode into the struggling mass. The Scots rushed down upon them and the battle became a furious slaughter.

The English had begun to waver, when they saw a fresh army come racing over the hill towards them. This new army was really only the servants and camp-followers, who, tired of watching, came rushing down

English horses plunging into the pits at Bannockburn

with clubs and knives, and with banners made of sheets tied to poles. The English lost heart and fled.

The battle of Bannockburn, the greatest English defeat for centuries, brought English rule of Scotland to an end. Scotland was free; Robert the Bruce was king of all his country at last, and the great soldier now became a wise ruler of his people.

QUEEN PHILIPPA
and the men of Calais

JUST over six hundred years ago, Edward III was King of England. He was a famous soldier who liked fighting better than ruling his country peacefully.

Edward wanted the throne of France as well as England, so he crossed the Channel with an army of longbowmen and knights to fight King Philip. With them was his eldest son, soon to be known as the Black Prince.

Edward left England in the care of his wife, Philippa, who was beautiful and generous. But as soon as the English army had gone, the King of Scotland decided that it was an excellent time to attack the North of England.

Queen Philippa was reading in her apartment at Windsor Castle when a noble entered and bowed.

" My lady Queen," he said, " news from the North ! David of Scotland has attacked your realm. He is laying waste the countryside with fire and the sword. What shall be done ? "

" Done, my lord ? " answered the Queen calmly. " Why, drive him back again."

" But, my lady," said the noble, " do you forget ? King Edward is in France. We have no army or leader."

The Queen rose.

" England is filled with good men who will fight for their Queen," she said.

Quickly she collected an army and marched north. She found the Scots at Durham and, at Neville's Cross, her soldiers fought so fiercely that they put the enemy to flight and captured King David. Philippa brought him back to London where he was sent to the Tower. Then

Queen Philippa at the head of her army

she asked for news of her husband and son.

It was good news. The English army had won a great victory at Crecy, and her fifteen-years-old son had been made a knight after the battle. Edward had marched on to capture the important town of Calais, which stands on the French coast, opposite Dover. When Queen Philippa heard this news, she took ship and crossed the Channel to join her husband in the English camp.

In those days, it was far from easy to capture a town. The defenders, from behind strong walls, could watch the enemy advance. They could fire at them from the arrow-slits without being seen. When battering-rams and scaling-ladders were brought up, they could hurl down stones and boiling lead on to the heads of the attackers. The walls of Calais were so strong that it would cost many English lives to capture the town.

So Edward made up his mind to surround Calais, and to starve its people into surrender. He placed his army all round the town, so that no one could enter or leave it. No food could reach the citizens and soldiers.

At first, the people of Calais did not worry. They had big stores of food; King Philip would come to their aid and his ships would bring food by sea.

But Edward's fleet chased away the French ships. Philip came near, but he found the English army so strong that he dared not risk a battle. The people of Calais began to use up their stores.

Weeks and months passed. The shops became empty, for there was no food left to buy. The people became pale and weak, but still they would not surrender. When every scrap of food had gone, they were forced to eat dogs and rats. The English king grew more and more angry with the brave people who had kept him waiting for so long.

At last, the citizens became so weak that the Governor of Calais knew they could hold out no longer. He sent one of the soldiers up on to the walls with a white flag. This was a sign that he would surrender.

"No!" thundered the angry king

King Edward was in his striped tent when Sir Walter Manny, one of his bravest knights, came back from his visit to the Governor of the starving town.

"Sire," said Sir Walter, "the Governor bids me to say that Calais is yours, if you will let its people go free."

"Upon my life, no!" thundered the angry king. "For a year they have kept us waiting. They shall die, every man, woman, and child. Then France shall know the fate of a town which will not open its gates to my army."

Sir Walter and the knights tried to make the king change his mind, saying:

"The French will kill every Englishman they capture."

"Remember, sire," said Sir Walter, "they have fought well. Men hold you for a gallant knight. Will you let them call you a butcher of women and children?"

The angry king turned away, pacing up and down. Then he said:

"Tell them to send six of their chief townsmen, bare-footed, and clad only in their shirts, with ropes around their necks. Let them bring me the key of Calais, and I will do to them as I please. Then may the rest go free."

The great bell of Calais clanged, and the townsfolk, thin and hollow-cheeked, gathered in the market square. Their Governor told them of the English king's reply. There was silence. How could they find six wealthy men ready to die for all the others?

Eustace, the richest merchant of the town, stepped forward.

"'Tis better for six to die, than all the town," he said. "I have had a long life and I will gladly go."

*Ready for death, the merchants take the key
of Calais to the English camp*

John Daire, cloth merchant, stepped forward to his side, then Peter Wesant and his brother, then two more of the aldermen.

Without a word, the six took off their velvet robes and their shoes. They stood barefoot, dressed only in long linen shirts, as the ropes were put round their necks. Then the gates were opened and the six burghers walked slowly across to the

"For the love I bear you, I cannot refuse you"

English camp, carrying the great iron key of Calais.

The soldiers watched silently as the six men were taken to the King's tent. There they knelt down, and Eustace offered Edward the key of their town. The King took it.

"Now, hang them in front of the walls, before the eyes of their stubborn townsfolk," he said.

At that moment, Queen Philippa entered the tent. She knelt at the King's feet, and looked up at him, weeping.

"My lord and husband," she said, "for you, I have held your kingdom. I have crossed the sea to you in great peril. But I have asked no reward. Now, I beg you on my knees, to grant me one wish, for love of the Son of God. Be merciful to these six men of Calais."

The angry King looked at her for a while; then he sighed, and said:

"Ah, lady, I wish at this moment that you were far from here. But, for the love I bear you, I cannot refuse you. Take them, and do with them as you please."

Joyfully, the Queen rose and led the six burghers from the tent. Her servants fetched clothes and food for them. Later, she sent them back to their homes, with gifts of food for the hungry townspeople. In the market square, they were welcomed with joy and wonder.

"We have given the key of Calais to the English King," said Eustace, "but from Queen Philippa we have had great mercy."

WAT TYLER
and the Boy-King, Richard II

WHEN Edward III died, his son the gallant Black Prince was already dead, so the prince's son, a boy of eleven, was crowned King Richard II. Because Richard was too young to reign, his uncle, John of Gaunt, ruled England. The people hated him.

England was an unhappy land at this time. Money was needed for the French wars and taxes fell heavily upon the poor.

In the country, the peasants had very low wages and many had to work two or three days every week on the land of the lord of the manor. They also had to pay him money at certain times. They were called serfs or villeins, and they were not even allowed to leave their village without permission.

Richard II and the rebels

About this time, a poor priest, named John Ball, went round the country preaching. On Sundays, as the people were coming out of church, they would see him standing on the green by the village cross.

"My good friends," John Ball would say, "why should there be lords and masters? God made us all, but they dress in velvets and silks, yet we have only rags. They have fine castles and palaces, yet we have only a draughty cott. God made Adam and Eve. He did not make lords and gentlemen. So I say to you:

When Adam delved and Eve span,
Who was then the gentleman?"

The peasants often said this little rhyme among themselves. They hated being serfs, and they loved fearless John Ball. But the Archbishop of Canterbury put him into prison for stirring up trouble.

One summer day in 1381 a group of peasants stood outside the ale-house of a village in Kent. They were grumbling about the Poll-tax, which everyone had to pay. Even the poorest family had to pay between fourpence and a shilling, which

"When Adam delved and Eve span..."

was a great deal of money for a poor man. Suddenly, a neighbour came running breathlessly across the green.

"What news, John Carter?" they asked.

"Great news!" he cried. "Over the hill past Hartdown, the tax-collectors have been beaten and ducked in the river. Some say Wat Tyler killed one of the thieving dogs with his hammer. All men are marching to Maidstone with clubs and bows!"

"To Maidstone? What for? Tell us, man, speak up." More and more villagers crowded round and others came running from the fields.

"Wat Tyler says arm yourselves and march to Maidstone Prison to set John Ball free. He says he will lead all true men to London to tell the young king our troubles."

"Hurrah!" roared the crowd, "to Maidstone! To London! Tell the King to overthrow the lords!"

They rushed off to collect scythes and clubs, while those who had served in the wars brought out their bows and rusty swords. Soon they were clattering out of the village towards Maidstone. Some stayed to beat the lord's bailiff and to burn the Manor rolls which showed every man's duties and debts.

John Ball was set free. Rochester Castle was captured. Canterbury was seized, and men of Essex, Kent, Surrey, St Albans, and Norwich were marching to London.

They gathered in a great camp on the open moor called Blackheath. Across the river was London, where the lords and merchants put up their shutters in fear and trembling. The young king and his nobles shut themselves in the Tower.

There was only one bridge across the Thames in those days. It was London Bridge, one of the wonders of the world. A highway ran between a double row of shops and houses, right across the river, but the last arch was a drawbridge. This had been pulled up by order of the Lord Mayor. How could the rebels cross?

They had friends in the city, poor men like themselves, wild apprentice boys and even a few aldermen. These friends lowered the drawbridge and the great mob of peasants poured across into London.

At first they stood and gaped with open mouths at the huge city, the endless streets and alleys, the great houses and churches. Wat Tyler told them to steal nothing, for they were true men, come to talk to the king.

Suddenly they caught sight of Savoy Palace, the magnificent home of John of Gaunt. It was the richest house in England. With a roar, the crowd burst in and began flinging its beautiful furniture and treasures into the street, and into the river. Then they set it on fire.

The drawbridge is lowered for the angry mob

Next day, the young king and his barons rode out from the Tower and met the peasants in Mile End fields, outside the city. There they listened to the country folk and promised that no one should be a serf again, and that everyone should be pardoned. These promises so pleased the peasants, that many of them at once started to go home.

But while they were talking, some of the

The peasants break into the Tower

mob broke into the Tower. They dragged the Archbishop from his prayers and cruelly killed him and the Lord Treasurer. Then they tore through the streets, killing, burning, and stealing.

Next day, there was another meeting, but this time the nobles wore armour under their robes and had daggers in their belts. They met at Smithfield, a market-place, just outside the walls. Wat Tyler had drawn his men up in ranks and they gave a cheer when they saw the boy-king come riding up, with his nobles and the Lord Mayor.

Wat Tyler cantered his horse forward

to meet the royal party. He shook hands with the king and spoke to him roughly.

"We are all true Commons here, and I am captain," he boasted. "Lords and masters—bah!"

One lord nearby cried out:

"I know you, Wat Tyler, for the biggest rogue and thief in Kent!"

This made Wat Tyler so angry that he drew his dagger. The Lord Mayor, Walworth, at once struck him down with his sword. Wat Tyler's horse turned and galloped back, dragging his lifeless body. A great shout went up:

"They have killed our captain!"

And a thousand bows were bent at the king.

Then Richard did the bravest thing in his life. He spurred his horse and rode out into the open alone, crying:

"Will you shoot your King? I will be your captain and leader. Follow me, good sirs!"

With a cheer, the ranks parted, and they followed the boy out to the fields beyond the city.

There Richard told them that all the promises would be kept if they went home. So, believing their brave young king, the men of Kent, and Essex, and Surrey, turned and made their way back to their homes.

Richard did not keep his word. With his barons, judges, and soldiers, he travelled through the countryside, hanging the rebel leaders at every cross-road and town-square. All who had made the great march to Blackheath were punished. John Ball himself was captured and executed.

"Serfs you are and serfs you shall remain," said the King. But, in time, the country folk were better treated, for the lords never forgot John Ball, Wat Tyler, and the Peasants' Revolt of 1381.

GEOFFREY CHAUCER
and "The Canterbury Tales"

THE Tabard Inn, at Southwark in South London, was crowded. All day visitors had been arriving. The stable boys were kept busy fetching water and hay for the horses. The serving maids hurried to bring ale and meat from the kitchen. By evening, a whole company of more than twenty persons was gathered in the big room of the inn.

The landlord of the inn, a great, red-faced man with a loud voice, stood beaming round at his company. He looked and sounded as happy as a schoolboy, for he was starting a holiday the very next day, leaving the inn in care of his stout wife, Mistress Joan.

His holiday was really a journey to

Canterbury, fifty-five miles away, where he would say his prayers at the tomb of Saint Thomas, and leave a gift at the shrine. Everyone in England tried to go as a pilgrim to Canterbury, at least once in his life, and the landlord of the Tabard had been twice already.

Of course he would not go alone; that would be very foolish in days when the woods on each side of the dusty road were full of robbers. He was going this time as leader and guide of the company of pilgrims, who were now gathered round the fire of his inn.

Clapping his hands for silence, the landlord stepped forward.

" My good friends," he began, " are you well served ? Have you ale in your pot ? Boy, fetch my lady Prioress a glass of our best wine.

" Now, my friends, tomorrow we set out for Canterbury. In truth, we go to ask the Holy Saint to forgive us our sins, but let us be merry on the way. 'Tis a long journey and slow, if we do not know how to pass the time merrily. But, listen well ;

The Pilgrims at the inn

The pilgrims riding across the Downs in the Spring

every man and woman loves a good tale that is well told. What think you of this plan of mine?"

He went on to explain that each pilgrim in turn should tell two stories on the way to Canterbury, and two more on the way home. The teller of the best tale should be rewarded with a splendid dinner.

Next morning, the pilgrims started out

on the road to Canterbury. There were men and women of every kind in the company—a brave, gentle knight who had fought on a Crusade ; his squire, a rosy, handsome lad ; an honest yeoman ; a cook ; a fat friar who was better at begging than praying ; a dainty Prioress ; a poor scholar from Oxford on a bony horse ; a doctor who was rather a fraud ; a poor parson who was truly good ; one or two rascals ; a miller ; a tax-collector ; a sailor ; a nun ; a fat, cheerful lady known as the Wife of Bath ; and a man with twinkling eyes and a little pointed beard.

This last man was Geoffrey Chaucer, a person of some importance at the King's Court, and also a poet and lover of good stories. He had made up his mind to join this company of pilgrims on the way to Canterbury. The landlord, however, did not think much of him :

" Who are you ? " he roared in his great voice, " don't look down on the ground as if you were searching for a hare or a rabbit. There's no need to be shy ; come on, my lad, cheer up, and let us have

Chaucer writing the Canterbury Tales

your tale. Here he is, friends, he's a bit shy, but he's nearly as fat round the middle as I am!"

Chaucer began his tale in the sing-song rhyme that was the fashion of the time, but the landlord soon had enough of it.

"Good sir," he grumbled, "this rhyming stuff's a waste of time. If you can't do better than that, let us have another's story in your place."

So Chaucer fell back and let someone else tell a tale. But he went on listening and remembering the people who rode in twos and threes along the rutted way to

Canterbury. When the pilgrimage was over, he went home and wrote down, not only some of the stories, but, best of all, a very clever and funny description of the pilgrims themselves. He never finished all the tales, so we do not know who won the splendid dinner, but his famous book, " The Canterbury Tales " has been read for over 500 years since that journey to Canterbury.

Geoffrey Chaucer was always lucky; his father was a rich wine merchant of London, so young Geoffrey was able to go to one of the old grammar schools of the city. Then he became a page in the household of a royal prince, Lionel, Duke of Clarence, who greatly liked his clever, merry page, and took him on his travels about the country.

At this time, the Hundred Years' War was still dragging on, and, as a squire, Geoffrey went to France in the Prince of Wales's force. It was not a very glorious campaign, for provisions were short, the weather bad, and the enemy would not give battle. Young Chaucer had one ad-

Young Chaucer amusing his friends at school

venture; he was riding ahead with a small troop to scout the land, when his party was surrounded by a strong French force and all were captured.

When Edward III learnt that this bright young squire was a prisoner, he paid a ransom of £16 (a large sum of money in those days) to have him set free.

This good fortune caused Chaucer to enter the King's service and he was made Yeoman of the King's Chamber. He had to look after the comfort of his royal master and to see that the servants, pages and Court messengers carried out their duties.

Chaucer in Italy

As he grew older, he was given more important work. He was sent on secret business for the King to France, Flanders, and Italy. We know he went to Genoa and Florence to arrange for Italian merchants to trade with London. Some of his secrets were so well kept that we still do not know the reason for his journeys. He was very happy in Italy, for he found a great love of poetry and stories among the people of that country.

Though he was a trusted messenger, Chaucer was also a merry, careless fellow. The King gave him many rewards for his services, but he was always short of money, for he loved books, good clothes, wine and feasting. As soon as Henry IV became King, Chaucer was granted a pension of 40 marks (worth about £600 now). But only a few days later, he had lost the paper giving permission to draw this money from the Treasury, and he had to ask for another copy!

Once, he was going from Westminster to the royal manor at Eltham, outside London, to pay the King's servants. Four robbers leapt at him from behind an oak tree, and snatched the bag containing £10 from his saddle. Feeling very cross, Chaucer rode back to Westminster.

obtained another bag of money and started out again to Eltham.

In the woods of New Cross, the same robber, Richard Brerelay, with three of his band, was watching the track which led from London. For the second time that day, they espied a well-dressed traveller approaching on a fine horse. As he drew level, the robbers sprang out at him with cudgels, knocked him from the saddle and this time made off with the horse as well as the money-bag. Poor Chaucer, robbed and bruised twice in one day, was left to find his way back on foot.

That evening, when, as was his custom, Chaucer was reading to the King, he made up a merry tale about his own sorry adventure with the robbers.

" Master Chaucer," laughed the King, " it seems that money can never stay long with you ! Find another messenger for Eltham, I cannot have the greatest poet in Europe cudgelled by the same knaves twice in one day."

HENRY V
at Agincourt

HENRY V was loved by his people more than any English King, except perhaps Alfred. Tall and strong, with dark, smooth hair and bright eyes, he seemed to be the perfect knight. He was brave, generous and kindly to everyone. Though he made it his rule to be polite to all men, he himself spoke little. He would listen carefully when his nobles spoke to him about taxes or the army, and then would either say, " It is impossible " or " It shall be done."

Henry sent a herald to the Dauphin, as the eldest son of the King of France was called, claiming the throne of France. But the Dauphin sent back a present of a barrel of tennis balls, which was his way of saying that he thought the English King was better at playing games than going to war. Henry laughed and said:

" He'd best beware, lest we turn them into cannon balls."

Then he began to gather an army together. Parliament voted him some large sums of money, so that he could offer his archers sixpence a day, which was more than a man could earn working on farmland. Soon he had the pick of the best bowmen in England. He promised them a good share of any booty that might be captured. But he made strict rules against the plundering and cruelty to women and children which were common in warfare.

When all was ready, Henry and his army set sail from Southampton and landed on the French coast. They at once laid siege to the strong town of Harfleur, using their three new cannons, which they nicknamed " The London," " The King's Daughter," and " The Messenger." Though they bombarded the fortress for weeks, the French held out and fought bravely. At last, the English captured the

Henry laughing at the tennis balls

town, but most of Henry's soldiers were weak from wounds and from the sickness which had broken out in camp.

This disease was so bad that Henry was in a difficult position. His army was no longer big enough to fight battles, but he did not want to go home after capturing only one French town, lest men should say he was afraid of the French. He decided to lead his men on the long march through France to Calais. This should show that Englishmen had no fear of the enemy. He sent the sick and wounded home by sea, then he gave the order:

"Straight to Calais!"

The little army of archers, foot-soldiers, and some mounted knights set out from Harfleur. As they marched, the French people fled before them, burning or hiding all the food. Soon they were so hungry that they were forced to eat berries and walnuts. The weather was cold and wet, but the soldiers were encouraged by their King, who shared the same hardships.

After several days, they reached the river Somme. But the bridges were broken down and a strong French force was camped on the far side. So Henry led his men several miles along the bank until they found a ford they could cross. Then once more they turned their faces towards Calais. But scouts, riding ahead, brought back the news that a big French army was advancing towards them, right in their line of march. What was to be done? Should they turn aside and try to avoid the enemy? What were the King's orders?

"Straight to Calais," was all that Henry answered.

He knew that his men were ragged and

The starving English army marching in the rain

hungry; he must fight or surrender, so he made up his mind to fight.

"Let every archer cut a six-foot stake from the woods, and sharpen both ends," he ordered.

When this had been done, he halted his army and calmly made ready for the battle. First, he listened carefully to the reports of his scouts. They told him that the French army, made up chiefly of knights in armour, was seven times as big as his own. They were camped across a valley between two woods, so they must attack him on a narrow front. He also learnt that they were spending the night feasting, and playing dice for the important prisoners they would capture next day.

The English had no food, but they passed the night resting and praying. Henry went among the soldiers bidding them to be of good cheer and to keep stout hearts. One of his knights looked round at the tiny army and turned to the King.

"In England, Sire, tomorrow is a holiday. I would we had one ten thousand of all the men who will do no work this day."

"Nay, Sir Walter," said the King, "I would not have one man more. If we win, there are few of us to share the glory. If we lose, England will not suffer a great loss."

During the night, it began to rain heavily, but the English archers covered their bowstrings to keep them from the wet. Next morning, Henry ordered the bowmen to stick their stakes in the ground, so that they slanted towards the enemy with each sharp point at the height of a horse's chest. Then each archer took off

King Henry cheers his men on the night before Agincourt

his left shoe to get a good grip on the wet earth with his bare toes, and the men-at-arms rolled up their ragged sleeves to have free play for their weapons.

Mounted on a small grey horse, Henry rode along the ranks ; over his armour he was wearing a loose coat with the leopards of England and the lilies of France, and, on his head, a magnificent gold crown round his helmet. The weary, hungry men raised a cheer for their hero.

"Today, lads," he cried, "God and our arms will bring us victory and great glory. Today, England shall pay no ransom for me!"

By this, the men knew that he would die rather than be taken prisoner. Then Henry dismounted and joined his soldiers. He had placed his archers first, with the sharp wooden stakes for protection. Behind the horsemen were men-at-arms on foot. In the woods on each side he placed mixed companies of archers and horsemen.

The French did not begin to attack, so Henry ordered:

"Banners advance!"

The little army went forward, and, at once, five thousand French knights thundered towards them. The English archers halted, their sharp stakes planted in the ground. When the French cavalry reached them, after floundering through the newly-ploughed earth, the stakes did their work well. Then, from behind them, the archers

*The French cavalry charge is broken by the
English stakes and arrows*

fired their terrible, yard-long arrows into the dense, struggling masses of horses and men. As fresh waves of cavalry charged, the English, rushing down from the woods, attacked their flanks.

When all their arrows had gone, the archers flung aside their bows, and bore down upon the enemy with swords. A furious struggle took place in the narrow valley, and the English line was almost broken. Prince Humphrey of Gloucester was struck down. Henry went into the thickest of the fight to defend his brother, and he himself was beaten to his knees by a tremendous blow from a French knight. His helmet saved him, and he continued fighting alongside his soldiers.

Then, for the last time, the English archers and horsemen charged from the woods at the French flanks. Terrible slaughter took place, and the battle was won. The enemy was completely defeated and hundreds of noble prisoners were taken, including two royal dukes.

When the fighting had ceased, Henry mounted his grey horse and rode slowly across the battle-field. A French herald was being led in as prisoner by an English foot-soldier.

King Henry rides in triumph through the streets of London

"The victory is yours, Sire," he said to the King.

"Nay, not mine," said Henry. "God gave us victory today. But, stay, herald, what tower is that?"

"That is the castle of Agincourt, Sire," replied the herald.

"Then men shall call this battle the fight at Agincourt," said King Henry.

Next day, the tired English army continued their march to Calais, taking with them the prisoners and captured banners. They crossed the sea to Dover, in a storm so fierce that the French knights said that they would rather fight another battle than face such another voyage.

England gave Henry a tremendous welcome. The streets of London were lined with wildly cheering people as the King, clad in plain dress, rode at the head of his men to offer prayers at St Paul's and Westminster Abbey.

When he was asked to put his helmet on show, so that the people could see the tremendous dent it received in battle, the modest king refused, saying with a laugh:

" Nay, we were brothers that day and we all took some stout blows. No man fought better than the next, that day at Agincourt."

WILLIAM CAXTON
Wool-Merchant and Printer

IN the year 1438, a company of wool-merchants left the town of Tenterden to make the two-day journey through the orchards and fields of Kent to London. As well as the sober merchants, there were servants armed against robbers, and, striding along between the pack-horses, a merry-faced lad of sixteen.

The travellers rested that night at Rochester and came next day into the city of London. They halted outside a big house which seemed to be shop, store, and house all in one.

While the servants were unloading the pack animals, and carrying bales of cloth from the narrow street into the yard, one of the merchants called the lad over.

"Come, William, boy," he said, "your father bade me hand you into the care of your master."

He led the way through the open shop and upstairs to a large upper room overlooking the noisy street. A grey-bearded man in a long gown of rich, dark material looked up and greeted them kindly. After he had read a letter which the merchant handed him, he looked the lad up and down, and said:

"So you are William Caxton, eh? You are welcome for the sake of my old friend, your father. He writes that you have been to school and are a good scholar at your Latin and French. Do you like hard work, William?"

"Yes, sir," answered young Caxton respectfully.

"Well, you shall work hard as my apprentice for seven years. You shall live here and share my table. I will teach you the cloth trade, how to buy and sell, how to keep your books, and bargain with the Flemish merchants.

"But now, lad, seek out Mistress Goode

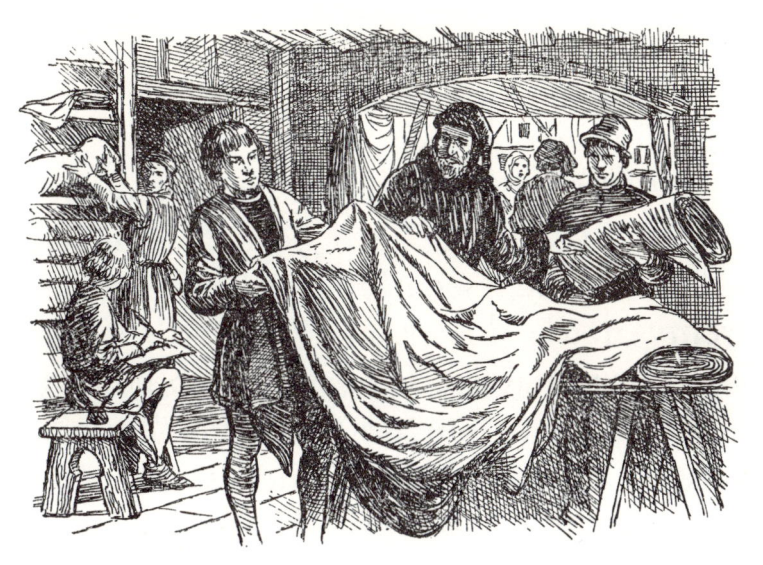

Young Caxton bargains with the merchants

and she will find you something to eat. We can start making a mercer of you tomorrow."

So young William served as apprentice to Sir Robert Large, cloth merchant, or mercer, of the city of London. For seven years he learned to judge cloth, to buy wool from English farmers and to bargain with the Flemish traders for silks, damasks, and cloth of gold. His master became fond of the quick, clever apprentice.

One day Sir Robert fell ill of the sickness which came each summer to the narrow, dirty streets of the city. He sent for

William, who came sadly to the side of his great four-poster bed.

"William," he said, "I fear I have not long to live. You have been a good lad and your time is nearly served. I give you twenty marks in silver. Take them and pay your passage to Bruges, the cloth city of the Lowlands. There is much money to be made by an English mercer in that city. My sons will send you business. Farewell, lad."

Soon afterwards, the mercer died and Master William Caxton went, as he had been told, to Bruges, in Flanders. Though he was young, he set up as a merchant, selling English cloth and wool and buying beautiful materials from the merchants of France, Venice, and Genoa. Because he was honest and hard-working, he did well. He grew rich, he travelled, he came to London on a visit and was honoured by the Mercers' Company. In Bruges, he was made chief English merchant of the Low Countries.

As he grew richer, Master Caxton had more time for his hobby. Ever since he was a boy, he had loved reading. He never missed a chance of seeing one of the

The dying merchant says farewell to Caxton

beautiful books copied out with loving care by a monk or clerk. Only the richest people had books of their own. A noble who had twenty of these beautifully written books was said to possess a famous library.

There were few English books in Bruges, so Caxton read French stories. One of his favourites was the story of Troy; he liked it so much that he turned it into English, and then copied it out for his friends.

About this time, an English princess came to Bruges to marry Charles the Bold, Duke of Burgundy. William Caxton was chosen to give her a message of welcome from the English merchants. He found that the Duchess was not only beautiful but was also fond of books.

"I hear already, Master Caxton," she said, "that you are as skilful with your pen as with a bargain. Duke Charles has many fair books in the library. Come, let us choose one for you to copy."

Soon, Caxton was spending more and more time in the library copying books for the Duchess. They became great friends and, presently, he gave up being a merchant and went to live at the palace.

One day, the Duchess Margaret found her friend in the library resting his head wearily upon his hands.

"Good-day, Master William," she said. "What is amiss?"

"I cannot copy any more, my lady," replied Caxton. "My pen is worn down with all this writing. My eyes are dim from looking at the white paper. Yet every book takes so long, so very long to copy. I would there was some quicker way."

"Now, listen," said the Duchess, "I have heard that a Master Gutenberg in

*Margaret, Duchess of Burgundy, with her friend
William Caxton*

Germany has printed many Bibles by some strange means. 'Tis said he can print many times faster than a man can write. Take a journey, my good friend, and see this thing for yourself."

Caxton went to Cologne and stayed there for several months, learning the secrets of this new printing. He made friends with a printer called Colard Mansion and brought him back to Bruges. Caxton gave the money to buy all that was needed and, together, they set up a printing press. The first book they printed was Caxton's favourite "Story of Troy," which he had translated into English. This delighted Margaret and her friends. The next book was "The Game and Playe of Chesse," because chess was a popular game of noblemen at this time.

Now Caxton made up his mind to go back to England and spend the rest of his life printing books for English people to read. Duchess Margaret wrote a letter to her brother, Edward IV, King of England, who gladly agreed to allow Caxton to set up his press near Westminster Abbey.

Caxton took his pupil, Wynken de Worde, with him, and they made all ready in their printing house. Then they hung out their sign. It was a white shield with a wide red stripe, called a "pale," down the middle. This told people that Caxton the Printer lived at "the sign of the Red Pale."

When everything was ready, the King,

Printing the Story of Troy

with ladies and gentlemen of the Court, came to see the wonderful new machine which printed books quickly.

They watched young Wynken arrange metal letters into words, which he fitted into a wooden frame. When he had made a whole page, he put the frame into the press. Next, Caxton took two big pads and inked all the letters, then he turned a large screw which pressed a sheet of paper on to the inky letters. In this way, a whole page was printed at once. After many copies of the page had been printed, the metal letters were used again to make up another page. Later, all the pages were sewn together and made into a book, the first book ever printed in England.

The King and the nobles crowded round to see the white paper which Caxton used instead of vellum ; they picked up some of the little metal letters which were made to look like the handwriting of the time. They were delighted to find that the new books would have a few pictures, skilfully carved from blocks of wood, and inked in the same way as the letters.

Everyone wanted his favourite story or poem made into a printed book, instead of having to pay a man to make a copy which

The King and nobles visit Caxton's printing press

would take him weeks. So Caxton printed stories, poems and ballads. He printed Aesop's Fables ; the stories of Reynard the Fox and of King Arthur and his Knights ; and also Chaucer's Tales which the pilgrims told on the way to Canterbury. Many of these stories were written in French, so Caxton translated them into English. Altogether he printed copies of 99 different books and, though he lived more than 450 years ago, many of his books still exist. Some are in the British Museum, and there are others at Manchester, Oxford, and Cambridge.

William Caxton, the boy from Kent, who became rich as a wool-merchant and famous as a printer, ended his days happily at the sign of the Red Pale. The Wars of the Roses were over, and Henry VII was King of England, but Caxton had done more for his country than all the barons and knights who fought in those wars. He had brought printing to England. Books were still rare and very expensive, but now there would be more printers and presses, until there were books for everybody.

BACKGROUND TO THE STORIES IN PART TWO

King Harold having defeated his brother, Tostig and Harold Hardrada, at Stamford Bridge, near York, hurried south to meet *Duke William* at Hastings. The battle was fought between two armies of not more than 10,000 men each.

Hereward led a rising against William. William was fatally injured at Mantes, in Northern France, and died at Rouen. Lanfranc was a great Archbishop.

William the Conqueror
1066–1087

Edgar Atheling, heir to Harold's throne, escaped to Scotland. His sister, *Margaret*, married Malcolm Canmore.

Malcolm fought against William I and William Rufus; he was killed at Alnwick, 1093.

Saint Margaret's Gospel Book is in the Bodleian Library, at Oxford.

Saint Margaret
Queen of Scotland
1066–1093

Following the troubled reign of King Stephen, *Henry II*, great-grandson of the Conqueror, curbed the power of the barons. He had vast lands in France. He became overlord of Ireland, after Strongbow's invasion, and overlord of Scotland by homage of William the Lion.

Thomas Becket, Archbishop of Canterbury was murdered, 1170.

King Henry II and Thomas Becket
1154–1189

Richard I spent only six months of his reign in England. He gave the rest of his time to the Third Crusade and to fighting for his lands in France.

[The First Crusade, in William II's reign, founded the Kingdom of Jerusalem.

The Second Crusade, 1147–1149, was a failure.

The Third Crusade, 1189–1192, failed to recapture Jerusalem from Saladin.]

Richard the Lionheart
1189–1199

Edward I, "The Lawgiver," was an able ruler. He added Wales to his kingdom by defeating *Llewelyn the Last*. He made himself overlord of Scotland, capturing John Balliol at Dunbar.

The Scots revolted under Wallace, who was defeated at the Battle of Falkirk, 1298.

The Welsh Prince, Llewelyn

Robert Bruce stabbed Comyn, nephew of Balliol, and had himself crowned King of Scotland. He led a new revolt against the English and, after years of varying fortune, he united his countrymen and utterly defeated Edward II at Bannockburn, 1314.

Robert the Bruce
of Scotland
1314

Edward III claimed the throne of France, and thus began the Hundred Years' War.

The Battle of Sluys was our first great sea victory.

The Black Prince gained fame in the victorious battles of Crecy and Poitiers. In 1347, Calais was captured.

In 1348-1349, about one-third of all the people in England died from the Black Death.

Edward III,
1327-1377, and
Queen Philippa

Richard II, son of the Black Prince, was eleven years old when he became king. The Peasants' Revolt, 1381, was led by *Wat Tyler* and *John Ball*. John Wyclif translated the Bible into English and sent his 'Poor Preachers' throughout the country.

Wat Tyler and the Boy King, Richard II
1377-1399

Geoffrey Chaucer completed the Canterbury Tales in the reign of Richard II. After Richard was deposed, his cousin, Henry IV, became king, and he too showed favour to Chaucer.

Geoffrey Chaucer
1340-1400

Henry V reopened the Hundred Years' War, and won an amazing victory at Agincourt, 1415, where, it is said, the French lost ten thousand men and the English one hundred.

Henry made wide conquests in France. He married the French King's daughter and was to gain the throne, but he died suddenly from camp fever.

While Henry VI was a child, Joan of Arc won her great victories, which led to the loss of all our French possessions except Calais. During Henry's reign the Wars of the Roses broke out after quarrels between the houses of Lancaster and York.

Henry V
1413–1422

In the reign of Edward IV, *William Caxton* set up his printing shop at Westminster. Among his customers were three kings, Edward IV, Richard III and Henry VII.

He printed and translated nearly 100 different books during the last fourteen years of his life. His books were printed in Gothic lettering, with no title-pages and little punctuation, but some were illustrated by woodcuts.

William Caxton, Wool-Merchant and Printer
1422(?)–1491

PART THREE

PART THREE

GREAT TUDORS AND STUARTS

SIR THOMAS MORE
Scholar and Saint

IN the reign of the Tudor kings, there stood in Threadneedle Street, London, a building known as the Hospital of St. Anthony. It was the home, not of sick people, but of twelve old men who were cared for by kindly monks. One room of the house was also used as a school.

The boys who came to this little school at 7 o'clock each morning were sons of merchants and lawyers. Most of their time was spent in learning Latin, and the monk who taught them would beat those who did not work hard enough. Among them was a merry, talkative lad named Thomas More, but he was so quick at his lessons that he usually managed to escape the birch.

When he was only 13 years old, Thomas More's father took him away from St. Anthony's, and sent him to be a page in the house of the Archbishop of Canterbury, a great house, filled with visitors, scholars and priests. He still had lessons to learn, which, besides Latin, included waiting at table, polite behaviour and holding the basin of scented water in which important guests dipped their fingers after dinner.

The clever little page, with his gay, charming manners, soon won the notice of the archbishop.

" Mark that boy," he said to a guest one day, " for he will grow into a marvellous man. He will surely be one of the greatest men in England."

The good archbishop sent young More to college at Oxford, where he quickly made a name for himself as a scholar, not only of Latin, but also of Greek. Better still, he made many close friends, who loved him for his clever wit and generous spirit.

When the time came to leave Oxford, Thomas went back to London to become a lawyer, like his father. In those days, many lawyers and judges were far from honest, so it was little wonder that people began to talk about the young man from Oxford, who cared more for justice than for money. His fame spread until even the King himself, Henry VIII, came to listen to him explaining law to students. Men began to say that More would become the foremost judge in the kingdom.

Thomas himself was far from sure that he wanted to become a famous lawyer. Beneath his gay manner, he was serious at heart, and he thought deeply about his duty to God. At one time, he

Thomas More as a page in the house of the Archbishop

almost decided to become a monk at a monastery called the Charterhouse. Unknown to his friends, he always wore a harsh hair-shirt next to his skin, to remind himself not to be proud or over-fond of comfort and riches.

King Henry VIII did not forget the brilliant young lawyer, and he gave him several important posts, as well as sending him abroad upon royal business. He made him a knight and would often talk to him about State affairs and religion, walking up and down with his arm round More's shoulders as though the lawyer were his dearest friend.

Sir Thomas bought a piece of land in the village of Chelsea, outside London. There he built a delightful house for his four children, Margaret, Elizabeth, Cicely and John. When they were very young, their mother died and Sir Thomas married a widow named Mistress Alice. The children thought their step-mother was sharp-tongued and not at all pretty. Worst of all, she could never see a joke. Luckily, their father usually found some way to make her laugh, and he persuaded her to learn to play the harp and the flute, so she could join in the family music and games, which filled the house with noise and laughter.

Thomas More was not stern with his children, as were most fathers of the time. He loved to play with them, to invent new games and funny sayings. Strangest of all, he believed that girls should go to school like boys.

The children were wonderfully happy at Chelsea, playing in their beautiful garden by the river, and looking after their collection of pets, which included a monkey, many birds and a tame fox. Friends, scholars, even the King himself, came to visit them. Master Erasmus of Rotterdam, the greatest scholar in Europe, was often at the house, and this is what he wrote about Sir Thomas:

"his talk is charming, full of fun, but never unkind. He is fond of animals, and likes to watch their habits. All the birds of Chelsea come to him to be fed. He has never made an enemy or become an enemy. His whole house breathes happiness."

But alas, trouble was drawing near, not only for England, but also for the family at Chelsea.

Henry VIII had grown tired of his Spanish wife, Catherine of Aragon, and he longed to marry

The King visits More at Chelsea

a lady of the Court, named Anne Boleyn. The Lord Chancellor, Cardinal Wolsey, suggested that the Pope might grant him a divorce, but when the Pope refused, Henry was so angry that he sent Wolsey away in disgrace. He called for Sir Thomas More and made him Lord Chancellor.

Thus, More became the greatest man in England, after the King. His wife, Dame Alice, enjoyed being a great lady, but Thomas himself had no love of power or riches. He knew full well that Henry could quickly turn from a friend into a ruthless enemy.

At first, More hoped that the King would give up all idea of marrying Anne Boleyn. He believed with all his heart that the Pope was appointed by God to be the leader of Christian people everywhere, and therefore no man should disobey him. When he realised that Henry was determined to have his own way, he knew he could serve him no longer. He gave up his position of Lord Chancellor, his wealth and power. He sorrowfully sent away his servants, clerks and watermen, and went back to his pretty house at Chelsea, hoping to be left in peace.

No one could stop Henry now. He caused Parliament to pass a law declaring that he was Head of the English Church. Disobeying the Pope, he sent Catherine away and married the beautiful lady Anne Boleyn. Then he ordered everyone of importance to swear an oath that the Pope was no longer Head of the Church and that Anne was the true queen of England.

When the King's officers arrived at Chelsea to summon More to take the oath, he told them calmly that he was a loyal subject but he did not believe that Parliament had the power to make Henry Head of the Church. He was arrested and imprisoned in the Tower of London on a charge of treason. He knew that unless he took the oath, he would lose his life.

Dame Alice came to visit him in prison. She reminded him of all the wealth that he had given up and told him that she and the children would be very poor.

" 'Tis well known," she pleaded, " that the King will give you free pardon if you will but take the oath. Then you shall come back to us at Chelsea and we shall be merry again. Think, husband, of your wife and children, and of your own dear home. The great ones of the kingdom have sworn the oath. Why must you stand alone ? "

More answered her gently and cheerfully, telling her that he could not do what he knew to be wrong.

" As to my house," he said, " is not this prison house as near to Heaven as mine own ? "

The King's officers came to reason with him ; the Duke of Norfolk told him what must happen, if he refused to obey the King.

" Is that all, my lord ? " Thomas answered lightly. " Then it only means that I die today, and you tomorrow."

Dame Alice and his many friends beseeched the King to accept More's loyalty without the oath, but Henry VIII had no mercy. More was found guilty of treason and was sentenced to death. Though he was ill, he remained wonderfully calm and cheerful throughout his trial. On the way back to the Tower, his favourite daughter, Meg, burst through the guards and flung her arms about him in a last farewell.

During the last few days in the Tower, he was quite alone ; even his writing materials were taken from him. Using a piece of coal to write with, he sent a message to Meg.

Meg bids farewell to her father

"Farewell, my dear child, and pray for me. I shall pray for you and all your friends, that we may merrily meet in Heaven."

Next day, he spoke cheerfully to the people who knelt round his scaffold. As he mounted the steps, he made a joke with the executioner.

"I pray thee help me safely up, but for my coming down, let me shift for myself."

He knelt down and placed his head upon the block, being careful to move his beard clear, "Since this beard," he said, "has never committed treason." His last words were, "I die, the King's loyal servant, but God's servant first."

Thomas More died as he had lived, one of the wisest, bravest and most gracious men in our history.

RICHARD CHANCELLOR
Merchant Adventurer

ONE May morning in the year 1553, there was great excitement along Thames-side. Prentice-boys and stout citizens hurried down the narrow alleys which led to the river-front; watermen and sailors on the wharves cheered and waved their caps, shouting " God speed ! " as three ships passed slowly down the river.

Opposite the Royal Palace at Greenwich, the ships dropped anchor. The boy-king, Edward VI, was too ill to leave his room, but gaily-dressed ladies and gentlemen of his Court sauntered down to the water-side to bid good fortune to the three captains. Guns were fired, the anchors raised, and to the cheers of courtiers and sailors, the little fleet set sail for the North Sea.

What was this expedition that aroused such excitement and high hopes? The Merchant Adventurers of England had fitted out three ships to try to find a new sea-route to India and Cathay, as China was then called. The Londoners, who had given them such a rousing farewell, were filled with hope that the ships would bring back gold, silks and spices, and the promise of rich trade.

Aboard the *Bona Esperanza* (the " Good Hope "), was Sir Hugh Willoughby, leader of the expedition,

Willoughby and Chancellor set sail from the Thames

His chief officer, a young man named Richard Chancellor, sailed in the *Edward Bonaventure*. They planned to sail north into the icy seas, and then to steer eastwards, in the hope of finding a sea-way round Europe which might lead them to India. Their ships carried stores for eighteen months, and the commanders bore letters from King Edward VI. Each letter, written in several languages, was addressed " to the Kings, princes and other Potentates inhabiting the north-east parts of the world," and asked for free passage and permission to trade for Edward's merchant sailors.

After a slow start, because of contrary winds, the voyage went well. The three ships crossed the North Sea and sailed up the coast of Norway until they reached the Lofoten Islands. Here Sir Hugh Willoughby called a meeting of his captains, and told them that they must try to sail close together.

"In the unknown waters that lie ahead," he said, "we may well encounter storms that cause us to part company. If that should come to pass, let us resolve to meet at the harbour of Vadsö, known to our seamen as the Wardhouse. Thus, gentlemen, I do command you."

Hardly had the captains returned to their ships, when a furious storm burst upon them. They raised anchor and ran before the gale. In the darkness and driving rain, Richard Chancellor lost sight of the other ships and, when daylight came, they were nowhere to be seen.

The storm died away, and the *Bonaventure* sailed on, steering a course for the Wardhouse harbour. Chancellor expected to find his friends waiting for him there. It was high summer when they reached Vadsö, and, as happens in those northern lands, the sun's light was still strong at midnight. There was no sign of Sir Hugh Willoughby and his companions. A week passed and still they did not arrive. Though the seamen did not know it, they were never to see their commander again. The storm had driven him far from his course and, long afterwards, the bodies of Sir Hugh and his two crews were found frozen to death on a distant shore.

Chancellor summoned his sailors to the deck:

"Men," he said, "I do greatly fear that ill-fortune has befallen our Captain-General. Perchance he has returned to London to repair the damage of the storm. Shall we wait longer or shall we go forward? What say you?"

A sturdy seaman answered him:

"Master Chancellor," he said, "we dare not tarry in these northern waters. I say let us go forward."

"Well spoken, Martin," cried Chancellor, "we are bound on a great enterprise, bearing letters from our Sovereign. Let us put our trust in God and sail on!"

The sailors readily agreed to their leader's plan,

A small fishing boat was sighted

and the little ship sailed on alone. After many days, the *Bonaventure* entered the great bay which is called the White Sea. They were close to the shores of Russia, or Muscovy, as it was then called. As they neared the land, they espied a small fishing boat.

A boat was lowered from the *Bonaventure,* but the fishermen, terrified at the sight of a ship far bigger than any they had ever seen, made for the shore at top speed and tried to escape.

When the English sailors overtook them, the fishermen fell upon their knees in terror. Chancellor gently raised them up and showed by friendly signs that he meant no harm, but had come to trade peaceably.

The fishermen quickly spread the news that men from a great nation, strangely courteous and gentle, had reached their shores. The Englishmen were greeted with kindness and hospitality by the countryfolk, who fetched their merchants and nobles to admire the goods which the strangers had brought with them.

Chancellor soon made himself understood, and he learned that he had reached the almost unknown land of Muscovy. Unfortunately, the merchants dared not trade with him until they had obtained permission from their all-powerful ruler, the Grand Duke of Moscow, who was also called the Tsar. It appeared that his palace lay more than a thousand miles away.

Messengers were sent off to Moscow, craving permission to trade with the strangers, but, as days and then weeks went by without an answer, Chancellor grew impatient.

"We have waited long enough," he said, "let us set out with a small company to see this great Emperor for ourselves, and show him the letters from our own Sovereign King."

The nobles, or boyars, begged him to wait a little longer, but, when they saw that he had made up his mind, they gave him horses, sledges and fur rugs for the long journey. Chancellor made sure that his crew was comfortably housed ashore, then, with prayers for a safe return, he set out for Moscow with a few companions.

It was midwinter; the Englishmen had never known such bitter cold, nor seen snow lie so thick. Yet, on fine days, the sun shone brilliantly from a cloudless sky, and the sledges ran swiftly over the frozen ground, or faster still along the ice-bound rivers. At night, the travellers were given shelter in the huts of peasants or in the wooden houses of friendly boyars.

After many days, they drew near to Moscow, and Chancellor was astonished at the sight of the rounded domes of its churches, gleaming gold, green and silver in the winter sunlight. Inside the great city, he was disappointed to find that its streets and houses were far meaner than those of London. The Royal Palace, known as the Kremlin, was a gloomy, shabby building of brown stone, more like a fortress than a palace.

But when he received permission to visit the Grand Duke, Chancellor was even more surprised by all that he saw within the walls.

A hundred nobles, dressed to their ankles in robes of gold cloth, stood waiting in an outer hall. They greeted him gravely, and led him forward into the audience chamber. Here, on a high throne, flanked by a company of magnificently robed attendants, sat Ivan the Terrible, Tsar of Muscovy. In his hand, he held a sceptre that glittered with precious stones; he wore a gold robe and, on his head, a tall diadem encrusted with jewels. Around him, in silence, stood bearded nobles, each wearing a high pointed cap, the height of which indicated his rank of nobility.

Striding between the boyars, Chancellor advanced to the throne and bowed low. He presented the King's letter with its great royal seal. Ivan accepted it, read it carefully and passed it to one of his attendants; then he smiled graciously to the visitors and told them they were invited to dine with him that afternoon.

The dinner was a strange and gorgeous affair, lasting from the afternoon until far into the night. First, the Tsar, dressed now in silver, made a solemn entrance; he greeted every guest by name, giving him a piece of bread from an enormous gold platter, as the High Steward called out:

"The Grand Duke of Moscow, Emperor of Russia, Ivan Vassilivitch doth give thee bread!"

As the hundreds of guests seated themselves, the Chief Gentleman Usher entered the Hall, leading one hundred and forty serving-men, who carried plates, dishes and goblets of gold. Eight roasted swans on gold plates were taken before the Tsar, who bowed his head to signify that the banquet might begin. Then the swans were taken to the carvers, who cut up the meat for servants to distribute to the guests. Dozens of courses followed, each more magnificent than the one before, but, as each was brought in, the same ceremony recurred of presenting the dishes to the Grand Duke. After several hours, he rose, again named each guest in turn, and gravely withdrew.

Richard and his men stayed for three weeks in Moscow, noting that the country was rich in furs, hides, wax and tallow, all valuable goods for trade. As soon as the Grand Duke gave him a letter to the King of England, Chancellor made all speed to return to his ship's company by the White Sea.

Chancellor presents the King's letter to Ivan

They joyfully welcomed him back after his long absence. It was now Spring, and the ice on the sea was melting. Stores and merchandise were taken aboard, and no time was lost in setting sail for England.

More than a year had passed since the three ships made their way so bravely down the Thames. As she came up to her wharf, news went along the river-front that the *Bonaventure* had returned alone, without having found a sea-route to India. Yet the voyage had not been in vain.

The merchants of London gave Chancellor a ready welcome, for he not only brought back valuable goods, but he had opened a way for trade with a vast, new country. The Muscovy Company was formed to continue this trade with Russia.

Before the year was out, Richard Chancellor sailed again in the same ship for the White Sea.

Once again, he made a successful trading voyage, but on the way home, the stout little *Bonaventure* was wrecked on the coast of Scotland. With most of his crew, Master Chancellor, resolute merchant-adventurer, was drowned.

Like many another voyager, Richard Chancellor had set out to find a new route to the East and had stumbled by accident upon a new land. Not dismayed by hardship or fear, he had carried out his mission of finding fresh markets for English goods, and, like so many of our seamen, he lost his life in this double quest for trade and adventure.

THE PRINCESS ELIZABETH

AS the procession left the gates of the palace, the trumpets blared, and, down the river, came the dull booming of cannon and the sound of bells pealing. Behind the trumpeters, along garden paths strewn with green rushes, walked the lords and ladies of the Court, brilliantly dressed in fur-lined silks, embroidered damasks and jewelled velvets. The Lord Mayor of London and the aldermen, in long gowns and gold chains, followed two by two.

In the Church of the Grey Friars, just beyond the palace, a Duchess handed a tiny child, wrapped in a purple mantle, to the Bishop of London. On either side of the silver font were Archbishop Cranmer and the Marchioness of Somerset, godparents of the baby princess; behind them stood the King's Council, with the Barons, Earls, Bishops, and the Gentlemen and Esquires of the Kingdom.

When the christening was over, the Garter King at Arms cried aloud:

" God send a prosperous life and long, to the high and mighty princess of England, Elizabeth ! "

The trumpets sounded and the procession, lit now by the fires of five hundred torches, returned to Greenwich Palace, where the three-days-old child was taken to the Queen's Chamber, and placed in her mother's arms. As she looked down at her baby, the Queen's dark eyes were filled, for a moment, with fear.

The Queen was Anne Boleyn, the dark lady, with great slanting eyes set in an oval face, whose beauty had captured the King of England. Looking at her child, she murmured, " Ah child, I would you had been a son."

For she knew that, unless she gave the King a son, all her power as Queen would vanish. She knew well enough that the great nobles hated her for an upstart, and that the people of England whispered that she was a witch, who had cast a spell upon the King. Had she not a sixth finger on her left hand, a sure sign of a witch?

Less than three years later, Anne was dead. Disappointed and angry at the arrival of another daughter, Henry readily believed stories of wickedness spread by her enemies, and he ordered her execution. On the day after Anne was beheaded, the King, dressed all in white, married his third wife, Jane Seymour.

The little princess, Elizabeth, was only two years old when her mother died, and she was already being brought up in a separate mansion with her half-sister, Mary, a girl of nineteen. At first, Mary refused to call this little girl " princess," for she remembered how cruelly her own mother had been treated because of the King's love for Anne Boleyn. But gradually Mary came to love the bright child with the red hair of the Tudors. The two princesses were very much alone, and no one could tell what their royal father's next mood might be.

Lady Bryan, Elizabeth's governess, was greatly worried about the little girl, for she did not know if she was still to be considered a princess, nor how she was to be brought up. Worse still, no money had been provided for the household, not even enough to buy clothes for the King's daughter.

In despair, Lady Bryan sent a letter to the Lord Privy Seal :

" My Lady," she wrote, " has neither gown nor petticoat, nor any manner of linen, nor pinafore, nor nightgowns nor biggens (night-caps). All these her Grace must have."

Another thing that worried the kindly governess was the behaviour of Mr. Shelton, head of the household. He insisted that the little princess should dine in state, seated at the high table and waited upon by servants, as if she were a grown lady.

" Alas," wrote Lady Bryan, " it is not right for a child of her age to keep such a rule yet. She sees meats and fruits and wines, and it is hard for

The Princess at dinner with Lady Bryan

me to forbid them. She is too young to punish greatly."

So the governess begged permission to give the little girl her meals in her own room, especially as she was cutting her baby teeth—" my Lady hath great pain with her teeth and they come very slowly forth."

Although he had many faults, King Henry loved children, and he ordered that Lady Bryan should have all she asked for. When his son, Prince Edward, was born to Jane Seymour, he remembered his two daughters, and both princesses came to London for the christening. Mary was lady godmother, and Elizabeth held the christening robe, but she was so small that one of the lords of the Court carried her in the procession.

As they grew up, Prince Edward and Elizabeth

became fond of each other; they had the same teachers, and they sometimes sent each other little letters in French and Latin, as well as presents at the New Year. All Henry's children were clever, and when Elizabeth was only six, she embroidered a cambric shirt for her brother, and had already learned her alphabet from a horn-book of silver filigree that was tied by a string round her waist. At ten years, she was learning French and Latin, and was able to write a letter in Italian to her new step-mother, Queen Catherine Parr, Henry's sixth and last wife.

Like her father, Elizabeth was musical, and she practised every day upon the lute and the virginals, her favourite instruments. Chess, needlework, beautiful handwriting and dancing were her pastimes, though she also read far more books than most men of her rank. The Court dances were extremely difficult, so Elizabeth would practise for at least an hour a day, dancing with her maids-of-honour to the music of a pipe and a drum, under the careful eye of the dancing-master. Out of doors, she was a splendid horsewoman, who loved hunting, and, it is said, she was a very fine shot with the bow.

When King Henry VIII died, the thirteen-year-old princess went to live with Catherine Parr at Chelsea Palace.

The new king, her brother, was Edward VI, a pale, clever little boy, but so delicate that it seemed certain that his reign would be a short one. If he died, who next would occupy the throne ? Mary, whom the Catholics favoured ? Or Elizabeth ?

As Elizabeth romped in the palace gardens with Catherine Parr and Lord Seymour, she little knew that she was caught in the web of a plot that would put her life in danger.

Lord Seymour, Admiral of the Fleet, was a gallant, handsome man, with amusing manners and a great chuckling laugh, that hid an eager thirst for power. Soon after Henry's death, he married the King's widow, Catherine Parr, but she too died. Admiral Seymour, standing by the diamond-paned window of his country house, watched a slim girl with red hair come running up the steps from the garden. He suddenly realised that, with her, he could reach the power he dreamed about. He would marry Elizabeth ; he had always been kind to the lonely princess and he knew that she liked him. Then he would claim the money due to her as daughter of a king, buy wide lands next to his own in the West Country, strengthen his castle, and then . . . when Edward died, or even before, one swift move would put Elizabeth on the throne, with himself at her side, the real ruler of England.

Seymour began to make friends with his nephew, young Edward VI, giving him pocket-money and sly presents ; he gathered noble friends and a small army ; he began to pay court to Elizabeth. But he talked too much, too boastingly. Tongues wagged at Court ; his friends tried to warn him, but he only roared with laughter . . . was not the King his nephew, and his friend ?

Suddenly, the Council took action ; Seymour was arrested, sent to the Tower and executed for high treason.

But what of Elizabeth? Surely she must know of this plot to seize the throne, to overthrow, perhaps, her own brother and the claims of her sister, Mary? The Council sent Sir Robert Tyrwhitt to Hatfield Palace to worm out the truth from the frightened girl. She was quite alone, since her gay, talkative governess, Kate Ashley, was already in the Tower. Hour after hour, day after day, Tyrwhitt and his wife questioned her, trying to trap her into saying one sentence that would send her to the executioner's block. Try as he would, Sir Robert found that the young princess had the same iron will as her father. "And yet," he wrote to the Council, " I do see it in her face that she is guilty . . . she hath a very good wit, and nothing is gotten of her, but by great cunning."

At last the tormentors left Elizabeth alone ; she was trembling and her eyes were red with angry tears, but she had won.

Soon afterwards, young Edward VI died, and Mary became Queen of England. As she entered London, Elizabeth rode next behind her sister. The cheering Londoners stared curiously at an eager girl of nineteen, who was handsome rather than beautiful, with golden hair, dark shining eyes and beautiful hands which she loved to display ; already she rode with the dignity and pride of a Tudor.

Without delay, Mary set to work to make

Elizabeth rides into London behind her sister

England a Catholic country once more. Priests were brought back, the Church services were altered, and, in all things, the Queen turned for advice to her Spanish friends. When it was rumoured that she meant to marry Philip of Spain, the people began to mutter that a change of queen would be better than a foreign king. The Spanish ambassadors, who came to arrange the wedding, were pelted with snowballs by an angry crowd, and a dead dog, dressed like a

Catholic priest, was flung through a window of the Court.

A Protestant gentleman, Sir Thomas Wyatt, raised the men of Kent, and marched on London to put Elizabeth upon the throne. Mary's courage in this moment of danger came to her aid; the rebellion collapsed and dreadful punishment was dealt out to all who had taken part.

Elizabeth was arrested. This time there could be no doubt that she was guilty of treason. One grey wet morning, a State barge carried her down the river to the Traitors' Stairs of the Tower. Elizabeth sat silent in the stern.

"Lady, will you land?" said one of the lords, offering his hand.

"No," said Elizabeth, "I pray you all, good friends and fellows, bear me witness that I am no traitor."

Presently, however, she rose and stepped on the stairs, saying : "Here landeth as true a subject as ever stood on these steps."

Her guards had great difficulty in getting her into the Tower, for she seated herself in the courtyard, refusing to move another step, despite the pouring rain. But at last, she was taken inside and kept a close prisoner for two months, while the long questioning went on. She said she knew nothing of the rebellion, and, though she was in great peril, her courage and sharp wits again saved her.

Nothing could be proved against her, for the death of Seymour had taught her to guard every

The Princess at the Traitors' Gate

word she spoke. One day, she scratched with her diamond ring on a window-pane:

"Much suspected by me,
Nothing proved can be."

Mary believed her guilty, but because of her popularity dared not keep her in the Tower any longer, though to set her free would be an invitation for fresh plots. So Elizabeth was taken from one great mansion to another—Woodstock, to Hampton Court, to Greenwich and on to Hatfield—always heavily guarded, she was not a prisoner, but she certainly was not free.

On a November day in 1558, a mud-bespattered rider spurred his way towards Hatfield Palace. He found the little town bustling with servants and retainers of nobles who had already made their way into Hertfordshire, when it became clear that the unhappy Queen was dying in London. Thrusting past their questioning faces, the messenger rode into the great park, towards the many-chimneyed house that had belonged to Henry VIII. Ahead, he saw two grooms leading a pair of handsome horses.

"I seek the lady Elizabeth," he cried.

One pointed with his whip, not towards the great house, but to the left, among the trees, and there he saw the princess. She was seated under a large oak-tree, reading aloud to two of her ladies-in-waiting.

The messenger dismounted, bared his head and knelt before her.

"My lady," he said, "I bear news from London!

"The Queen, your royal sister, is dead.

"Long live the Queen!

"Long live Queen Elizabeth of England!"

Young Drake on the Medway

DRAKE'S REVENGE

(i) Treachery at San Juan

AN old ship lay moored to the bank of the River Medway; a line of washing fluttered between her bare masts, and a wisp of smoke from the stern showed that a meal was cooking in the galley. Seven or eight children played along the decks and scrambled up and down the ladder which ended on a grass-grown wharf.

Two of the children paused in their game and pointed towards the river-mouth, where the Medway joins the Thames Estuary. A tiny boat, heeling over in the wind, came scudding towards them. As it drew near, the sail was lowered and the skiff was brought alongside with the skill of expert hands. A moment later, a brown, smiling boy, in a tattered shirt, sprang nimbly on deck, and hurried across to where his frowning father was waiting with a Bible in his hand.

"Ye are late, son," said his father, "I would ye could learn to read as easy as ye learn sailing."

The boy was Francis Drake, fourteen years old and eldest of twelve children. His father, a Devon man and a sailor-turned preacher, had brought his family to Gillingham, Kent, after the local Catholics had chased him from his farm. Since they had no house and little money, the Drake family made their home on an old ship in a backwater of the river. It was small wonder that young Francis loved boats better than the lessons that his father gave him.

When he was fifteen, he went to sea with the captain of a little coasting vessel. It was rough, hard work, but the boy was eager to learn all he could about the craft of sailing a ship. The old skipper took great pains to pass on his knowledge, for he realised that Francis was a born seaman, with more brains and courage than most lads. After some years, the captain died and left his ship to his pupil.

Barely twenty, Francis Drake was captain of his own ship, but it was not long before he began to wish for a more adventurous life than sailing a little trading vessel up and down the coast. He **sold the ship and went to Devonshire.**

At Plymouth, he joined his cousin, John Hawkins, who was fitting out a slaving expedition that promised both adventure and riches. Wicked as it seems to us today, we must remember that no-one at this time saw anything wrong in the slave trade. The Queen herself lent two ships, the *Jesus* and the *Minion*, which, with four smaller ships, made up Hawkins' fleet.

With Drake as one of his officers, Hawkins sailed to West Africa. Plying along the coast, he bought and captured 500 negroes, who were then crowded below decks. Supplies of fresh water were taken on board, and a course was set for the Spanish Main, across the Atlantic Ocean. Drake, by this time, had been put in command of the *Judith*.

When they reached the Spanish settlements, Hawkins found that the King of Spain had forbidden all trade with Englishmen, though the two countries were supposed to be at peace. Philip II claimed, with the Pope's blessing, that the lands and riches of the New World belonged to Spain, and to Spain alone.

The Spanish settlers were in a difficult position. They did not wish to anger their King, but they badly needed black slaves to work in their fields and sugar plantations. At first, they pretended that they would not buy the slaves at all, thinking they would get them cheaply. Hawkins landed 200 men, armed to the teeth, and marched to the Governor's house :

" You *will* trade with me, Don Costellanos."

he said, fingering the hilt of his sword. " You will pay my price, and find it a fair one ! "

The Spaniards quickly agreed, and it was not long before Hawkins and Drake were ready to sail for England, with a cargo of Spanish goods and bar silver, as their profit from the voyage. Suddenly, a terrible storm arose, which so damaged the English ships that they needed repair before they could undertake the long Atlantic crossing.

The little fleet limped into the harbour of San Juan. Here Hawkins struck a bargain with the Spanish Governor ; he would not attack the treasure fleet which lay at anchor, but would act peaceably, and pay for all goods, while he repaired his ships.

The bargain was agreed, with friendly promises and courtly speeches on both sides, and the English sailors set to work. Under cover of night, however, the Spaniards made a treacherous attack from all sides. Hawkins and his men fought desperately in the darkness, cutting down the boarding party and sinking the Spanish flagship. Hawkins himself fought like a madman, roaring all the time.

" God and Saint George ! Upon the traitorous villains ! "

Four of his ships were lost, including the Queen's ship, *Jesus,* and the best part of his men were butchered ashore or killed in the fighting. Drake, in the *Judith* was hard-pressed ; he saw Hawkins steer the *Minion* out of the harbour, so he cut his own cables and followed him to the open sea.

Hawkins fought like a madman

After a dreadful voyage, both ships reached Plymouth. Only a handful of men were alive, and they were near starvation. Most of the fleet and all of the silver had been lost. All England was in an uproar when the story of Spanish treachery became known. Drake never forgot the disaster of San Juan, and he vowed to have his revenge.

(ii) The attack on Nombre de Dios

Francis Drake had done well on his first ill-fated expedition, but he knew that he still had much to learn. With Hawkins' help, he made two short voyages to the New World to obtain information about its harbours, islands and bays, and also to find out how the Spaniards brought so much gold to Europe.

In the centre of the Spanish Empire was the Isthmus of Panama, a long, narrow neck of land joining North and South America. The Spaniards shipped the treasure of Peru up the West coast to the city of Panama; here it was loaded on to mules and carried across the Isthmus to Nombre de Dios ("Name of God"). The treasure was stored in this town until a strong fleet of galleons arrived to take it across the Atlantic to Spain.

Drake made another important discovery. In the mountains and forests of the Isthmus lived hundreds of negroes, called the Cimaroons. They were runaway slaves, who so hated the Spaniards that they would help anyone against them.

Back in England, Drake quietly made his preparations. He carefully chose seventy-three mariners for the expedition; all were young men, hardy and bold, and, among them, were two of his own brothers, John and Joseph. In May, 1572, they sailed from Plymouth in two tiny ships, the *Pasha* and the *Swan*. Below decks, were stowed the parts of three pinnaces, low swift boats, that were to be fitted together in the New World.

By July, Drake had reached a hidden bay, not far from Nombre de Dios; he landed his men and set them to build a fort for defence against a surprise attack. Next, they fitted together the pinnaces, and when these were ready, Drake called a council of war, at which he unfolded his plan. It was unbelievably simple and daring.

"Comrades," he said, "my plan is to capture the whole treasure of the Isthmus! At this very moment, the treasure-house of Nombre de Dios is stuffed with gold, awaiting the fleet that comes each half-year. Capture Nombre de Dios with one bold stroke and, with God's help, the treasure is ours!"

Manning the pinnaces, the Englishmen set out along the coast. After three days of rowing, they reached the Isle of Pines, close to the treasure city. Hiding in the woods until dark, they heard bad news from a friendly negro. He told them that the

Cimaroons had recently attacked the town, and the Spaniards were well armed and on the alert.

"Never fear," said Drake, " 'twill make our victory the more glorious. Follow me, for God and the Queen!"

In darkness, they rowed towards the sleeping town. A single gunner sighted them, fired one shot and ran to give the alarm.

Drake's plan was ready. Though he had never set foot in Nombre de Dios, he had so closely questioned prisoners and slaves, that he knew every inch. He sent a party of eighteen men under John Drake to the far side of the town, while he led the attack from the other side, with trumpets blaring, drums beating and fire-torches blazing!

The Spaniards, believing themselves to be attacked by a large force, fired one volley and fled. Drake was wounded in the leg, but he knew he must act swiftly, before the Spaniards discovered that they had been tricked by a handful of men. He led the way to the Governor's house, where bars of silver were stacked from the floor to the ceiling.

"Nay, lads, do not touch it," he cried, "we are here for gold. To the treasure-house!"

They found the treasure-house across the marketplace, but it was securely locked. As they set to work to beat down its doors, a tropical storm delayed them, putting out the torches and making the muskets useless. A cry went up that the boat party was attacked, that the Spaniards had rallied and were closing in. Drake sprang forward, but fell fainting to the ground. Unknown to his comrades, his leg had been bleeding for an hour. They raised him up and began to carry him to the shore. He opened his eyes and cried :

" Hold, hold, where do you bear me ? "

" To safety, Captain," replied one of the men.

" Set me down," he cried, " back, my lads, back to the treasure-house ! "

But he fainted again, and they carried him to the pinnaces, preferring his safety to all the gold in Nombre de Dios.

By morning, the town was heavily guarded at all points. Drake's plan had failed, but he was not beaten yet. On board ship, he quickly recovered from his wound, and steered down the coast, capturing one or two ships, so the Spaniards would think that he had left the Isthmus to work along the Spanish Main.

After some weeks of successful attacks on shipping, which gave him ample stores but little treasure, Drake returned to his secret bay and went ashore to question the Cimaroons. The runaway slaves told him that the Spaniards would not move any gold during the rainy season. It would be several months before the mule-trains set out from Panama.

" We can wait," said Drake.

All through the rainy season, he kept his men in good heart. They found another quiet bay, where they amused themselves playing bowls and quoits and practising archery. Every now and again, to obtain fresh food, they sallied out and captured a Spanish ship. Unfortunately, in one of these attacks, Drake's brother, John was killed. Soon afterwards, Joseph died of fever.

At last, the Cimaroons brought word that treasure was massing in Panama and mule-trains would soon start carrying gold across the Isthmus. Leaving a party to guard the ships and the sick men, Drake chose eighteen Englishmen and some Cimaroons to march inland. The negroes led the way through 100 miles of wild country and over the range of mountains that runs down the Isthmus. As they toiled towards the summit of the ridge, Drake saw ahead a giant tree, with steps cut in its side. The Cimaroon leader took him up the tree to a platform wedged in the upper branches. He gazed spellbound at the forests and valleys before him, at the distant town of Panama and, beyond it, the shining waters of the Pacific Ocean. No Englishman had ever seen it before. Drake gazed silently, then he bowed his head.

"Almighty God," he prayed, " grant me life and leave to sail but once in an English ship upon that great sea."

They left the tree and cut their way through the forest until they were near to Panama. While they lay hid, a Cimaroon spy went into the town. He returned with the news that, next day, eight mules loaded with gold and one with jewels would leave for Nombre de Dios.

Drake posted his men on either side of the mule-track, ordering them to wear their white shirt-tails outside their coats, so each man would know his friends in the darkness. After several hours,

The Attack on Nombre de Dios

tinkling mule-bells could be heard in the distance, and, nearer, the thud of a horse's hoofs. One rash Englishman darted out from the bushes, the rider swerved and galloped back. The rest of Drake's men crouched, waiting. When the mules came level, the ambush rose like one man, scattered the guards and captured the whole train. With eager shouts, they ripped open the packs. Inside, there was only food and a small amount of silver. The horseman had given warning of a stranger in his path, and the commander had sent his baggage mules ahead of the treasure!

Once again, ill-fortune had robbed Drake in the moment of success. Behind him lay Panama, alarmed and ready; ahead was Venta Cruz, a fortified town, half-way across the Isthmus. Drake, as ever, made a bold decision. He ordered a swift advance along the track and a sudden attack upon Venta Cruz. He drove out its garrison, and captured the town, but treated the terrified ladies with the greatest courtesy. Gathering all the treasure they could lay hands upon, the Englishmen made all speed to the coast, where they rejoined their comrades.

Though he now had only thirty-one men left of the original seventy-three, Drake put to sea to rob coasting vessels of food and small quantities of gold. Presently, he fell in with a French ship, whose captain agreed to join him in one more attempt upon the mule-trains.

Again, Drake found a safe anchorage and rowed up the coast in the pinnaces, with a party of fifteen Englishmen and twenty Frenchmen. Putting into a creek near Nombre de Dios, he landed most of his men, and sent the rest back with orders to return in four days' time. Then he led the way inland through the forest, until they reached the track leading to the town.

All night the adventurers waited; soon after dawn, a train of 190 mules, guarded by soldiers, came slowly up the path from Panama. Suddenly, the shrill note of Drake's whistle signalled the attack. Hidden men sprang from the bushes, there was a sharp struggle and the Spaniards fled. The French captain was badly wounded, but the mule-train was in Drake's hands. The silver, fifteen tons of it, was hastily buried. Then, with every man shouldering as much gold as he could carry, the attackers moved through the trees towards the coast.

When they reached the meeting-place, there was no sign of the pinnaces!

In a few hours, the Spaniards would begin to comb the coast with hundreds of soldiers, and little mercy would be shown any Englishman who fell into their hands. Unless the pinnaces arrived, they were all lost.

Danger always brought out the best in Drake. With furious speed, he lashed logs into a raft, and hoisted a crazy sail made from biscuit sacks. Taking three men with him, he set off down the creek, steering the raft with a single oar. After hours of desperate battling, they sighted the pinnaces some miles down the coast, making slow headway against

Drake and his men ransack the Governor's house

a strong wind. Drake pretended to be exhausted and at his last gasp, when they hauled him aboard the leading pinnace. Then, looking up with a great grin, he pulled a piece of gold from his shirt and cried: "Thanks be to God, our voyage is done!"

He drove the crews to row as they had never rowed before, and, with little time to spare, they reached the creek and took off their comrades, who waded out carrying the precious gold above their heads.

Even when he was safe aboard the *Pasha*, Drake insisted on going back to rescue the French captain who had been wounded. They found him dead, and two of his men who had stayed with him; but they brought back one Frenchman who had managed to escape the Spaniards.

At last, Drake was ready to sail to England. He said farewell to his faithful friends, the Cimaroons, giving them presents and pieces of iron for arrowheads. The *Swan* had been sunk and the *Pasha* was in no condition to cross the Atlantic, so Drake coolly captured a fast Spanish frigate and made the voyage home in twenty-three days.

He reached Plymouth on a Sunday morning, and, it is said, the news of his arrival spread so quickly that people flocked out of church to meet him, leaving the preacher alone in his pulpit!

Drake had taken his revenge for the treachery of San Juan.

The Queen's Company arrives at Stratford

MASTER WILL SHAKESPEARE

"TRR-RUMM ! trr-rumm ! trr-rumm !" went the two drums, beating time together, and, every few yards, the trumpets brayed out their harsh brave music. Behind them, some dressed in hose and trunks, short leather cloaks and feathered hats, others in long gowns, spangled to hide their shabbiness, came the men and boys of the Queen's Company.

Alongside the procession, two boys, dressed as clowns, and another as a hobgoblin, ducked and bowed, turned cartwheels and slapped each other with blown-up pigs' bladders. At the end of the procession, came three bony nags, with baskets of stage costumes strapped to their flanks.

Every citizen of the little riverside town of Stratford-on-Avon had turned out to watch the arrival of the actors, or to run alongside, gaping at the fine costumes and the comical antics of the clowns. It was the first time that a company of real London actors had ever come to Stratford, and no one was going to miss the show.

With a fine flourish of trumpets, the company reached the Inn, and began to prepare for their play, before the admiring eyes of half the town.

The Inn was built round a courtyard, and the upstairs rooms opened on to a balcony from which there was a first-class view of the stage. Seats up there cost a whole sixpence, but there was plenty of room in the yard for all who could pay a penny to come in. The stage was soon put up, along one side, for it consisted merely of planks laid across ale-barrels.

When all was ready, and the yard and galleries packed with townsfolk, the leading citizen, Alderman John Shakespeare, held up his hand for silence.

On this important occasion, he made a long-winded speech, ending with: "And thus, in the name of the aldermen, worthy burgesses and honest gentlefolk, I, your Bailiff, welcome the Queen's Players to Stratford. Proceed."

The leading actor bowed his thanks, and the play began. How polished, how skilful were the London actors, compared with the strolling mummers and jugglers who trudged into town from time to time!

Among the eager crowd, none was more

fascinated than William, the little son of Alderman Shakespeare. Peering through the wooden rails of the balcony, he clutched his mother's skirt when the dragon appeared, and clapped his chubby hands when brave St George killed him. He laughed as loud as any at the antics of the clown and the comical doctor.

When the first play was ended, it was followed by another, this time about kings and princes, with men-at-arms, fighting the French, with what looked like real swords. At last, all was over, and young Will, with his parents and the people of Stratford, trooped happily home to supper and bed.

Later that year, the Earl of Worcester's Men came and acted in the same yard to the same rapturous audience. Afterwards, scarcely a summer passed without a visit from one or another of the London companies.

When they came, Will Shakespeare, the Alderman's son, was missing from home. He was down at the inn-yard, talking to the players, fingering their costumes and watching, always watching, how they walked and spoke their lines upon the stage, or fell down dead in a " battle." His younger brother, Gilbert, was often sent to fetch him home to finish his lessons or help his father, who sent promises of a beating if he did not obey.

The boy who, at four, had been so thrilled by the Queen's Company, was now at the town Grammar School, where Master Roche taught him Latin, a little Greek and just enough of arithmetic to be able to buy corn or sell a house.

William's father, the Alderman, was one of the chief business men of the town. Some spiteful people said he had enough trades for six men. He was corn-merchant who also dealt in wool, malt and leather. He made and sold gloves, as well as being a butcher. His fellow townsfolk had elected him, not only Alderman and Bailiff, but official ale-taster, which meant that he had to test the quality of Stratford's ale, malt and bread.

But the alderman had one weakness; he wanted to become rich too quickly. He loved buying and selling houses. He also lent money and was quick to take a man to court if he thought he had cheated him. He began to get tangled up with lawyers and court-cases, which took a lot of his time, when he should have been in the market looking after his business.

All at once, Alderman John's luck changed. He made some bad bargains in the year when the harvest failed. His cellars were flooded by a sudden tempest and valuable goods were lost. His friends grew tired of his short temper, business grew slack and he had to borrow money.

Master Will was thirteen when his father's business began to fail, so he left school to help with the corn and malt, the butchering and tanning. But things went from bad to worse, for his father appeared in court for debt, much of his furniture was sold, and, deepest disgrace, his alderman's coat was taken away.

Young William did his best to help, but he

Young Shakespeare imitates the players

hated being a shop keeper. He loved to be out in the fields and woods, or practising archery with his friends on the green. Best of all, he loved to be down at the inn-yard when the actors came. Then, after they had gone, he would entertain his friends with imitations which, they said, were every bit as good as the players themselves.

He was a wild, adventurous lad, at this time. Sometimes he went poaching for hares and pheasants—going at night with the older men, for the sport and danger of it. He was always full of tales that he picked up from pedlars and actors, bubbling with laughter, as he re-told them to the lads and lasses down on the green.

Then, just before he was nineteen, he fell in love with a pretty, dark-eyed lady, named Anne Hathaway. He had no real trade and no money, but nothing and no-one could stop him from marrying Anne, least of all his grumbling, bewildered father.

For two or three years, William tried to keep his wife and, presently, his babies, Hamnet and Judith, but they barely had enough to eat. Something had to be done. Anne must go back to her father's farm, while he would go to London.

" I shall make my fortune and mend my father's," he said. " Then I shall come back and buy the finest house in Stratford ! "

So, at twenty-one, like many another country lad, Master Will set off for London. Down at the inn, the older citizens shook their heads. " Will's a wild boy," they said over their mugs of ale, " he'll come to no good, like his father."

But William, though he told no-one, knew quite well what he was going to do. The visits of the actors, and his own skill with a tale, made him certain that he could join a company of actors, even if he had first to hold horses' heads outside a theatre.

Dusty and footsore, when he reached London, he went straight to the lodgings of Richard Field, a Stratford man, who had come to London some years earlier. Field was in the book-trade and he might know some of the actors.

At this time there were only two theatres in London, the "*Curtain*" and the "*Theatre*," which were shared by several companies of actors, who named themselves after various famous men of the day. Field took William along to James

Burbage, owner of the " *Theatre* " and asked him if he could give the young man a job.

" What dost thou know of the actor's trade ? " asked Burbage.

" Little enough, sir," replied Will, " but try me, for my heart is set upon it."

Burbage looked at his eager face and offered to give him a trial, but first he must make himself generally useful about the theatre.

For several years, William struggled to make his way, though there was little or no money to send back to Stratford. He was given small parts at first, and then, as he grew experienced, more important roles in the Lord Chamberlain's Company.

He lived in the poorest lodgings, and often went hungry and threadbare in winter, when bad weather prevented the Londoners from watching the play. In summer, he trudged the dusty roads from town to town, playing many parts on town greens and in inn-yards, as the actors had done in Stratford, when he was a boy.

Slowly, steadily, his fortune began to change. He was a good actor, though not perhaps a great one, like his friend, Richard Burbage, son of the theatre-owner. But the Lord Chamberlain's Men discovered that Will Shakespeare had one gift which would bring fame to them all.

The acting companies were always short of material to act. Few plays were written down, but most were made up from old stories and legends, into which the actors would introduce popular happenings of the day. It was found that young Shakespeare had a wonderful way of polishing up these old tales and adding new verses and characters.

Presently, he began to write whole plays of his own for the company to act. Sometimes he used old romances and histories, or stories about famous Romans and kings. Then too, there were the Italian stories which were becoming so popular, and tales from travellers that one might hear in the London taverns. For these stories, he invented comical or tragic plots, and he filled them with people who held the audiences spellbound. For them, he wrote wonderful poetry, since plays were expected to be in verse. Nothing like these plays had ever been heard before.

At first, he received only a few shillings for a play, but later, as much as five pounds, or even ten. He had no right to ask for payment for every performance as playwrights do today.

But things began to look up for the Lord Chamberlain's Men. Word went round that they acted new plays, much finer than any in London. The Elizabethan audiences, quick to hiss a bad play, were just as ready to roar their approval and to throw their hats into the air when they were pleased. The new plays were so good that a rival playwright, Richard Greene, wrote some spiteful verses about the upstart actor from Stratford.

Business in the theatre became so good that Will and his friend Burbage came to a great decision. They were seated with some friends in the " Mermaid " tavern one day, when Burbage said :

Shakespeare at the " Globe "

" Will, we must build a new theatre of our own ! "

" Thou knowest, Dick," laughed Henry Condell, " that there is not a yard of land in the city of London for building a dog kennel ! "

" True," replied Burbage, " but I mean to build across the river at Bankside, where there is land in plenty."

" Bankside ? " said another. " But will the citizens cross the river to the play ? "

"They go across for the bear-baiting," answered Burbage, "and by Harry, they'll cross for Will Shakespeare's plays!"

In 1599, Burbage built the famous "Globe" theatre across the river at Bankside, not far from the end of London Bridge. Will Shakespeare was one of his chief supporters and shareholders.

The "Globe" was not round, but eight-sided. It was built of wood, and the centre, like the inn-yards, was open to the sky, and here, on the ground, stood the stage. Its front part jutted out into the "pit," and there were curtains across the back, in case an "inner room" was needed. Above the stage was a balcony, and higher still, an upper room, called the "hut." When the play was ready to begin, a flag was flown, and a trumpeter leaned out of the hut and blew a fanfare. If the play included a thunderstorm, old cannon-balls were rolled to and fro across the floor of the hut to make the rumbling sound overhead. All round the pit ran balconies, like those of the inns, where the wealthier playgoers sat under shelter, since the top gallery was roofed over.

Across London Bridge to the "Globe" at Southbank came the London citizens with their wives and sweethearts. Men of fashion took boat from Whitehall Palace, and the well-to-do merchants and lawyers of the city came across in wherries. The richer folk paid a shilling to sit in the galleries, or as much as half a crown for the lowest balcony next to the stage.

The common people, or "groundlings," paid a

At the " Mermaid" Tavern

penny to come into the pit, in front of the stage. There they ate apples and nuts, quaffed ale and smoked pipes that were passed from hand to hand, keeping up a fire of jokes and cat-calls if the play was bad. But, if it was good, as was usual at the " Globe," they wept and cheered, and threw their apple-cores at the gallants who sat on the edge of the stage and sometimes blocked their view.

These were the people for whom Will Shakespeare wrote his wonderful plays—" A Midsummer Night's Dream," " The Merchant of Venice,"

"Henry V," "Twelfth Night," "Macbeth" and many others—and into them he put some of the things that thrilled him when he was a little boy—kings, queens, soldiers, countryfolk, witches, fairies and clowns.

So that he might be near his beloved "Globe," Master Shakespeare took lodgings in Southwark, next to the Bear Garden. He was no longer shabby and hungry, for he had money in his purse, and money now to send home to Anne, whose temper had not improved during the years when she had had to struggle alone. Will Shakespeare was becoming very well known. He had good friends, some of them noblemen, and, at Christmas, he acted with Burbage and others at Greenwich Palace before the great Queen Elizabeth herself.

One day, his brother Gilbert came up to London to see one of his plays, and, when the summer came, he persuaded Will to make the journey back to Stratford. Anne preferred the countryside to the stench and bustle of London, so William now divided his time between the theatre at Bankside and his home in Stratford, where, as he had promised, he bought New Place, the finest house in the town. He paid his father's debts, and so set him up again that the old fellow took new heart and actually tried to recover his lost dignity by applying for a coat-of-arms !

The reign of Queen Elizabeth is rich in great names, but the greatest of them, honoured in almost every country of the world, is that of the glover's son from Stratford-on-Avon, William Shakespeare.

SIR WALTER RALEIGH

LIKE so many of Queen Elizabeth's seamen, Walter Raleigh was born in Devonshire. His family had been squires and landowners for many years, and young Walter grew up in a long, thatched farmhouse, from which fields and woods sloped down to the sea.

When lessons were over, the boy would run down to the shore to play among the boats, or better, to learn sailing and navigating from his older half-brothers, Adrian and Humphrey Gilbert.

Sometimes, he would sit on the sea-wall, listening to the sailors, as they spun tales of voyages to the Indies, and of desperate attacks upon the forts where treasure of Mexico and Peru awaited the galleons from Spain. Young Walter and his friends vowed that they, too, would sail to the Americas one day to discover new lands, and rob the Spaniards of the riches which they claimed for themselves alone.

In Queen Elizabeth's days, a man who would

be known as a gentleman and courtier, had to be educated and well-mannered, but he must also have travelled abroad and have acquitted himself bravely in battle. As soon as he left Oxford, Walter Raleigh made his way to France to fight in the French wars, and then he crossed to Ireland to serve with the Queen's forces. His courage and skill soon attracted the notice of his commander, who chose him to carry despatches to the Royal Palace at Greenwich.

One story tells how Raleigh won the Queen's favour by spreading his rich cloak across a muddy puddle in her path. It is more likely that his good looks and charming manners captured Elizabeth's fancy. When he first appeared at Court, Raleigh was the very picture of the perfect courtier. He was tall and exceptionally handsome, with dark, curling hair, a high forehead and the fashionable pointed beard.

He was skilled in all the things which Elizabeth admired in her courtiers. He was a poet and a writer, a gay and witty companion, as well as a man of action whose courage was already proved. The red-haired Queen loved to have handsome, elegant men about her, and she showered Raleigh with her favours. She made him a knight, and gave him lands and offices which brought wealth and honours. He became Captain of the Guard, a rich appointment which enabled him to be always at Her Majesty's side on the royal journeys through her Kingdom, and at the balls and masques in the Palace at Greenwich.

Raleigh dancing with the Queen

But, much as he loved the brilliant glitter of the Court, Sir Walter could never forget the tales of adventure which had fascinated him when a boy. The Court was for ever humming with the story of some new voyage of discovery or piracy. His own half-brother, Humphrey Gilbert, perished most gloriously on a voyage home from America, after he had claimed Newfoundland for the Queen. This disaster only increased Raleigh's longing to go himself in search of lands and riches across the Atlantic Ocean.

" I wish above all things," he told the Queen, " to discover a land for Your Majesty, richer in gold than Peru, a better Indies than any that the King of Spain hath."

Elizabeth smiled at him, but she would not allow her favourite to leave the Court.

Raleigh could not disobey his proud, vain Queen, but he had friends ready to sail. With his own money, he equipped two ships and sent them to seek a new land which could be claimed for England. The first reports of his adventurers told of a splendid new country in America, with rich soil and friendly natives. Raleigh named this colony Virginia, in honour of Elizabeth, who was sometimes called the Virgin Queen—the queen who never married.

It was not long, however, before the colonists quarrelled with the Indians and among themselves. Some were killed and the rest returned to England.

Sir Walter did not despair. He felt certain that many stout-hearted English folk were ready to make their homes on the rich plains of America, where they could live comfortably and happily, as loyal subjects of their Queen. He sent out new expeditions—one under the command of that fierce sea-dog, Sir Richard Grenville, and another under John White—but they also failed. The settlers wanted gold and easy riches, not the slow toil of farming. Quarrels, desertions and fighting put an end to every venture.

One of the men who returned from Virginia wrote about a strange herb called " Uppowoc," or " tobacco." " The leaves," he said, " are dried and brought to powder, and the Indians used to take the fume or smoke thereof, sucking it through pipes made of clay. We ourselves used to suck it after their manner, as also since our return."

Raleigh seems to have taken to the smoking

habit, which quickly became popular. He certainly introduced another American plant, called the potato, on his estates in Ireland.

Though some of the expeditions to the New World failed, and many an English adventurer came home ragged and penniless, men never ceased to believe that somewhere lay a land of fabulous riches. This hidden land of the Inca people was known as El Dorado, which means " the Golden One." No one had ever discovered El Dorado, but travellers were always bringing back new stories of its wealth. This golden land was supposed to lie somewhere up the Orinoco River, in Central America, and its capital city, built all of gold, was called Manoa.

At long last, Raleigh found the opportunity to go himself in search of El Dorado, not merely for the gold, but also to please the Queen, since he had somewhat lost her favour.

In 1595, he sailed with four ships, capturing the island of Trinidad from the Spaniards on the way. When he reached the Orinoco, Raleigh found that he could not take his ships up the fast-flowing river, so he decided to make a perilous journey of exploration in an oared galley.

The explorers rowed upstream between dense tropical forests and dank marshes. Natives attacked them with poisoned darts, they were sick, weary and hungry, but they went on. At length, they came to a most beautiful country, which stretched in broad plains on either side of the river.

" I never saw a more beautiful country," said

Raleigh, " all fair, green grass, deer crossing our path, the birds singing on every tree with a thousand several tunes, herons of white, crimson and carnation perching on the river side, and every stone we stooped to pick up promised either gold or silver."

But the winter rains came on, drenching the exhausted explorers, and turning the river into a furious torrent. They were four hundred miles from their ships; all were weak and many were ill with fever. Sadly, Raleigh gave the order to return. They had not reached El Dorado, but he felt sure it was not far distant.

Back in England, the Queen restored Raleigh to favour, but she listened coldly to his glowing tale of a wonderful land. He had not brought back enough gold to win support for a new expedition.

A few years later, the great Queen died, and it quickly became clear that James I had little liking for her one-time favourite. Raleigh's witty tongue and high position had earned him many enemies, and now they seized their opportunity to bring about his downfall. They accused Raleigh of plotting to overthrow the King, and, after an unfair trial, he was found guilty of high treason.

For thirteen years, under sentence of death, Sir Walter was a prisoner in the Tower of London. Fortunately, his wife and children were allowed to visit him, and he was able to take a walk every day in a little garden. He passed the time writing his *History of the World*, and in making experiments

Raleigh in the Tower

in science and chemistry. His friends often sent him news of new voyages and explorations in the New World. He himself offered again and again to make a voyage in search of lands and treasure for his Sovereign.

One day, when his wife was reading to him, a servant arrived with a letter from the King's secretary. He read it, and turned joyfully to his wife.

" At last, my dear Bess, at last ! " he cried. " The King is graciously pleased to give me leave to search for El Dorado. 'Tis well known that his greed for gold is equalled only by his fear of the Spaniard. I am ordered not to fight or make war upon the Spaniards, or else I lose my head. But, think, Bess, when I return laden with gold, we shall have my freedom ! "

In 1617, with a fleet of fourteen ships, Sir Walter sailed westwards once more. But his enemies had warned the Spaniards, who were awaiting him. Long years in the Tower had wrecked his health, and he was too ill to leave his cabin when the fleet reached the Orinoco River. But he was still gay and full of hope that this time El Dorado would be discovered. He gave his men careful instructions, and a strong party set off up the river.

Several weeks passed while Raleigh waited for news. One evening, a tired, ragged messenger reached his cabin and stammered out the tale of disaster. The Englishmen had come across a Spanish settlement, and, against orders, had attacked it. The Spaniards were prepared, and the Englishmen were heavily defeated and put to flight. Raleigh's own son was among those killed. The rest had struggled on, but no gold had been found.

Once again, Raleigh had failed, but the perfect courtier did not fail to keep his word. He might have escaped, but he returned to England and the Tower. King James showed him neither mercy nor forgiveness, but ordered his execution.

Though he was ill, Raleigh met his end with dignity and cheerfulness. He wrote a poem on the night before his death, ending with these words:

" But from this earth, this grave, this dust,
 My God shall raise me up, I trust."

Next morning, he stepped briskly into the Old Palace Yard at Westminster, and greeted the bystanders: " I have a long journey to make and I must bid the company farewell."

He ran his thumb along the keen edge of the axe and remarked, smiling: " It is a sure cure for all diseases."

He knelt down and prayed ; then he placed his head upon the block. A moment later, the strange, varied life of the poet, courtier and adventurer was ended.

PRISCILLA MULLINS

Of the "Mayflower"

"PRISCILLA! Priscilla!" called Mistress Mullins from the hatchway. "Do stop gossiping with Mary Chilton and Humility Cooper, and come and help with the bedding."

"Yes, Mother," answered Priscilla gaily. "But let the bedding wait a little longer. Come on deck, dearest, and wave farewell to our friends, with Father and Joey."

Protesting that she did not know that the ship, after so many delays, was at last ready to sail, Mistress Mullins joined her family on deck, as the sailors cast off the last rope from the quayside.

Captain Jones, master of the *Mayflower*, gave orders to his crew, as the stout ship moved away into deep water, but his passengers had eyes only for a group of people on shore.

"Farewell, farewell. God keep you!" they cried from the quay. Some fell upon their knees and prayed aloud for the safety of their friends, others waved and shouted last messages of hope, while the women wept quietly.

Priscilla, holding the hand of her little brother Joseph, looked round at the company crowding against the ship's rails. Her father, Master William Mullins, clasping the hand of his gentle, anxious wife, stood with John Carver, pious leader of the party, and William Bradford, with his beautiful young wife, Dorothy May. Close by, her own friends, Mary Chilton, Constance Hopkins and Humility Cooper, were weeping as they waved their cambric handkerchiefs to their friends. Apart from the rest, his arms folded across his broad chest and his legs straddled like a fierce little gamecock, stood Miles Standish, the only soldier of the party. With him, Priscilla noticed, was a tall young man who had but lately joined this company of men, women and children who were about to leave England for ever. The tall young man stared at her so steadily that Priscilla turned away.

It was September 6th, 1620, when the *Mayflower* put out to sea from Plymouth and headed westward to the new land of America. Priscilla Mullins, just twenty years old, was a pretty, brown-haired girl, whose gay smile and merry tongue had already made her a favourite on the ship, and the sailors had named her their own little " mayflower." With her parents and many friends, Priscilla was setting out for the New World, where Puritans might worship God in their own fashion.

Joseph was tugging at her hand.

"How long will it take to reach Virginia, sister?" he asked.

Priscilla shook her head, smiling.

"No one can tell, Joey," she answered, "six or seven weeks, perhaps, if the winds are kind."

Then she went below decks to help her mother and their servant, Robert Carter, to stow their baggage and to prepare the family's bedding in the cramped hold of the ship.

At first, the wind was kind to the Pilgrims, as these Puritans called themselves. For several days, the *Mayflower* rolled steadily westward upon a gentle sea, but suddenly the weather changed and the full force of Atlantic gales burst upon her. For days on end, it was impossible to hoist a sail, and the little ship wallowed desperately in the mountainous seas, as the captain strove to ride out the gale.

Below decks, 102 Pilgrims were crowded in the dim, stuffy hold. They were sick and frightened. The rolling of the ship made it impossible to cook any food, and those who were not too ill to eat lived on salt horse-flesh, hard biscuits and beer. The pounding seas opened the seams of the ship, and the passengers were continually soaked in icy water. John Carver, Bradford and Master Wilmslow led the Pilgrims in prayers and hymns, while Samuel Fuller attended the sick as best he could. Priscilla was always at his side, or helping the frailer women, like Rose Standish, wife of the fierce little soldier. Priscilla comforted the youngest children by singing nursery rhymes and telling them stories about Holland, where she had lived for several years.

One day, John Howland, unable to stand the stuffy atmosphere any longer, went up on deck and was immediately swept overboard by a mighty wave. He managed to hang on to a rope which was trailing over the side and was miraculously rescued by two sailors with a boat-hook. Next day, with a sound like a musket shot, the main beam of the ship cracked, and even Master Jones, the captain, could not conceal his fears for the ship's safety. Fortunately, someone had brought a great iron screw aboard, and John Alden, the tall young man whom Priscilla had noticed at Plymouth, managed to force the cracked beam back into place.

November came, and the Pilgrims were still at sea, but at last, through the icy mist, the look-out man sighted the shores of America. As the ship rounded Cape Cod and dropped anchor in a large bay, the Pilgrims learned that they had been driven several hundred miles north of Virginia. Yet they fell on their knees and thanked God for deliverance from their perils at sea. The voyage had taken ten weeks; one of the Pilgrims had died at sea, and a baby boy had been born, named Oceanus Hopkins.

All the Pilgrims were anxious to leave the ship, but Governor Carver reminded them of the dangers that might lurk in the woods. Sixteen armed men, under the command of their grim little captain, Miles Standish, were put ashore to explore the neighbourhood and to bring back badly-needed

An armed party went ashore

supplies of fresh water and wood. They returned with news that it was a wooded country, with large grassy clearings and fresh streams, but, strangely enough, there was no sign of Indians.

Next day, therefore, the women and children went ashore, and the wives at once set to work to wash their families' clothes, dirty and salt-caked from the voyage. The children who were placed in Priscilla's care, played wild games up and down the shore, in their joy at being able to run about again, but they were forbidden to go into the woods.

For several days, armed parties explored the land in search of a suitable place to build their new homes. In all these expeditions, Miles Standish, who had fought in Holland against the Spaniards, was the leader, with John Alden as his right-hand man. Returning to the shore one day, the exploring party noticed some strange heaps of sand at the foot of a steep hill. Digging into the sand, they uncovered a large basket, " very handsomely and curiously made," which was filled to the top with corn. It was maize, or Indian corn, which not only helped out their food supplies, but would provide seed for planting, which they seem to have forgotten to bring from England. All this time, the Pilgrims kept anxious watch for Indians. Not one was seen, though signs of their dwellings were found in the woods.

In December, the Elders decided to build a settlement at a place called Thievish Harbour, which was re-named New Plymouth. Snow was falling as the men unloaded the ship's boats, and Priscilla and the other brave women carried ashore the first bundles of household goods. The settlement was to be built along the bank of a stream, known as Town Brook, and plots of land were soon marked off for each family. The " street " rose steeply to a Fort Hill, where Captain Standish was already mounting his cannon and drilling some of the settlers, because Indian war-cries had been heard in the woods and a sudden shower of arrows had kept them on the alert.

The first task, after felling trees, was to build a Common House of rough-hewn planks, with a thatched roof, which could shelter the whole company. Here, as carpenter, John Alden naturally took the lead, for he was liked and trusted for his skill by the men. But he was so shy that the younger ladies, especially Priscilla, had great sport in teasing him.

Food supplies were so low that hunting parties went off each day to bring back game and fish for the common larder. Venturing too far, one hunting-party was forced to spend a bitter night in the open, and, on their return, two of the men fell sick. Next day, several others were taken ill and the disease spread rapidly among the Pilgrims, all of whom were weary from their hardships and half-starved.

The Common House became a hospital where those who were sick tended those who were dying. Samuel Fuller, with Susanna White and Priscilla Mullins worked unceasingly, but their friends died one after another. Among the first who died were Priscilla's own father and mother, and then her dear brother Joey. They were buried on Fort Hill, where Captain Standish levelled the earth over the graves, so that prowling Indians should not discover how weak the garrison had become. Priscilla bravely brushed away her tears, for there were only six Pilgrims left who were strong enough to tend the sick. She and Susanna nursed them through that first terrible winter, when food was desperately short and wolves howled in the darkness; when Standish and John Alden alone mounted guard against the Indians on Fort Hill.

When spring came, only half of the company that had sailed from England remained alive; many of the children were orphans, for all the

"Welcome! Me Samoset"

wives, except four, had died. Priscilla made her home with Master William Brewster and his good wife, Mary, and, as the days grew warmer, she had her first opportunity to look about at her new country. One day, walking beyond Fort Hill, she noticed that the woods were filled with wild fruit trees and bushes, strawberries and herbs; and she caught sight of several wild turkeys, ducks and deer. As she returned towards the settlement, she heard a sound behind her. Turning, she saw to her horror, a tall Red Indian in full war-paint, armed with a bow and arrows.

To her astonishment, he smiled and said in English: " Welcome ! Me Samoset."

Hiding her fear, Priscilla led him to the Common House, where Standish and the rest seized their muskets and leapt forward. With a broad grin, the Indian asked for beer, which they brought him, together with a red coat which he put on with vast delight. He explained that his name was Samoset and that he had learned some English from traders and fishers along the coast. Next morning, he departed with gifts, promising to bring some beaver skins in return.

Presently, Samoset came back with another Indian, named Squanto, who was the sole survivor of the tribe which had buried the maize and which had perished from a plague four years earlier. Squanto quickly made friends with the white men, showing them how best to plant Indian corn with three fishes wrapped round each root to enrich the soil. He showed them where to hunt deer and wild fowl, and where the boys might catch eels and cod ; he also taught the women how to brew an Indian drink from strawberries and a plant called sassafras. Squanto and the Pilgrims liked each other so well that he lived with them for several years and, most important, he arranged a treaty of peace and friendship with the powerful chief Massasoit.

Miles Standish remained always on his guard against the Indians, and when a northern tribe sent, as a war-threat, a sheaf of arrows tied up in a rattle-snake skin, Standish filled the skin with powder and shot and sent it back to show that the settlers were not afraid. On another occasion, Chief Massasoit warned the white men of a plan to massacre the whole colony.

As the summer lengthened, the hearts of the Pilgrims grew lighter. Their crops were thriving, and there was time to build seven small houses, as well as four " common buildings " for stores and meetings. Several exciting incidents gave Priscilla and the women plenty to talk about, as they fetched water from the brook and washed their worn, patched clothing. Two of the men, out hunting, had been frightened by the roaring of " lions," but these turned out to be wolves. The roof of the Common House caught fire one day. One of the harum-scarum Billington children ran away to the woods and was found many days later by Standish, living among the Nauset Indians. John Carver died suddenly of sun-stroke and Master Bradford was elected Governor in his place. One of the most exciting events for the womenfolk was

The first Thanksgiving Day at New Plymouth

the colony's first wedding, that between Susanna White and Edward Winslow, who once went quite alone to pow-pow with an Indian tribe.

At the end of the summer, the Elders decided to hold a holiday feast in thankfulness for the harvest and the peace with the Indians. To this Thanksgiving Day (which is still kept as a holiday in the United States), came Chief Massasoit with ninety braves. Fortunately for the larder, they killed five deer; and the womenfolk set about cooking venison, wild duck, goose, turkey, eels, shellfish, corn-bread, leeks, wild plums and cranberries for a mighty feast that lasted three days. The Indians listened astonished to the prayers and hymns of the Pilgrims, who were equally impressed by the strange dances and savage whoops of their guests. Captain Standish put on a military show which ended with the firing of his cannon, to the terrified delight of the boys and the Indians.

On the third day of the feast, Priscilla was preparing a large fruit pastry in Mistress Brewster's cottage, when John Alden appeared in the doorway.

" Good-day, John," said Priscilla, with a smile, for the tall, red-haired, young man was not often bold enough to come to talk to her.

John looked up and down; he rubbed one deerskin boot against the other, fidgetted with his hands and cleared his throat.

" Come, John, speak out. What have you to tell me ? " asked Priscilla in a teasing voice.

Gradually, with much help from Priscilla, the story came out. John had come to speak for his friend, Captain Miles Standish. The gallant and fierce little captain was minded to marry again and, if Priscilla was willing, the captain would be honoured to make her his bride.

Poor John mumbled out his message and stood silent, gloomily staring at the floor. He had done what his friend had asked, even though he himself had loved Priscilla from the moment that he had seen her waving good-bye at Plymouth. Shyness, and the fact that he was only a carpenter, had prevented him from telling her of his love.

"Why don't you speak for yourself, John?"

Priscilla went on with her pastry; she knew well enough that John always flushed scarlet when she spoke to him, and she had long guessed the reason. But, though she loved him for his strength and his shyness, how could she, a modest maiden, make the first advance? As for Standish, she smiled to think that the fierce little gamecock was not courageous enough to come and woo her himself. Looking at John's unhappy face, she suddenly made up her mind; if he was shy, then she must be bold: "John," she said softly. "Why don't you speak for yourself, John?"

A few weeks later, John Alden and Priscilla Mullins were married in the Common House by Governor Bradford. All the colony was there to greet them; even Captain Standish put a brave face on his disappointment and wished them well.

The rest of their story is a happy one, for they lived together through many more hardships and dangers, bringing up eleven children and moving out to a farm at Duxbury, a few miles away.

John became one of the chief men of the colony, being assistant-Governor, soldier, magistrate and treasurer. He lived to be almost ninety, and was buried beside Priscilla near Eagle Tree Pond, Duxbury. Between them, they had not only helped to found a new town, but also the new country of America.

The story of the brave, dogged Pilgrims has never been forgotten, and, in 1913, the Alden family, descendants of John and Priscilla, placed the Pilgrim Fathers' Memorial at Southampton, and on it is written :

To the Glory of God
in lasting memory of John Alden, a
citizen of Southampton,
who joined the Pilgrims on this quay
1620.
" Youngest of all was he of the men
who came in the *Mayflower*."

Born 1599, he married Priscilla Mullins,
the " mayflower of Plymouth,"
who, according to story, when he was
pleading suit for his friend Miles Standish,
archly said,
" Why don't you speak for yourself, John ? "

MONTROSE

The Great Marquis

AS the Dean, clad in a white surplice in place of the customary black gown, ascended into the pulpit, the huge congregation of St. Giles' Church, Edinburgh, quivered with anger and indignation. The Dean opened the new Prayer Book, which King Charles I had ordered to be read that day in every Scottish church. As he began to read, murmurs from the congregation rose to a hubbub, until an old woman, Jenny Geddes, cried out: " Ye false thief! Wilt thou say Mass in my ear?" and, with that, she hurled her stool at the Dean's head.

Pandemonium broke out in the church; stools and books were flung at the hapless Dean, who fled to safety with his white surplice torn to ribbons. At length, soldiers had to be summoned to close the church and restore order.

In many parts of Scotland, similar disorders clearly showed that the Scots would have no interference by the King in their religious worship. In Edinburgh, they drew up a great parchment, called the Covenant, which was spread out on a flat gravestone in Greyfriars Churchyard and signed by thousands of indignant Scots, who bound themselves to fight for freedom to worship God in their own manner.

Those who signed the parchment were known as Covenanters and, like the Puritans in England, they heartily disliked Catholics, bishops, and any set form of church service. Among the leaders of the Covenanters was James Graham, Marquis of Montrose, only son of a Scottish Earl.

Young Montrose signed the Covenant because he thought the King might be persuaded to change his mind about the Prayer Book. When Charles sent an army to teach the Scots obedience, Montrose captured Aberdeen for the Covenanters, and gave his countrymen their first glimpse of his brilliant military skill.

King Charles quickly made peace with the Scots, for he had far worse quarrels with his Parliament in London. By 1642, things came to such a pass that Charles unfurled his Standard at Nottingham. The Civil War had begun.

At first, the Scots took no part in the war, but the Covenanters, led by the Earl of Argyll, were soon planning to take sides against the King. Argyll was chief of the Campbells, a powerful clan hated by many of the Highlanders.

Although Montrose had signed the Covenant, he had come to believe that Argyll was using religion as a cloak for his own ambition. He quarrelled with the Covenanters, for he would never agree that the authority of the King should be overthrown.

Thus, Montrose was already in the royal camp at Oxford when news came that the Scots were marching on Parliament's side. Charles now turned to the brilliant young marquis and sent him north to raise troops from among the Highlanders and

Signing the Covenant

the enemies of the Campbells. Plans were also made to bring over from Ireland a force of Macdonalds, who had been driven out by the Campbells and were thirsting for revenge.

Montrose went to York, where he found the Royalists so hard-pressed that only one hundred horsemen could be spared for his mission. How could he invade Scotland with only a hundred men?

Difficulties never dismayed Montrose, and he set about raising recruits in the north-west with such energy that he soon had a force of 2000 men. Unfortunately, the defeat of the Cavaliers at Marston Moor compelled him to offer his newly raised troops to Prince Rupert. The invasion of Scotland now seemed to be only a hopeless dream.

But nothing was hopeless if one had courage. Montrose had friends in the Highlands, and, if he could but cross the Lowlands held by Argyll, he might yet strike some shrewd blows for the King. A small force would be cut to pieces by the Campbells, but could he not slip through alone ? Or better, with a couple of trusted friends ?

He chose two friends, grey-haired Colonel Sibbald and young William Rollo, who dressed themselves as plain country gentlemen and rode quietly northwards from Carlisle. At their heels, leading a spare horse, was Montrose, disguised as a groom, with the King's Commission and the Royal Standard hidden in the lining of his saddle.

In such troubled times, they passed few travellers on the road, only a couple of farmers and a party of Lowland soldiers, who warned them to keep a look-out for the traitor Montrose who was somewhere in the district ! A little further on, the road narrowed and a trooper, coming up to rejoin his companions, reined his horse to let the gentlemen pass. As they drew abreast, he looked keenly into the groom's face and, startled, said :

" Good-day, my lord Montrose ! "

The Marquis calmly patted his horse's neck, and answered : " You are mistaken, my friend."

The trooper, who had earlier served under Montrose, said : " What ? Do I not know my lord Montrose well enough ? " He looked from one traveller to another, and a strange look, of both cunning and admiration, came over his face.

" But go your way, gentlemen," he said, adding in a low voice : " and God be with you wherever you go ! "

The trooper must have kept their secret, for, in four days, they reached the home of Patrick Graham, on the edge of the Highlands. He was known as Black Pate, from a gunpowder explosion which had left dark scars on his face, and he served his kinsman, Montrose, faithfully through the struggle that lay ahead.

For a few days, Montrose lay hidden, while Black Pate took word to the clans. Then he returned with the great news that the Irish Macdonalds had landed and were marching towards them. But this was followed by an alarming report that the Stewarts and Robertsons were gathering in arms to drive off the invaders, for long experience had taught them that strangers came to raid and plunder.

Montrose left his hiding-place, and hurried with Black Pate to greet the Macdonalds. They were just in time to prevent a pitched battle between the clansmen.

The charm and reputation of Montrose speedily won over the chieftains, and when he slit open his saddle and shook out the crumpled Royal Standard, the Highlanders and the Macdonalds stood together as comrades in one force.

Since shock and surprise must be his chief weapons, Montrose decided to act swiftly. He ordered a march towards Perth, which was defended by a Covenanter army of 6000 well-armed troops, with cavalry and guns. Montrose had 2000 men and only enough ammunition for one shot each; he had exactly three horses. The enemy was sighted at Tippermuir, drawn up in correct battle order.

Without hesitation, Montrose gave his orders. His men fired their one volley, and, under cover of the smoke, charged with all the fury of Highlanders, armed with dirk and claymore. The ferocity of the charge shattered the Covenanters' line and, in the savage hand-to-hand fighting that followed, the shocked citizen-soldiers had no chance. They broke and fled in all directions. By dusk, Montrose entered the city of Perth.

Staying long enough only to secure food and ammunition, he left Perth and marched north to Aberdeen. Here, a strong garrison came out to drive off the wild rabble of Highlanders, but, as at Tippermuir, one savage charge routed the Covenanters, who fled headlong into the town.

After a battle, it was always Montrose's first anxiety to see that prisoners were honourably treated and that ordinary townsfolk did not suffer the slaughter and plundering which were the usual customs of war. Chivalrous and generous, he hated unnecessary bloodshed, but on this occasion, the wild pursuit through the streets could not be checked, for his Irishmen were maddened by the shooting-down of a drummer-boy, during a parley before the battle.

Following the violent capture of Aberdeen, Argyll himself, at the head of a large well-equipped army, marched up from the south to put an end to these unexpected victories. When he drew near, Montrose made off to the hills, with Argyll after

Montrose enters Perth

him. There followed a long game of hide-and-seek, as Montrose's force moved swiftly about the Highlands, followed by the Covenanters, plodding along in full equipment, with stores, baggage and heavy guns.

Montrose was not to be caught; his aim was to exhaust Argyll's army and then to fight on ground of his own choosing. His men had no baggage or stores, for they could exist on a few handfuls of oatmeal, raw if need be, helped out by any game they might kill. At night, they slept in their thick plaids, which served as cloaks and blankets. Immensely hardy, they could march for days on little or no food, moving at great speed across the wildest parts of the Highlands, normally considered impassable for troops.

During the bitter Scottish winter, only the

hardiest of his troops remained with him, but it was in the worst of weather that he undertook the daring exploit of attacking Argyll in the heart of his own Campbell country, where the Covenanters felt secure until the spring. Cutting across country, Montrose inflicted great punishment upon the Campbells, but was himself well-nigh trapped in a narrow pass, sealed at both ends by strong forces. He escaped by leading his men up the precipitous mountain sides and through the snowdrifts and icy gullies of the lower slopes of Ben Nevis. Marching all night in bitter weather, he brought his starving, tattered force, by daylight, to a point above the enemy's camp on flat ground at Inverlochy.

His exhausted men never hesitated when he ordered the charge. Like a torrent, the Macdonalds poured down the slopes and fell in fury upon their hated foe. Fifteen hundred Campbells fell that day at Inverlochy, though Argyll, their chief, escaped by boat down the loch.

The grim game of hide-and-seek went on, with Montrose always the master, slipping away into the mountains when he chose, and attacking when the ground and opportunity were right. He broke the fighting power of the Campbells, defeated General Baillie at Alford, and routed him at Kilsyth.

In one year, the disguised groom, who had crossed the Border with two friends, had become master of all Scotland.

Montrose entered Glasgow and Edinburgh in triumph. He released his friends from Tolbooth

Prison, but, although they had been shockingly illtreated, he refused to allow revenge to be taken upon his own prisoners, who were given honourable treatment.

There was a day of glory for his Highlanders, when he paraded them at Glasgow, and knighted huge Alasdair Macdonald in the name of the King. But triumph was swiftly followed by disaster.

Montrose had secured Scotland for the King. What must he do next? General Leslie, with a Scottish army, was marching back from England to help the Covenanters. King Charles, desperately near defeat, urged Montrose to smash Leslie and then bring help to the Royalists in England.

Brave though they were, Montrose knew that his little force could not hope to defeat a regular army in the field. His proper course would be to draw Leslie into the Highlands, to harry and exhaust him until he was ripe for the kill. But such a plan would take time, perhaps another winter, and the King was in desperate need.

Recruits by the hundred and thousand were wanted, and Montrose himself hurried off to the Border country upon promise of large numbers of new troops. Meanwhile, by swift marching, General Leslie cut him off from his Irish foot-soldiers, who were surrounded and utterly out-numbered. Offered honourable terms, they surrendered. Then, to the horror of every decent soldier, Montrose's heroic clansmen were slaughtered in cold blood. Argyll and his party were triumphantly back in power.

In sorrow and bitter anger, Montrose made his

way once more to Black Pate, and again set about building up a Highland force, when dreadful news arrived. The King, defeated by Parliament, had given himself up to the Scottish army, and he now sent orders that Montrose must disband his forces. Charles, fated to trust his enemies more than his real friends, believed that he could recover his fortunes with the help of Argyll.

Montrose was still strong enough to secure terms, and so, with a heavy heart, he left Scotland and went into exile in Holland.

His fame had spread throughout Europe; he was honoured and decorated, and offered a field-marshal's baton in foreign service. But he remained with Queen Henrietta Maria, herself in exile for safety's sake, ready to give his sword and his life for the Royalist cause.

Then came news from England that so stunned the exiles, that, it is said, Montrose himself fell unconscious to the ground. The Scots had handed the King over to Parliament and, in January 1649, upon the order of Cromwell, Charles I was beheaded in Whitehall.

Gallant and determined as ever, Montrose at once prepared to invade Scotland. Armed with the commission of the new King, eighteen-year-old Charles, he gathered ships and men and set sail for his own land.

A storm scattered Montrose's ships before he landed in the Orkneys, and, when he reached the Scottish mainland, rumours had already been spread that the young King in Holland had given

The exiles learn of the King's execution

his support to Argyll. While the clansmen hesitated, Montrose's small force was broken up by Covenanters under Colonel Strachan. Montrose cut his way out, and escaped to the mountains with a price of £30,000 on his head.

Across the moors and mountains, from lonely farms and crofts, Strachan's troopers hunted him. Days later, exhausted and ill, Montrose staggered into the little Highland castle of Ardvreck. Its chieftain gave him food and shelter and he fell asleep from utter weariness.

In the morning, Strachan's soldiers marched in and took him as he lay asleep. He begged them to give him a clean death with the sword, but, obeying orders, they bound him and took him away.

Though he was ill from the hardships of his campaigns, Montrose received no mercy from his enemies. His arms bound, and his feet tied under the belly of a shaggy pony, he was led from town to town through Scotland, with a halter about his neck, to be spat on and derided as a traitor and murderer. As shame and dishonour were heaped upon him, his calm gaze and courageous smile never left his face. Even his captors grew weary of their shameful task, and looked away when old friends kissed his hands as he passed.

The Edinburgh mob, egged on by Argyll's agents, lined the streets of the city to complete his humiliation, but, as the hangman's cart drew near, and they saw the bound, ragged marquis with his head erect and an expression of serene courage upon his face, they fell silent. The cart moved slowly down the streets, not through a torrent of jeers and abuse but through an awed silence for a brave man.

Argyll was not to be cheated of his revenge by the tribute of the mob. Montrose was condemned as a traitor and sentenced to be hanged like a common criminal, his head to be stuck upon the gate of the Tolbooth and his severed limbs to be nailed to the gates of Stirling, Glasgow, Perth and Aberdeen.

When they told him his sentence, Montrose answered lightly: "They have designed lasting monuments to four of the chiefest cities of this realm."

One small thing troubled him, as his end drew near. He had enough pride and vanity to hate to go to his death ragged and unkempt. A friend,

Montrose on his way to execution

Lady Napier, contrived to send him a comb and a suit of clothes. His jailers would not allow him the service of a barber, but he managed to comb and arrange his handsome curls. As he did so, an enemy jeered:

"Why is James Graham so careful with his locks this morning?"

"My head is still my own," answered Montrose with his usual courtesy; "I will arrange it as I please. Tonight, when it is yours, you may do with it as you please."

As he stepped into the street, handsome, elegant and smiling, he noticed that he was heavily guarded. "Do you fear me still?" he asked. "My ghost will defeat you yet!"

At the scaffold he was not allowed to speak to the silent crowd, but he said to those around him;

"I fear God and honour the King! I pray that he be not betrayed as his father was. I leave my soul to God, my service to my Prince, my goodwill to my friends, my love and charity to you all."

Eleven years later, when Charles II had regained his throne, and Argyll had been brought to trial, the limbs and head of Montrose were given solemn burial in St. Giles' Church. The coffin, carried by fourteen Scots lords, was followed by Black Pate of Inchbrakie and by those friends and followers who had escaped execution. This time, the people of Edinburgh lining the streets paid an honourable farewell to Montrose, the great Marquis.

MR SAMUEL PEPYS

And the Fire of London

JANE was tired, for she had been sitting up late with the other maids, making preparations for a dinner-party which her master had planned for the next day.

There had been sauces to make, a goose pie and a great venison pasty to prepare for the cookshop, where Will Hewer would carry them in the morning to be baked, and brought home later, all hot on a tray. Little Jane had been cleaning silver and pewter most of the evening, for the master was very particular about his plate, and more than a little proud of his tableware. But it had been pleasant work, with Mercer and Susan singing so merrily. The master and his wife came and took Mercer out to the garden. There, in the warm September evening, they had sung several of the delightful songs which her master had himself written.

When she reached her attic bedroom, long after midnight, the night was so warm and breathless that Jane opened her window, and stood for a moment looking out at the sleeping city. Suddenly, her attention was caught by a light some distance off, not a steady light, but flickering and glowing red. As she looked, she could see clouds of dark smoke billowing away, and she realised that there was a fire in the city, and no ordinary fire at all.

Alarmed, Jane ran downstairs and tapped at her master's bedroom door.

"Mr Pepys! Mr Pepys!" she called. "Come quickly. There's a great fire, burning down all the city!"

Mr Pepys was out of his four-poster bed in a twinkling, and, night-cap on head, mounted the stairs two at a time to Jane's window. The maids and Tom, the house-boy, crowded behind him.

It was no great affair, decided Mr Pepys, and he told them not to alarm themselves but to go to bed peacefully. The fire, he said, was a great way off and would doubtless be out by morning; for his own part he would go back to bed.

Next morning, the whole household was up early and, while Mr Pepys was arranging his books and papers in a new book-case, Jane came in with fresh news about the night's happenings.

"There's no other talk at the cookshop but the fire," she said. "They do say that above three hundred houses have been burned down. Nor is it out yet, but all Fish Street is a-burning, and the fire running faster than any can stop it towards London Bridge."

Though he was still a young man, and a merry one too, Mr Samuel Pepys was already becoming an important citizen. He was Clerk to the Navy, and his work was to provide His Majesty King Charles II's ships with ropes, stores, men, pay and,

Mr Pepys sees the fire for the first time

in fact, everything needed by a growing navy. Therefore, he thought to himself, if the fire was really as bad as Jane reported, he must see that the King's property was safe. So he put on his hat and walked out towards the Tower of London.

Knowing the Lieutenant of the Tower, he was able to go up into the Keep to obtain a good view of the city, taking with him, in his usual kindly way, the little son of a friend. From their high viewpoint, they could see only too clearly that Jane's report was true. Under a dense pall of smoke, the fire stretched like an angry sea across the city, and the houses at one end of London Bridge were already alight.

Really alarmed, Mr Pepys came down to have a word with his friend.

" They say it all started in Faryner's house, the

King's baker in Pudding Lane," said the Lieutenant. "Like enough some will say 'tis the work of Catholics or French spies. But 'tis spreading, Mr Pepys, and I know of no man who can stop it."

Mr Pepys was a man of energy, who possessed a great fund of common sense, so he hurried off to the waterside and looked about for a boat. Watermen were scarcer than usual at this time, owing to the Plague and the Press-Gang, but he soon hailed a boatman whom he knew, and went on the river, in the company of a gentleman who was also anxious to see the fire.

Flames had now reached houses and alleys along the waterfront, and Pepys could see people running to and fro, frantically trying to save their goods and possessions, flinging bundles down into waiting boats, handing down children and old people. They stayed in their precious homes until the last minute, and then they rushed down the steps into boats, as the flames swallowed their houses.

No one seemed to be making any effort to stop the fire itself, but only to save what little they could carry away. A rising wind began to sweep the flames towards the centre of the city.

Mr Pepys made up his mind.

"To Whitehall," he ordered the boatman.

Along the river lay Whitehall, that great rambling palace, more like a town than a royal residence, where, at this time, privileged persons could walk in and out. They could even watch the King sitting at dinner, or strolling with the Court beauties who surrounded him.

The fire swept along the waterfront

Mr Pepys bustled along to the King's apartments, where the usual crowd of idle gentlemen was lounging and chatting. His first-hand news of the fire roused them from their boredom, and word was taken in to the King, who sent for his energetic Navy Clerk.

Charles II was dallying over a late breakfast with his brother, James, Duke of York, when Mr Pepys entered and bowed. Charles turned his dark, handsome face towards the man whom he already knew to be one of his most loyal and diligent servants.

"Ah, Mr Pepys," said the King, " to whom, brother, we are already vastly obliged for his service to our ships. Now what of this great fire, Mr Pepys? Tell us all you have seen."

Mr Pepys gave a full account of the damage

which had occurred in the night and of the danger to the whole city, if drastic steps were not taken to check the fire.

"Your Majesty knows," he said, "that after this long drought, the houses are as dry as tinder. Therefore, unless Your Majesty commands houses to be pulled down, nothing can stop the fire, until the whole city be burned to the ground."

The King listened attentively and then commanded Pepys to order the Lord Mayor to destroy houses in the path of the fire. The Duke of York added that he would provide soldiers if they were needed for the work.

Leaving Whitehall, Pepys met another of his many friends, a sea-captain, who offered him a lift in his coach, and they drove to St Paul's, enquiring on every side for the Lord Mayor. The streets were crowded with people trundling carts, lugging great bundles on their backs, and even carrying sick folk in their beds away from the fire.

At last, in Canning Street, they found Sir Thomas Bludworth, the Lord Mayor, mopping his face with a kerchief, and looking as if he were at his wits' end. When Pepys gave him the King's orders, he flung out his hands in despair.

"Lord, what can I do?" he wailed. "I am done : people will not obey me. I *have* been pulling down houses, but the fire overtakes us faster than we can do it."

Mr Pepys thought he was behaving more like a feeble woman, than as Lord Mayor of one of the greatest cities in Europe, and he did not hide his contempt for Sir Thomas, who continued to bemoan his lot. No more soldiers were needed, declared the Lord Mayor, and, as for himself, he must go home and take some breakfast, for he had been up all night, not lying a-bed like some other folks who now came giving advice and orders!

So Mr Pepys made his way home, to receive his guests for the dinner-party; there were Mr Wood and his wife, Mr Moone, Mr Shelden and pretty Mistress Barbara Shelden, for whom Mr Pepys could not hide his admiration. There was also, of course, Mistress Pepys, his own pretty little French wife, who was cross with him when he eyed the ladies. They sat down to a handsome dinner, with Jane and Susan waiting at table. Everyone tried to be merry, but the fire filled their thoughts. Then, in the middle of the meal, a neighbour came in to ask news of her relations whose house was said to be burned down.

So, instead of entertaining the ladies with his flute and songs after dinner, Mr Pepys and Moone went out again and found people full of distress and the fire still spreading, so that goods which had been moved to safety in the morning were again in danger.

Presently, they decided to go on the river, and this time Pepys took his wife and friends. The wind was now so strong that showers of sparks fell all around their boat and forced them into the middle of the river among other boats, crowded and so laden with household goods that some fell into the water and were lost. All this upset Mrs Pepys, so they went across to the far bank and took wine at a little tavern, and stayed until dark watching the fire, which was now a great arch of flames more than a mile long. They could see churches, shops and houses burning furiously, and all the time the fire made a terrifying, roaring, crackling sound, mingled with the crash of falling buildings.

Back home, they gave shelter to a neighbour, poor Mr Hater, who was so distressed by the loss of his house and furniture that they had to put him to bed. But there was little sleep for anyone that night. The news from every side was so alarming that it was time to begin packing up their own goods. Mr Pepys carried an iron chest full of money down into the cellar, while the servants took the best plate and linen into the garden. Fortunately, it was a warm, moonlit night. At four o'clock, someone sent Mr Pepys a cart, which was soon loaded with furniture and wheeled round to a friend's house in a safer quarter. Mr Pepys rode on the cart, in his nightshirt.

" Lord ! to see how the streets and highways are crowded with people," he cried, " running and riding, and getting of carts at any rate to fetch away things."

All that day, and the next, Mr Pepys worked tirelessly, hurrying here and there, sending away his goods by cart and boat, yet not neglecting the Navy Office where he kept his precious papers concerning the fleet, and the plans for new ships.

Pepys and Admiral Penn bury their wine

As the fire drew nearer his home, he and Admiral Penn dug a big hole in the garden in which they put their best wine and a great Parmesan cheese.

Tired from the digging, they sat awhile in the garden.

"This is a melancholy business, Mr Pepys," remarked the Admiral heavily. "All London burning and nothing to be done, save you and I to dig holes for cheese!"

"Sir William," said Mr Pepys with decision, "it seems certain that the Navy Office and all our records will be destroyed. You know how much such a disaster would hinder the King's business. Some extraordinary means *must* be found to stop the fire."

"True enough, but what means?" replied Penn.

"I will tell you," continued Pepys, growing excited, " call out every workman from the King's shipyards at Woolwich and Deptford to blow up houses round about the Navy Office. The seamen can be trusted to use gunpowder. If you yourself do but give the orders, it can be accomplished."

Admiral Penn agreed with the plan, and he left at once to collect workmen and sailors from the shipyards down the river. He would give them orders to carry out one task only : to blow up houses in the path of the fire, so that it had nothing to burn.

A little later, while Mr Pepys was writing a letter to the Secretary of the Navy to inform him and the Duke of York what they had determined to do, he heard the welcome sound of explosions, as the first houses, down by the Tower, were blown up by Penn's sailors.

But, in the middle of the night, as he lay trying to snatch some sleep under an old quilt on the floor, Pepys' wife in tears, shook him until he awoke.

" Samuel, wake up, wake up ! " she cried. " The fire is at the bottom of our lane ! "

There was no time to waste, but they must abandon their cherished home. Pepys had kept a boat ready, and now he put his man Will Hewer, little Jane and his wife into it, and he himself stepped down into the stern, grasping a bag containing more than £2000 in gold.

They rowed down the river to Woolwich to the home of a good friend who had promised to give them shelter, though, being a careful man, Mr

Pepys told his wife and Will Hewer that they were not to leave the gold unguarded by night or day!

When it was light, he went back to Seething Lane, and found to his joy that the fire had not quite reached their house, though it had been close enough. The good work of Penn's men was beginning to take effect, and the fire was at last being checked; everyone reported that the flames were dying down.

Now, after five days, he could think of washing and shaving and putting on clean clothes. Yet he could not find a shop left standing that could sell him a new shirt, so he borrowed one from Mr Creed, and went to dinner with a party of friends. There was only fried mutton, served on odd earthenware plates, as poor a meal as he had ever eaten, but it seemed like a feast, and they were as merry as schoolboys.

A week later, there were tremendous comings and goings at the Pepys' house—carpenters putting up four-poster bedsteads, curtains and shelves; workmen carrying in tables, chairs and books; and the servants scrubbing and polishing for all they were worth. Mr Pepys fetched his gold from Woolwich, and dug up his wine and the great cheese, but, as they were carried into the cellar, he hoped that the workmen would not notice the iron money chest which was still there!

In every direction London lay in ruins, the pavements still too hot for any man to walk upon. St Paul's Cathedral was destroyed, with scores of churches and many hundreds of houses. All would have to be rebuilt; and London *was* rebuilt in amazingly short time by the energy and determination of the Londoners, together with the genius of Christopher Wren.

As for Mr Pepys, that jolly, music-loving man who did more than any of his time to build up a strong navy, he wrote in his Diary on 15th September 1666, thirteen days after Jane espied the outbreak of the Great Fire :

"I to finish my letters and home to bed: and find, to my infinite joy, many rooms clean: and myself and wife lie in our own room again. But much terrified in the nights, now-a-days, with dreams of fire and falling down of houses."

JOHN AND SARAH CHURCHILL
Duke and Duchess of Marlborough

TOWARDS the end of Charles II's reign, there could be seen in the royal household and at the dances and functions of the brilliant and elegant Court, a young man named John Churchill.

"Handsome Jack" was the son of a Cavalier gentleman who had lost most of his money and lands in the service of his King during the Civil War, and whose reward was now to have his family placed at Court.

Young Churchill was first a page to the Duke of York, and then, like most young bloods, he joined the Army and served in the wars on the Continent, and in North Africa, against the Moors.

Now, at twenty-eight, Colonel Churchill was perhaps the most handsome and charming young man at Court, favoured by the King and the Duke, and vastly admired by the ladies. But, apart from his army pay, Churchill was penniless. If he was to make his way in the extravagant, pleasure-loving world that centred about the King, he must marry a lady with a rich fortune.

It was noticed, however, that he often danced at balls and parties with one of the maids-of-honour to the Duchess. He had eyes for no-one else. She was Sarah Jennings, a dazzling girl of seventeen, fair, with sparkling blue eyes, a pert, lively air—

and a temper like a wild-cat. Colonel John fell head-over-heels in love with her for the rest of his life. It was a stormy courtship, during which he was often in despair at Sarah's tantrums. Once he sent her a present, with a letter.

" I was last night at the ball," he wrote, " but I was not so happy, for I could see you nowhere. Pray see which of these two puppies you like best. They are above three weeks old, so that if you give it warm milk it will not die."

Despite her temper, Sarah loved John faithfully, and it was in vain that his father pointed out that she had no money. They were secretly married in the Duchess's house, and John remained in the service of the Duke of York, while Sarah became lady-in-waiting to his daughter, Princess Anne.

The princess was not particularly clever, but she was gentle and warm-hearted, and she was so devoted to her clever, lively Sarah, that theirs became one of the most famous friendships in history. Anne thought it silly that her dear friend must give her the titles and ceremony due to a princess, so she invented two ordinary names, which they could use in their private conversations and letters. Anne called herself " Mrs Morley," while Sarah was " Mrs Freeman."

The fortunes of the Churchills improved when the Duke of York became King James II. They could afford to build a house at St Albans, though Sarah continued as Lady-of-the-Bedchamber to sweet-tempered " Mrs Morley." John became Lord Churchill and was made a general.

John Churchill and Sarah Jennings at Court

Unfortunately, James II quickly showed that he meant to rule as he pleased and to impose his own Roman Catholic religion upon the people of England. Secret plans were made to depose him and to bring over his Protestant daughter, Mary, and her Dutch husband, Prince William of Orange.

"Dutch Billy" landed in Devon in 1688 and John Churchill, in charge of James II's army, went over to his side. He said that, although he would give his life to protect the King's person, his Protestant religion prevented him from fighting against the Dutch prince. James retreated to London, angrily ordering the arrest of Sarah Churchill.

But the ladies were prepared for flight. Unlike her father, Princess Anne was a sincere Protestant, and she said she " would rather jump out of the window than face her father," or lose her beloved " Mrs Freeman." Together, at night, they hurried down a wooden staircase at the back of Sarah's apartments and slipped out of an unguarded backdoor, at which the Bishop of London and Lord Dorset were waiting. In the muddy street, Anne lost one of her shoes but there was no time to look for it ; they were bundled into a coach and driven to the bishop's house. Next morning, they drove to a house in the heart of Epping Forest, and, after a rest from their bumping over the rutted roads, set off for Nottingham, accompanied by the Bishop himself, armed with sword and pistols !

In London, there was a hullabaloo at the disappearance of the princess, some saying that she had been murdered by Catholics. When James II reached Whitehall, the unhappy king cried :

" God help me ! Even my children have forsaken me ! "

He could find no support whatever, and he went into exile to the Court of Louis XIV of France, who treated him with royal generosity. James's daughter Mary, and her husband, " Dutch Billy," became joint-sovereigns as William III and Mary.

Though William rewarded Churchill by making him Earl of Marlborough, he did not like him very much, while Queen Mary ordered Anne to dismiss Sarah, whom she disliked for her power over the heiress to the throne. Anne was gentle, but she could also be stubborn. She absolutely refused to part with her dearest friend, and, after a public quarrel, the two royal sisters never spoke to each other again.

William's whole heart was devoted to the struggle to save his beloved Holland from Louis XIV, the " Grand Monarch," the gorgeous " Sun King " of France. William himself, an invalid and somewhat crippled, was an indomitable fighter and a patient, wily foe. His silence and surly manners, his dislike of women and greediness at table did not make him popular at Court. The ladies, whispering behind their fans, called him " a low Dutch bear." He favoured his Dutch officers and would not make full use of Marlborough's gifts as a general, for he did not fully trust him.

For a time, Marlborough was placed in the Tower, and while Sarah was striving furiously to secure his release, she was supported by Anne, who wrote :

" I hear Lord Marlborough is sent to the Tower ; and though I am certain they have nothing against him . . . methinks it is a dismal thing to have one's friends sent to that place. I am told by pretty good hands there will be a guard set upon the Prince and me. But let them do as they please, nothing shall ever vex me, so I can have the satisfaction of seeing dear Mrs Freeman."

Marlborough's chance arrived at last, when

Anne became Queen of England, for she was only too delighted to give the command of her armies to the husband of her dear friend.

Through ten campaigns, Marlborough commanded the English and Dutch armies against the might of Louis XIV, with a brilliance that places him with the greatest generals of all time, the equal of Caesar and Napoleon. He had only a small professional army, and he was constantly hampered by the Dutch rulers, who, quite naturally, did not want their troops taken far from Holland. But he was tirelessly patient and good-humoured with his allies, and his partnership with the Austrian Prince Eugene was always successful.

His greatest victory was at Blenheim in 1704, when, with breath-taking boldness, he marched his army across Europe at a speed which outwitted both his enemies and allies. Unless he could get between Vienna and the French army, he knew that the war was lost. Joined by Prince Eugene, he crossed the Danube and attacked the French with such perfect timing that he gained the greatest victory for British arms since Agincourt.

Blenheim saved Austria; the battle of Ramillies, where he nearly lost his life, saved the Lowlands, and further victories broke the enormous military strength of Louis XIV. Marlborough rode in triumph through London, with hundreds of captured French standards in the procession. He was rewarded with an estate and the vast house called Blenheim Palace; he became a Duke and a millionaire.

Marlborough on campaign

Marlborough was the best general we have ever had; " he never rode off any field except as a victor," for he never fought a battle that he did not win nor beseiged a fortress that he did not take. Moreover, he was modest and charming to all men; beloved by his soldiers as " Corporal John," he cared for their welfare as did few commanders at that time, seeing they had good boots, food and regular pay. On campaign, he travelled, not with a vast train of cooks, barbers, musicians and fashionable ladies, but as a plain man leading soldiers to victory.

No English general ever won such power over the minds of the French as did " Malbrouck." From Marshal down to drummer-boy, they felt him to be their master—that it was hopeless to resist him. They even made up a song about him:

"Malbrouck s'en va-t-en Guerre" (Marlborough has gone to war), which was sung to the same tune as "For he's a jolly good fellow."

Yet this greatest of generals was afterwards removed from his rank and dismissed from the army; vile stories were made up against his name, both then and for ever since. Why?

The reason lies in the bitter jealousies of the time. There were two great parties in England, the Whigs and the Tories, struggling for power and for influence over the Queen. Plots, lies, scandalous stories, false evidence and forgery were the weapons of both sides.

Marlborough was never happy as a party-man; the Tories hated him and the Whigs never loved him. As the war dragged on, some said he was prolonging it for his own glory and wealth, others feared he was so powerful that he would set himself up as another Cromwell, while Sarah, in her special position as the Queen's closest friend, was said to rule the country.

Worst of all, they said Marlborough was mean. Perhaps it was his early poverty that made him careful with money; at all events, he gathered a vast private fortune. When he was very rich, men said he had only three coats to his back, and he ordered his army servant to slit his old, muddy gaiters along the seams so they could be turned and re-made. They said that he would walk home to save sixpence on a coach, that he did not give banquets to his officers, nor drink nor gamble like any other fine gentleman. It was only to be

" Malbrouck s'en va-t-en Guerre "
(*Marlborough has gone to war*)

expected that so mean a man would take bribes and use the money for his troops to enrich himself. The writings of his beloved Sarah and, in our own day, of Sir Winston Churchill show how little truth there was in these vile taunts.

Yet it was Sarah's famous temper that brought about her husband's downfall. Even the gentle, patient Queen Anne grew tired of Sarah's rages, and she listened instead to the soothing, respectful voice of Mrs Masham, her new Tory favourite, who detested the Duchess Sarah. After some tremendous scenes, Anne turned completely from her " dear Mrs Freeman " and dismissed her for ever. Once she was out of favour and out of power, Marlborough's enemies were able to bring about his downfall.

But, despite her faults, he loved Sarah dearly; on campaign, he wrote to her constantly from his general's tent. After Blenheim, his first thoughts were for her, and he scribbled a note in pencil, handing it to an officer who rode night and day across Europe to give it to Sarah. At the foot of the letter, was added:

"I beg you to give my duty to the Queen and let her know her army has had a glorious victory."

Once, in a rage, Sarah cut off her beautiful hair to annoy her husband; he said not a word, but, years afterwards, she found her locks in a cupboard among his dearest possessions.

She herself was loyal and faithful to him all her life; and, after his death, when the Duke of Somerset asked her to marry him, she replied:

"If I were young and handsome as I was, instead of old and faded, as I am, and you could lay the empire of the world at my feet, you should never share the heart and hand that once belonged to John, Duke of Marlborough."

LADY NITHSDALE
The Story of a Famous Escape

IN 1715, Lord Nithsdale, a Scottish nobleman, was lodged in the Tower of London on a charge of high treason against His Majesty King George I.

The armies of "fat George" of Hanover had proved too much for the Jacobites, which was the name given to the supporters of the Stuarts after James II had been driven from his kingdom. Lord Nithsdale, with several more of the leading Jacobites, was captured and brought to London for trial.

His beautiful wife, Winifred, followed him to London, and, with her maid, Evans, found lodgings in Drury Lane. They were joined by Miss Hilton, a Jacobite lady.

Next day, Lady Nithsdale asked permission to visit her husband, but this was refused unless she was willing to share his imprisonment. Though she longed to be with him, she had no intention of giving up her freedom, because she had already made up her mind to do everything possible to secure his release.

Her maid Evans found out that Lord Nithsdale was occupying an upper room in the Lord Lieutenant's Tower. Lady Nithsdale went to the main gate, and managed to pass the guards by pretending that she was visiting the Lieutenant himself. The soldiers, seeing an aristocratic lady with her maid, let her pass.

When she reached the Lord Lieutenant's Tower, there was a great deal of bustle and noise in the courtyard, as some soldiers were drilling, while others were unloading heavy guns and baggage from field-wagons. Under cover of the commotion, Lady Nithsdale spoke quietly to one of the Yeomen.

" I am Lady Nithsdale," she said in a low voice. " I beg you to take me to my husband."

" I couldn't do that, ma'am," replied the astonished, but kindly, soldier. " No-one is allowed to see his Lordship. Strict orders, ma'am."

" I am his wife," she whispered beseechingly. " You have a wife, I am sure. If you were in prison, would she not wish to see you, perhaps for the last time ? It is such a little thing I ask. Look, here is some money. Let me see him just for a moment, I beg you."

The good-hearted Yeoman scratched his head. " I don't rightly know if I ought, ma'am," he said, " but be quick. I'll unlock the door and stand guard outside."

He led Lady Nithsdale up to the first floor, and unlocked the door. She stepped inside.

" Ah, William ! " she cried, embracing her husband.

" Winifred, my love ! How came you here ? "

" I bribed a good fellow to let me in. Listen, William, we *must* get you from here."

" My dear Winifred, it is quite impossible to

Lady Nithsdale pleads for her husband's life

escape from the Tower. Let us speak of something else."

"William, there is but one sentence for treason—death. Therefore we must find some way of helping you to escape."

"I am not afraid to die. Perhaps there is one hope and one thing you can do. Carry a petition to the King. I will permit you to ask for mercy for the sake of our children."

"Ah, William, we can expect little mercy from German George, but I will try; I will try anything."

They embraced again, and then Lady Nithsdale slipped out of the Tower, putting half a guinea into the hand of the Yeoman, who escorted her to the main gate.

In February 1716, Lady Nithsdale, dressed in black, waited at St James's Palace for the King's approach. When he drew near, she fell upon her knees, begging for her husband's life and holding out the petition for mercy. George did not pause to listen, but brushed the petition aside, refusing even to read it.

As her friends bore her away weeping, Lady Nithsdale decided that she would plan the escape of her husband, no matter what the risk.

First, she went to the Tower, where, pretending to be full of joy, she told the guards that Parliament was in favour of mercy being shown to the prisoners and that her husband was certain to be pardoned. Then she gave them some money to drink the health of the King, though she was careful not to give them too much, in case they became suspicious of her.

The next day was the 23rd of February, the day before the date of Lord Nithsdale's execution. That afternoon, at her lodgings, Lady Winifred called Mrs Mills, Evans and Miss Hilton the Jacobite lady.

"With your help," she said, "I am determined to effect my lord's escape. I have everything ready, but you must do exactly what I tell you. Now, listen carefully. . . ."

The ladies were so excited as she unfolded her plan that they did not stop to think of the dangers. All the way to the Tower, in the coach, Lady Nithsdale kept on talking, in order to hold their attention. Since she was allowed to take in only one visitor at a time, she left Mrs Mills in the coach and took Miss Hilton with her.

They hurried up a dim staircase, and through an outer room, where several guards and their wives were chatting round a fire. They had grown accustomed to the visits of the generous lady and they saluted respectfully when she explained that she was bringing some friends to say farewell to her husband.

Miss Hilton was wearing a cloak, beneath which she was hiding some similar clothes. Once inside Lord Nithsdale's room, she stayed only long enough to leave these clothes behind, and then was hurried out by Lady Nithsdale. As they crossed the outer room, she let the guards hear her tell Miss Hilton to send her maid to dress her, since she must go to Parliament that very evening to beg for his lordship's pardon.

At the top of the stairs, she met Mrs Mills on her way up. She was dressed in a blue cloak and hood, and was holding a handkerchief to her eyes as if weeping bitterly. The guards' wives murmured sympathetically as the poor lady came through.

Inside the apartment, Lady Nithsdale took off Mrs Mills's cloak and hood, and handed them to her husband.

"Put these on, William," she commanded. "Mrs Mills is as tall as you and the hood will help to hide your face."

She made him put on a fair wig, and she disguised his dark eyebrows with a yellowish paint, so that he would look like Mrs Mills in a dim light.

Meanwhile, Mrs Mills had dressed herself in the clothes left by Miss Hilton, which made her look like that lady. Then, no longer weeping, she was taken through the outer room by Lady Nithsdale, who kept talking very earnestly in the same way as before :

" My dear Mrs Catherine," she said, " I do beg you to go in all haste and fetch my maid. She certainly cannot know the time, and must have forgotten that she is to attend me when I go to Parliament. Tell her to make all haste to come to me."

The guards, probably confused by all this coming and going, politely opened the door for them, and Lady Nithsdale hurried back to complete her husband's disguise.

To hide his beard, she told him to hold a handkerchief to his face all the time. It was now almost dark and the most dangerous moment had come.

She opened the door and led him out. The guards, who had seen a weeping lady go into the room, now saw a weeping figure in the same blue cloak and hood being hurried across to the staircase by Lady Nithsdale, who pretended to be very anxious indeed.

" My dear Mistress Betty," she cried, " run and bring back my maid Evans for God's sake. You know my lodging. Go there and tell her to come at once. If you ever made haste in your life, do it now."

Keeping close behind, to cover his manly stride, Lady Nithsdale hustled her disguised husband down

Lady Nithsdale guides her husband past the guards

the stairs, where the faithful Evans was waiting to take him across the courtyard, into the street and away to a place of safety.

Lady Nithsdale returned to the empty room and shut the door behind her. She must give her husband time to get away, so she kept up a conversation, as if he were still there, talking loudly in her own voice and imitating his replies in a lower tone. She walked up and down several times, as though they were talking together.

After some time, she decided to go. She opened the door and, looking back, said most tenderly, but loud enough for the guards to hear:

"Goodnight, dearest husband. Some strange thing must have kept Evans, for she was never neglectful of me. I must go myself, for time is short. But if the Tower be still open, I will return here this night to bring you good news. I will come for certain in the morning. So farewell."

She pulled a cord that raised the latch and shut the door with a click, so it could only be opened from the inside, and began to leave the outer room. At that moment, a servant appeared, carrying candles for the prisoner's room! All would be lost if he tried to enter the empty room! Lady Nithsdale turned to him.

"No," she said, "not yet. My lord is at his prayers now, and will not have candles until he calls for them."

Then she went down the stairs and left the Tower.

There was still much to be done before her husband was safe. Evans, the maid, had found an attic in a poor lodging house, where Lord and Lady Nithsdale remained hidden for two days, not daring to move about, lest it became known that there were strangers upstairs. They had nothing to eat, except a little bread which the good Mrs Mills brought in her pocket.

Mr Mills had a trustworthy friend who was a servant to the Venetian Ambassador. He was ordered to take a coach to Dover to meet the Ambassador's brother, and he took Lord Nithsdale with him, disguised as a footman of the household. At Dover, a small boat was hired to take Lord Nithsdale to France, where he stayed with Jacobite friends, until he was able to join the Stuart Court in Rome.

Brave Lady Nithsdale had not yet finished her

adventures. King George was furious at the escape, and ordered her arrest, but she was determined to return to Scotland to protect her son and to put her family affairs in order, especially as she had buried her papers, jewels and plate in the garden, before she left for London !

"I had risked my life for his father," she said afterwards, "and I was resolved to run a second risk for my son. Though I had never ridden a horse, except on the journey down, I bought three saddle-horses and went a horse-back, with only my dear Evans and a very trusty man. We lodged at small inns, where I was sure not to be known, and, by this means, I got safe home."

After more adventures and narrow escapes, she crossed to France and joined her husband. She became a lady-in-waiting at the Jacobite Court and governess to the Royal children, including young Charles, known later as Bonnie Prince Charlie. Many years later, Lady Nithsdale died in Rome, "very old and greatly loved."

BACKGROUND TO THE STORIES IN PART THREE
SIR THOMAS MORE (1478–1535).
More was a friend of *Erasmus*, the great Dutch scholar. More's most famous book, *Utopia* (Greek for " nowhere ") describes an imaginary country with a perfect government. More died because he refused to agree that the King, not the Pope, was Head of the Church. He was made a saint in 1935.

RICHARD CHANCELLOR (*d.* 1556).
Sebastian *Cabot* (son of John, who discovered Newfoundland, 1497) founded the Company of Merchant Adventurers, which sent Willoughby and Chancellor on their voyage. Other famous travellers of the time were *Martin Frobisher*, *John Davis*, *Henry Hudson*, who tried to find the North-West Passage to India. *Ralph Fitch* (1583–1611) made an eight-year journey in the East which led to the founding of the East India Company.

THE PRINCESS ELIZABETH (1533–1603).
Henry VIII had three children—*Mary*, daughter of his first wife, Catherine of Aragon ; *Elizabeth*, daughter of Anne Boleyn (a Protestant) ; *Edward*, son of Jane Seymour (a Protestant). Elizabeth was well educated as a girl, but rather neglected by her father. She was in great danger during the reigns of Edward VI and Mary, because of suspicion of Protestant plots to put her on the throne.

FRANCIS DRAKE (1540–1596).
Following the events described in this book, Drake sailed round the world in the *Golden Hind* (1577–1580), on the greatest voyage ever made by an Englishman. When open war with Spain broke out, Drake was " General of Her Majesty's Navy," and made many raids against the enemy, including the famous attack on Cadiz, when he " singed the King of Spain's beard." In 1588, he was second-in-command against the Armada. Next year, he failed in an attack on Lisbon and retired to shore. After several years, he and Hawkins sailed against the Spaniards in the West Indies ; both commanders died, and Drake was buried at sea off Porto Bello. He was extraordinarily generous and brave ; even a Spaniard said he was " sharp, well-spoken, boastful and not very cruel."

WILLIAM SHAKESPEARE (1564–1616).

Little is known of his life, though town-records give some facts about his father. He seems to have gone to London to seek his fortune; he joined The Lord Chamberlain's Men (afterwards called The King's Men) and became a fairly good actor. He began to write plays for his company and became well-to-do. He bought a big house in Stratford and had a share in the Globe Theatre. He was much admired by the poets and writers of the day who met at the Mermaid Tavern.

SIR WALTER RALEIGH (1552–1618).

The most splendid of Elizabeth's courtiers—a poet, writer, soldier and explorer. Among the great Englishmen of his time were *Sir Humphrey Gilbert, Sir Philip Sidney, Sir Richard Grenville.*

PRISCILLA MULLINS OF THE *MAYFLOWER*.

In Elizabeth's reign, the Puritans separated themselves from the Church of England and were punished for holding their own plain services. One body of Puritans was driven from Lincolnshire to Holland; then they decided to go to America to worship God in their own manner. They left Southampton in the *Mayflower*, but had to put back into Plymouth, from which they sailed in September 1620. After dreadful hardships, they succeeded in founding New England. Later, they were called " *The Pilgrim Fathers.*"

MONTROSE (1612–1650).

The Civil War between Charles I and his supporters (Royalists or " Cavaliers ") and Parliament (" Roundheads ") broke out in 1642. At first, the Royalists were successful but could not capture London. The genius of *Oliver Cromwell* and the valour of his Ironsides defeated the King in two great battles (Marston Moor, 1644; Naseby, 1645). The Scots came in on Parliament's side because they feared Charles would force his hated Prayer Book on them. After Naseby, the King's last hope was Montrose, whose Highlanders were eager to attack the Covenanter Lowlanders. Montrose, after brilliant success, could not hold his clansmen together and fled abroad. Charles I surrendered to the Scots and was handed over to Parliament. He might still have gained his throne but for his trickery. Cromwell insisted upon his execution in 1649. Montrose made a last attempt to raise the Highlanders for young Prince Charles (afterwards Charles II). He failed and was executed by the Covenanters.

SAMUEL PEPYS (1633–1703).

Cromwell was a great ruler, but after his death there was no-one strong enough to take his place, and Charles II was invited to take the crown in 1660. Pepys, in his secret diary, described how the King came back, and the events of the next nine years, including the Plague, Great Fire and the Dutch Wars. Besides being a lovable, gay fellow, Pepys did much to build up our Navy. *John Evelyn* also kept a famous Diary at this time.

JOHN AND SARAH CHURCHILL.

Charles II died in 1685 and his brother, Duke of York, a fine soldier and sailor, became James II. In three years he lost his throne because he tried to make England a Catholic country. His daughter, *Mary*, and her Dutch husband, William of Orange, were offered the throne as *William III and Mary* (1689–1702). Next, James II's younger daughter became *Queen Anne* (1702–1714). In her reign, Churchill, *Duke of Marlborough*, won his great victories over the French armies of Louis XIV, who wanted to become master of Europe.

LADY NITHSDALE.

When Queen Anne died, the crown went to *George I* of Hanover, a Protestant cousin. He was a German of fifty-four years, unable to speak English. *James Edward Stuart*, (Anne's half-brother), son of James II, had a much better claim to the throne, but he was a Catholic. However, the "Jacobites," supporters of the Stuarts, rebelled against George I in 1715. They were defeated, and by the time James Edward appeared, all was lost. Many Scottish leaders were arrested and about fifty executed. Lord Nithsdale was one of the Jacobite leaders to be sentenced to death. The rising was known as "*The Fifteen*"; thirty years later came "*The Forty-Five*" (1745), when Bonnie Prince Charlie tried to win back the throne for the Stuarts.

PART FOUR

PART FOUR

GREAT PEOPLE
OF
MODERN TIMES

CHARLES EDWARD STUART
The Young Pretender (1720-1788)

ON the 23rd of July 1745, a bedraggled party of seven travellers struggled ashore on an island of the Hebrides. Making their way through mist and rain, they found shelter in a low thatched hut, and gratefully warmed themselves by the peat fire. Presently, they dined upon baked fish and oatmeal cakes. One of the party, a tall, pale young man, moved restlessly to and fro, from fireside to door, from door to the windswept beach outside. He seemed anxious, as if he were waiting for messengers to arrive, and all the time he kept coughing and spluttering in the peat-smoke that filled the hut.

At last, the host, Angus MacDonald, could stand it no longer :

" What is the matter with that fellow," he cried, " that he can neither sit nor stand still ? "

The young man laughed, and sat down upon a pile of peat by the hearth, and joined his friends at the humble meal. For the moment, no one dared tell Angus that the restless visitor was Prince Charles Edward Stuart, grandson of King James II. He had just landed from France with seven companions to try to win the throne for his father, James Stuart.

During the next few days, messengers were sent through the glens to summon the Highland chiefs to meet their rightful Prince. In twos and threes, they arrived to offer the same advice :

" Go home, sire," they said, " you can do no good here, without arms or French help."

" I *am* come home," replied Charles Edward, " and I will not return to France, for I am sure my faithful Highlanders will stand by me ! "

The chiefs tried to reason with him. It was true, they said, that most of the Scots longed to see a Stuart again on the throne ; but George of Hanover, as they contemptuously called the King, had arms and men and generals.

" Sire," warned the chief Lochiel, " without support from the French King and the English Jacobites, 'tis madness to raise the clans."

" In a few days," answered Charles in a ringing voice, " I will raise my standard and proclaim my father King James of Scotland and England ! Lochiel may stay at home and learn from the newspapers his Prince's fate ! "

The old chief gave in. " No, sire, not that ! " he cried. " I'll share the fate of my Prince."

In this way, with his eager charm and princely bearing, Charles Edward won over the Highland chiefs. He would not hear of danger or failure, so

The proclamation of King James VIII of Scotland

they stifled their doubts, and brought in their clansmen to the Stuart standard.

At first, one glorious success followed another. When it became known that the Scottish clans were gathering in arms, King George II sent an army against the Jacobite rebels and offered a reward of £30,000 for the capture of the " Young Pretender." But Charles and Lochiel, at the head of their Highlanders, marched south and entered Edinburgh.

At noon, heralds proclaimed Charles Edward's father James VIII of Scotland. Through the excited crowd rode Margaret, wife of John Murray. She carried a drawn sword in one hand; with the other she distributed the white cockades of the Stuarts.

Next evening, a great ball was held at Holyrood

Prince Charlie and his Highlanders enter Edinburgh

Palace to celebrate the return of a Stuart prince. It was a brave and splendid affair, and Charles Edward won the hearts of everyone, with his gay manners and disdain of danger. Though there were secret jealousies among the chiefs, no man of spirit could hang back. The lords brought their swords and their followers; the ladies sold their jewels to give Charles money for the great adventure. He looked every inch a prince, and they called him " Bonnie Prince Charlie."

Two days later, the Prince led his army from Edinburgh, to meet the approaching foe. Charles himself had spent the night on the field with his troops, who declared that " he could eat a dry crust, sleep on straw, take his dinner in four minutes and win a battle in five!" Next day, at Prestonpans, the Highlanders broke through the English ranks with one furious charge.

And now for England! Though the Highland chiefs did not wish to go, Charles knew that he must enter London to secure the throne. Once more, his charm and obstinate spirit won the day. The chiefs would not desert their Prince, so they followed him on a march which they believed to be hopeless.

With a small army, they crossed the Border and captured Carlisle. To the brave wailing of the bagpipes, they marched southward to Manchester, and then, cleverly avoiding the English armies, they plunged on towards the capital. On the march, the strength of Charles Edward amazed his followers. Scorning to ride, he walked at the head of his army through ice and snow, fording the rivers, eating rough meals with the men, sleeping in his clothes and rising before the rest at four o'clock in the morning. His men adored him and nothing could damp his high spirits, except quarrels with the jealous chieftains.

In December, they reached Derby, in the heart of England, little more than a hundred miles from London. Here the Scottish chiefs gloomily refused to go any farther. Where was the help promised by the English Jacobites and the French King? It was true that no one resisted them, but the English waited to see what would happen. Their own men were weary and footsore; many had deserted.

"We must go back," advised the chieftains.

In vain, Charles begged them to continue the march, but, on the next day, "Black Friday," he was forced to agree to the retreat. Riding a black horse, the Prince started on the long and bitter journey north; all his hopes and gay spirit had turned to despair. Had he only known it, London was in a panic when news arrived that the Scots had reached Derby. King George and his friends were packing their jewels and silver, ready to depart to Germany. Shopkeepers and merchants put up their shutters and counted their money-bags, as the London Jacobites prepared to welcome the Stuarts back to the throne.

But the rebels were retreating. A two months' march brought them to Glasgow with an English army under the Duke of Cumberland at their heels. He drove them into the Highlands and utterly defeated the gallant clansmen at the Battle of Culloden Moor. Charles himself escaped from the field, because two of his officers seized his bridle and led him away.

After the battle, Cumberland's troops dealt out terrible punishment to all who had taken part in the rising, "The Forty-five," as it was called. An enormous reward was offered for the capture of the "Pretender," and spies and soldiers hunted for him everywhere, burning farms and hanging rebels as they went. But, though the reward would have made any one of them rich for life, the ordinary Scottish people never betrayed their "bonnie prince" during the long weeks when he wandered from place to place in their ruined countryside.

With two or three loyal friends, he had numberless adventures and narrow escapes in the Highlands and among the Scottish islands off the coast. Sometimes, Charles Edward took shelter in caves or in tiny deserted huts, with only heather or a piece of old sail-cloth to lie on. He lived on fish caught in the streams, barley-bread, oatmeal or whatever food he and his companions could obtain.

Charles himself often acted as their cook, and once made a "cake" from oatmeal and the brains of a cow that they had killed. He was usually cheerful, far more so than when on the retreat from Derby, and he would encourage his friends with a song as they crouched all night under a ledge of rock or tramped through driving rain across the mountains.

Once, having had nothing to eat for two days, except some mouldy crumbs, found in the lining of a coat, he and O'Neill came to a hut where an old woman gave them two eggs and a piece of cake. Since she had no drink to offer, she pointed to the hillside where some girls had gone to milk the goats. Though his companion fell exhausted to the ground, the Prince ran nimbly uphill and cried to the girls :

"Come, my lasses, what would you think to dance a Highland reel with me ? We cannot have a bagpipe just now, but I shall sing you a reel."

And he danced for them, snapping and clacking his fingers to keep time and to cheer up his dispirited friend.

Hungry, ragged, often soaked to the skin, they were remorselessly hunted by Cumberland's soldiers. When capture seemed certain, a brave, sweet girl, Flora MacDonald, disguised Charles as her maid, "Betty Burke, an Irish girl." Though the tall "maid" took long strides and seemed to manage her skirts badly when crossing a stream, yet Flora took the Prince from under the very noses of the soldiers to a less dangerous place on another island.

At last, he secured a boat and reached France again, through the help of his friends and the loyalty of dozens of Scots, who had surely recognised him during his wanderings, but never said a word.

When Donald MacLeod was imprisoned for the help he had given to the Young Pretender, he was asked :

The Prince dances for the Highland girls

"Did you know what a sum of money was upon his head? A sum to make you and your children happy for ever?"

"What! Thirty thousand pounds!" answered stout-hearted Donald. "Though I could have gotten all England and Scotland, I would not have allowed a hair of his body to be touched."

The Scottish Jacobites loved the gallant lad who led "The Forty-five". The dress he had worn as "Betty Burke" was kept as a precious relic and its pattern copied for the ladies to wear. They made up songs about him which have never been forgotten, songs like " Charlie is my darling," " Over the sea to Skye " and " Will ye no come back again ? "

But Charles Edward never came back again. The cause of the Stuarts was lost on that day when he was forced to turn back from Derby. Many years later, he died in Rome, almost forgotten, The gay, handsome prince had become an unhappy. quarrelsome man, lonely and disappointed in all his hopes of a crown. Yet he might have been King of England and Scotland :

> " Speed, bonny boat, like a bird on the wing,
>   'Onward,' the sailors cry,
> Carry the lad that's born to be King,
>   Over the sea to Skye ! "

GENERAL JAMES WOLFE

(1727-1759)

IN the year 1740, a red-haired boy, with a pale, pointed face, lay on his four-poster bed, beating his pillow with anger and vexation. He managed to hold back tears of disappointment when his mother entered the bedroom with the family doctor, who told him that there would be no getting up for a week. Then, as soon as he was better, he must be packed off back to boarding-school:

"With no more running-away-to-be-a-soldier nonsense, my young fire-eater," remarked the doctor, as he left the room.

The boy was James Wolfe, son of an Army officer whose tales of a soldier's life had led the thirteen-year-old lad to enrol as a volunteer in his father's regiment of marines. Just as the regiment was about to embark on a dangerous expedition against the French, young James was taken ill, so, instead of marching to glory as a drummer-boy, he was sent home to his mother and put to bed.

But James had made up his mind to be a soldier like his father. Only two years later, when he was fifteen, he became an ensign, or junior officer, in the 12th Foot Regiment and went to Flanders to fight against the French. After his first long march, he wrote home, " my strength is not so great as I imagined," for he had had to share a horse with his brother Edward, also an ensign.

To tell the truth, young Wolfe was not strong enough to be a soldier, in those days when soldiers had to march all day and night and often fight a battle the next day. Even the officers shared great hardships with their men, but Wolfe's courage and determination never failed him, however tired, ill or sea-sick he might be. At sixteen, he fought at Dettingen, where George II was our last reigning king to appear upon a battlefield. Wolfe's regiment was in the middle of the first line ; his horse was shot and he carried out his duties through the long day on foot. Soon afterwards he was promoted lieutenant.

Next year, he was in the Highlands, fighting against luckless Prince Charlie at Culloden. Afterwards, he went back to the Netherlands, always on service, often ill, but loved by his men, though he trained them into a fine regiment by the strictest discipline. At twenty-three, he was a colonel, trying to improve his knowledge of foreign languages, of books and poetry, instead of playing dice and cards, like his brother-officers.

The Seven Years War broke out between France and Britain, the two greatest nations in the world.

They were rivals everywhere; in Europe, on the seas, and in their growing empires. Both countries had possessions in India and North America, where Canada was known as "New France."

At first, the war went badly for Britain. Colonel Wolfe took part in a "commando" raid on the French coast. Like so many of our affairs at this time, it was a miserable failure. Wolfe was in angry despair at the feeble way in which the war was being managed, and he felt that he would never have a chance to show that courage and well-trained soldiers could beat the enemy. But old Admiral Hawke had noticed the energy of this thin, red-haired officer and he mentioned his name to William Pitt, the great statesman. Pitt, on the look-out for young men of ability, persuaded the King to promote him to brigadier-general and to send him on the attack upon the great French port of Louisburg, the strongest fortress in America.

This sudden rise made people jealous. Officers complained that Wolfe was too young, he was stubborn and rude, he read books and even poetry. In fact, said the Duke of Newcastle to George II, the fellow was mad.

"Mad, is he?" said the old King. "Then I hope he will bite some others of my generals!"

Despite sickness, Wolfe served so splendidly at the attack and capture of Louisburg, that, after his return, Pitt offered him a dazzling opportunity to gain complete victory over the French. He was to command an expedition sent to capture Quebec, the fortress-town which the French had built on

Pitt offers the command of the Quebec expedition to Wolfe

the St Lawrence River. If it fell, all Canada would fall to Britain. Wolfe was promoted to the rank of major-general. He was only thirty-two.

In June 1759 (afterwards known as "The Marvellous Year," "The Year of Victories"), Admiral Saunders brought his fleet through the dangerous channels of the St Lawrence River by such wonderful seamanship that the French said, "the enemy have passed sixty ships of war where we dare not risk a vessel of a hundred tons by night or day." In the warships were Wolfe's soldiers, and from the deck, their general surveyed the situation.

He saw the towers, spires and barracks of Quebec gleaming in the sunshine, high up above the river. The town was perched upon a rock on the left bank and was fortified with more than 100 guns and 2000 men. Beyond the town, there were steep cliffs, with here and there a tiny beach at the river's edge. On this side of Quebec, the St Charles River joined the St Lawrence, and across a bridge of boats was Beauport, the huge French camp, where the French general, Montcalm, had 14,000 men and more than 1000 Indian scouts. It was impossible to attack the camp, except from the river, because its eastern side was protected by another river, the Montmorency. This river fell over a great waterfall, two hundred and fifty feet high, and joined the St Lawrence between the banks of a deep gorge.

General Wolfe could quickly see that the task of capturing Quebec was the most difficult operation he had ever met in his soldiering life. Though their food was low and they could not expect help from France, the French believed that it was quite impossible to take their city. From their lofty position, they could afford to watch the English landing troops on the opposite bank, but no army could ever scale their steep, well-defended cliffs. In any case, the terrible Canadian winter would force the enemy to go home when autumn arrived. As for their general, Montcalm was known to be one of the finest commanders in the world, who knew far more about warfare in this country than his gawky young opponent.

Wolfe landed his troops on the Isle of Orleans, four miles from the city; then he moved guns and men up to Point Levi, opposite Quebec, and began to bombard the city. He also made a camp on the left bank of the river, but the Montmorency

Gorge and its thunderous waterfall prevented him from attacking the enemy whom he could see clearly. Presently, he tried to land a strong force from the river, but his men were mown down by the guns at Beauport, and he was forced to order the bugles to sound the retreat, as the wounded and dying were carried back to the boats.

The hot summer wore on. The English guns bombarded Quebec, reducing its richest quarter to ruins. Some of the English ships managed to slip past the French guns to sail on the river above the city, but the cliffs were well guarded. There were sudden attacks, alarms and retreats, with the Indians always on the prowl to scalp the dead and dying. The French remained certain that the English must sail away before winter closed in.

Wolfe gave himself no rest; he went up and down the river examining the banks, inspecting his troops and arguing with his senior officers. They felt that the position was hopeless and even Wolfe began to despair. He wrote to his mother:

"My enemy has wisely shut himself up in his entrenchments, so that I can't get at him without spilling a torrent of blood. . . . Montcalm is at the head of a great number of bad soldiers and I am at the head of a small number of good ones. . . . But the wary old fox avoids an action."

Then Wolfe fell ill from fever and rheumatism. He knew that his men were losing heart without him but he lacked the strength to leave his tent.

THE CAPTURE OF QUEBEC

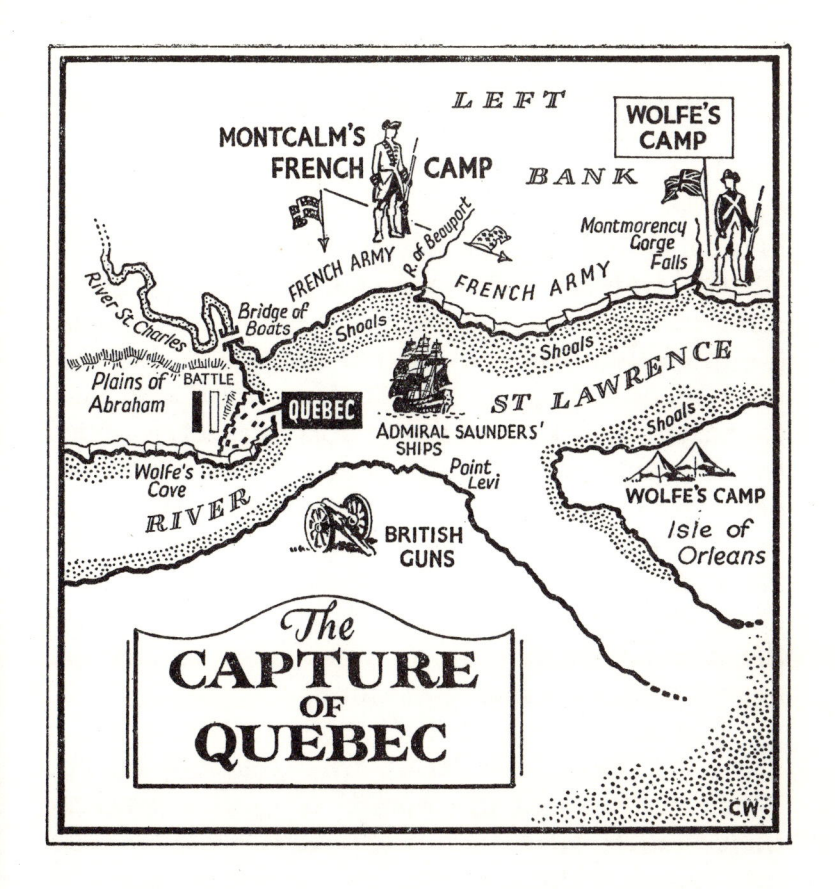

Tossing on his bed, he said to an officer, " I would give a leg to take Quebec."

But, as he lay there, a plan grew clearer and clearer in his mind. Quebec, he knew, could only be captured by surprise, by taking a risk, which, if it failed, would ruin him. But he already felt that his health was ruined :

" Patch me up," he said to the army doctor, " after that, nothing matters. I know you cannot cure me, but if you can fix me up so I shan't suffer too much pain for a few days, I can do my duty."

He began to move ships and troops about on the river, both above and below the city, so the French would not be certain of his plans. His officers wanted him to make a landing about eight miles above Quebec and then march upon the town, but Wolfe knew that Montcalm had sent 3000 men to face such a landing. In any case, a march of eight miles across densely-wooded country amid Indians and sharp-shooters, was not likely to lead to a successful attack. He had a better, more daring plan. He broke up the camp across the Montmorency River and kept Admiral Saunders' ships busier than ever, in order to make the French think that he was about to make a second attack on Beauport camp.

The attack was indeed about to come, but it was not to be eight miles up-river, nor at Beauport. Wolfe had noticed the women of Quebec washing their clothes on a tiny beach at the river's edge, and hanging them to dry at the top of the cliff. There must be a path by which the women came and went to the river. In a rowboat, he had scanned the bush-studded cliffs, murmuring to himself some lines from a favourite poem, " Elegy Written in a Country Churchyard." To an ensign, who raised his eyebrows at hearing the General recite poetry, he remarked with a weary smile : " I would rather have written that piece than take Quebec ! "

But he had seen what he wanted ; a tiny zig-zag path, winding from the little beach to the

A French sentry challenges Wolfe's boats

cliff-top, so steep that a hundred men there could stop a whole army. Therefore it was almost certainly lightly guarded.

On the night of September 12th, while Montcalm waited anxiously for an attack on Beauport, 1700 of Wolfe's men silently entered their boats, rowed with muffled oars and drifted down the river towards the little beach, which has, ever since, been called Wolfe's Cove.

As Wolfe said, it was a desperate plan, requiring fine seamanship and good fortune. As the boats passed close to the enemy's bank, a French sentry challenged them from the darkness:

" Qui vive ? " he shouted.

A Scottish officer who spoke French replied, " La France. Be careful lest the English hear you."

A convoy of provisions from up-river was

expected that night in Quebec, and the sentry allowed the dark line of boats to pass. A little farther on, a second sentry cried:

" Qui vive ? "

The Highlander hissed :

" La France ! Keep quiet, the provision convoy must go through."

Again the sentry allowed them to pass.

At the cove, Wolfe was the first to leap ashore. He looked up at the steep grim cliffs and, for a moment, his heart almost failed him. Quickly, twenty-four volunteers were chosen, who, with weapons strapped on their backs, began to haul themselves up the path, grasping bushes and tree-roots. Wolfe waited below, dreading lest a falling rock or stumbling soldier should raise the alarm. He heard a shout and muffled cries above, as the guard was overpowered. Then he gave the order to ascend. In his excitement, all thought of his fever and weakness was forgotten, and he led the main body of troops to the top.

In the darkness, the squadrons from upstream drifted down to the landing-point, while more troops were ferried across from Point Levi. By dawn, 4500 men, with two field-guns, were drawn up on the Plains of Abraham, a mile or so from Quebec.

The British ships on the river had been bombarding the French camp all night, and it was not until six o'clock in the morning that a breathless, white-faced messenger brought Montcalm the shocking news that the English army was across the river. Montcalm could not believe the man, but thought it was a wild rumour caused by the success of a small landing-party. He mounted his horse and went himself to see the truth of the matter. To his horror, he saw, not a handful of marines, but rank upon rank of British red-coats, marching in perfect order to the music of the bagpipes and the steady beat of the drums. Montcalm summoned his officers.

"We must give battle at once," he said, "before the enemy can bring up more guns and men. Order the whole army to advance to the plains. Place sharp-shooters in that wood to hold up the British."

Montcalm's fiery courage roused the spirit of his troops, many of whom were badly armed and unused to fighting in regular battle-order.

Wolfe's arrangements for the battle were perfect. His troops believed in him utterly; they halted and awaited his orders in silence. He put on a new uniform and moved everywhere, encouraging the men and pointing out the enemy's movements to their officers. He gave his last order:

"The officers and men will remember what their country expects of them. . . . The soldiers must be attentive to their officers and resolute in the execution of their duty."

At ten o'clock, the French attacked in three columns. The British stood waiting in silence. When the enemy was only forty paces away, the order was given, "Fire!" As though from a single gun, the volley roared out. Under cover of the smoke, the British re-loaded, advanced twenty paces and fired again. Then the Highlanders and red-coats charged the broken French ranks, which

The dying Wolfe gives his final orders

became a flying mob, except where knots of white-coated French regulars put up a desperate stand.

But the sharp-shooters had marked Wolfe. Early on, he was hit twice, but he hardly seemed to notice his wounds, as, with shining eyes, he pointed his regiment to charge. At that moment, he was hit in the chest. Struggling to keep up, he muttered to one of his officers:

"Hold me up! They must not see me fall."

Two or three grenadiers half-carried him a hundred yards to the rear. One ran for a surgeon.

"Don't grieve for me," gasped Wolfe, "I shall be right in a few minutes. Take care of yourself, man, I see you are wounded." He closed his eyes as the pain bore over him. Then, hearing shouts, he asked eagerly for news of the battle.

"They run!" cried a soldier.

"Who run?" he asked.

"The French, sir. They have given way on every side!"

Wolfe raised himself:

"Go," he said, "run quickly to Colonel Burton. Tell him to march Webb's regiment to the river. Tell him to seize the bridge to cut off their retreat."

His voice trailed away, and he turned on his side, as if to sleep, smiled, and whispered, "Now I die content." He died, as William Pitt said afterwards, "in the moment when his fame began."

Montcalm, the gallant French general, was fatally wounded as he strove to rally his men, and he died next day. He sent a last message to the British commander, begging him to treat the people of Quebec with mercy: "Do not let them feel they have changed masters," he said.

Fortunately, the French people were treated sensibly; they were allowed to keep their customs and religion. As a result, when the American colonies revolted against the English rule, the Canadians refused to join them. Today, the Province of Quebec retains its French character and language, though it is a proud part of the Dominion of Canada in the British Commonwealth.

THE STORY OF CAPTAIN COOK
(1728-1779)

JAMES COOK was born in a village among the Yorkshire hills, some distance from the sea. No one would have guessed that the little boy who drove the cows to the milking-shed with a stick longer than himself, was one day to become the greatest English explorer and navigator. His father was a farm-worker, and young James had little in the way of toys or books. Almost as soon as he could walk, he was busy scaring crows from the corn, and helping about the farm, in order to earn a penny or two a week to take home to his mother.

For a short time James went to the village school, where he showed himself to be so quick at arithmetic that it was decided that he must be a shopkeeper. He was only twelve years of age when he said good-bye to his mother and set out across the moors, with a spare suit and a clean shirt tied in a bundle. After several miles of rough walking, the road dropped steeply downhill into the fishing village of Staithes. From the top of the hill James saw the sea spreading away to the east like a grey crumpled sail-cloth. A ship was nosing its way into the little harbour, and far out on the horizon, a larger vessel was heading across the North Sea, perhaps to the trading ports of the Baltic. James Cook thought he had never seen anything so vast or fascinating in his life.

He made his way downhill, past the whitewashed and tarred cottages, to enquire for Mr Sanderson, who kept a haberdasher's shop. Next morning, he began his apprenticeship as a draper's assistant. He slept at the shop and ate his meals with the Sandersons; he opened the shutters, swept the shop floor and the front outside, ran errands and delivered parcels. During the next year or two, he learnt how to serve ladies with buttons, cottons and laces, to unroll a length of calico, to fetch down ribbons from a top shelf and to remember the prices of collars, shawls and darning-wool. He worked hard and did his best to please his master, but he hated the shop and was sometimes scolded for spending his time with the sailors and fishermen on the jetty.

"I don't know what to make of you," said Mr Sanderson at last. "You're honest, I'll say that, but you'll never make a harberdasher with your head full of rope, tar and rigging! Go to sea, then; that's what I say to you, and the taste of salt pork and foul weather will soon have you scurrying back home!"

So it was arranged that young James should be apprenticed to Mr Walker, coal-shipper of Whitby. At fifteen, he went to sea in a dirty, broad-beamed collier, or coal-ship, which was engaged in carrying coal from the northern mines to London, whose numberless chimneys and workshops demanded more and more coal every year.

It was a hard life on a collier, with vile food and damp bedding, and with long hours in freezing winds and bitter gales, as the sturdy ship battled her way through the seas that rage along the east coast in winter. There was danger too, for there were few lighthouses or buoys, and the captains kept as close to the shore as they dared, relying on their knowledge and skill to avoid the shallows and sandbanks along the coast. Yet James Cook was happy. He was strong and tireless and ever ready to learn. The boy who could not learn the haberdashery trade picked up every scrap of knowledge about seamanship as if it needed no effort at all. The master of the collier found himself teaching sailing and navigation to the tall apprentice with the calm, serious face. Mr Walker praised the lad when he came into Whitby after a couple of voyages and made him welcome in his own house.

In 1755, James Cook, now mate of a stout collier, brought his vessel into the Thames and tied up at the usual coal wharf. Presently, off-duty, he stepped ashore to take a walk and to hear the news of the day. There was war with France, and the Press Gang was busy all along the waterfront, entering taverns to seize any likely-looking fellow for His Majesty's Navy. Seamen were needed and none would go willingly, for the food was shocking, pay always behindhand and discipline as hard as iron. The Press Gang snatched men where it could, even from ships at anchor, or from merchantmen home after three years in the East Indies.

Cook pondered upon what he heard. Then he ordered a waterman to row him out to the *Eagle*, a warship of sixty guns, which lay at anchor. He went aboard and asked for the duty officer.

" Who the devil are you ? " demanded Lieutenant Stack of H.M.S. *Eagle*.

" James Cook, first mate of the collier *Friendship*, come to enlist in His Majesty's Navy."

" Great Heavens, man ! Are you mad, or escaping from the law ? " cried the lieutenant.

" Neither, sir," replied Cook stiffly, " I have a mind to see more of the world than from the deck of a collier. I would enlist rather than be pressed."

" Very well," replied the lieutenant, " you will ship as an able seaman. From the look of you, I shall see you join my boat's crew."

For the next four years, Cook served in the Royal Navy. He soon caught the eye of his captain who recognised in the silent Yorkshireman a born sailor, who was cool and painstaking in all his duties. He allowed Cook to study the charts and navigation books in the Chart Room.

In 1759, Admiral Saunders' fleet carried General Wolfe and his army towards Quebec, but the coast of Canada and the mouth of the St Lawrence River were almost unknown to English sailors. The master of a small vessel, the *Mercury*, was James Cook, and he it was who was given the task of sailing ahead to make charts of the river and its numberless shoals and sandbanks. Though this was his first serious attempt at the work, Cook provided the fleet with such perfect charts that the admiral was able to bring his ships to anchor below Quebec without loss of a single vessel.

Admiral Saunders sent for the master of the *Mercury*. " Cook," he said, " when, by the Grace of God and the skill of our army, Quebec has been taken, I shall see that you receive further employment for your talents. The Navy has need of many more charts like these."

The admiral was as good as his word. Cook went on with his chart-making and, in 1768, when the Admiralty wished to send a ship into the Pacific Ocean to study the path of the planet Venus, and also to make discoveries in those little-known waters, Lieutenant Cook was given command of the *Endeavour*. To his joy, he found that she was a sturdy vessel very similar to a Whitby collier. In August, he sailed with a crew of eighty-five, some scientists, artists and a famous collector of plants, on the first of his three great voyages.

The *Endeavour* rounded Cape Horn and reached the newly discovered island of Tahiti. Here the scientists observed the planet Venus, and the sailors enjoyed the company of the friendly natives of this most lovely island. Then, Lieutenant Cook decided to sail into almost unknown seas.

Very little was known about the Pacific Ocean ; it had been believed for many years that a vast continent, called Terra Australis, lay in the Southern Seas. Dutch sailors had touched here and there

Cook studying his charts

upon a barren coast which they called New Holland. One Dutchman, named Tasman, reached Tasmania and even New Zealand, but no one knew for certain if the great southern land existed, and, there were no maps or charts of this vast ocean with its thousands of islands.

The *Endeavour* reached New Zealand, which was found to be two large islands, with rich soil and fine trees, but no domestic animals. The natives, who called themselves Maoris, were warlike cannibals, so fierce that it was difficult to make friends with them. Writing in his diary, Cook said:

" They are a strong, well-made active people, of a dark-brown colour, with black hair, thin black beards and white teeth. Both men and women paint their faces and bodies with red ochre mixed with fish oil. They wear ornaments of stone, bone and shells at their ears and about their necks and the men generally wear long white feathers stuck upright in their hair."

After Cook had sailed all round New Zealand making careful charts, he sailed for Australia—or "New Holland"—and explored the east coast for 2000 miles, naming its capes, harbours and bays. There was the famous Botany Bay, where Mr Banks, the expert, found hundreds of new plants and flowers; there was Smoky Cape, where native fires were sighted, and Point Danger, where the ship had a narrow escape. Cutting the date and the name of his ship upon a large tree, Cook claimed the land for King George III by the name of "New South Wales."

The *Endeavour* sailed northwards, with the captain still making his charts and taking careful soundings of the depths of the sea. One night, as the ship was sailing quietly along, she suddenly went aground and stuck fast amid white surf. At once the sails were taken in and the boats lowered. At daybreak, it could be seen that the ship was wedged on a coral reef that rose almost to the surface from an enormous depth—it was the terrible Barrier Reef, which lies off the east coast of Australia but which was then quite unknown to sailors. It seemed certain that the ship must be destroyed and the crew stranded upon an unknown shore. After two days, however, in a high tide, the *Endeavour* slid off the reef into deep water. Though she was leaking, Cook managed to bring her into the mouth of a river where she was beached for repairs.

The " Endeavour " aground on the Barrier Reef

It was then found that a great lump of coral had broken off and remained wedged in the ship's timbers. Today, the town of Cooktown stands on the spot where the ship was mended.

Sailing on through dangerous waters and with his weary crew now stricken with illness, Cook left Australia. After months of anxiety, as man after man died of scurvy or fever, he brought his ship up the English Channel to drop anchor in the Downs.

The voyage had taken three years; great discoveries had been made and they were set down on accurate charts and in the captain's diary, but of the crew, thirty out of eighty-five had died. Most had died from scurvy, the dreaded disease of sailors ; three of the scientists had died, the surgeon, the first lieutenant and two midshipmen, the boatswain, both the carpenter and the sailmaker with their mates, a corporal of marines, the cook and more than a dozen seamen. Though this was not an unusual number of deaths on a long voyage, Cook shook his head over the waste of good men :

" I shall make it my business, Mister Mate," he said to one of his ship's officers, " to see that my men do not die in such numbers. When we sail again, I shall take strict measures concerning what they eat and what they drink."

Cook was a man of few words, though he had a sudden temper. He was strict with his crew and once had a man flogged with a dozen lashes on his bare back for disobeying an order not to eat salt meat. But the sailors looked on him as a father, though a stern one, and he never had a mutiny, or a refusal to sail on into unknown waters.

Scurvy was caused by the bad food which sailors ate, by lack of fresh vegetables on board and too much salt pork. Damp, dirty conditions below decks, as well as the sailors' love of strong drink, helped the disease. So Cook cut down the ration of salt meat, and took aboard stocks of fresh fruit, especially oranges and lemons, and also vegetables, even wild celery, whenever they touched land. At first the men disliked these new rations but they were made to eat them. Their sleeping quarters had to be scrubbed and kept dry, and the whole ship was regularly " smoked " with gunpowder mixed with vinegar, which acted as a disinfectant.

After his great voyage, Cook was promoted Captain R.N. and presented to the King himself, but he was soon eager to be at sea again. His second voyage proved that there was no continent lying south of Australia but only a vast land of ice around the South Pole. His stout collier-like vessel, the *Resolution*, sailed far into these icy seas and stood up to the pounding of the ice for months on end, as its captain tried to find a way through. Then he visited New Zealand again, crossed the Pacific to Cape Horn, and finally reached home after an absence of three years and eighteen days.

This time, of the crew of 118, only one man had died of sickness, but there was no case of scurvy. Cook had proved that a ship could stay at sea for years and still return home with a healthy crew.

Captain Cook was now famous. He could have retired to a comfortable life with his wife and their three sons, but the born sailor was soon restless for his ship and the strange, lonely life at sea. There was a new expedition being talked about; it was hoped that the mystery of the North-West Passage might at last be solved. Was there a way round North America, from the Atlantic into the Pacific? Captain Cook was offered command of the expedition and he chose his faithful old *Resolution*, with Captain Clerke in a second ship, the *Discovery*.

They sailed in 1776, with picked crews, good

provisions and a few cattle and sheep for the Pacific islands which lacked these useful animals. There were also vegetable seeds, and tools, knives, beads and ornaments as presents for the natives.

A long course was steered, by the Cape of Good Hope, to New Zealand again. Many new islands were discovered and visits were paid to friendly chiefs, to whom nails, beads and cloth were given in exchange for fresh meat and fruit. Cook was always careful to treat native peoples with kindness and generosity, and at Tahiti old friends greeted him with joy, almost as though a god had returned to the island. At Christmas 300 turtles were caught for food on an island which was suitably named Christmas Island. A new group of islands was discovered and named the Sandwich Islands, where the people were tall, handsome savages, who possessed splendid canoes and weapons, and long cloaks made of feathers.

From here, the ships bore away northward towards New Albion, which Drake had discovered 200 years earlier, and which is now California. Then they sailed further north into colder seas, where the natives, who came out in canoes to visit the ships, proved to be great thieves:

"Before we left the place," wrote Cook in his diary, "hardly a bit of brass was left in the ships. . . . Whole suits of clothes were stripped of every button . . . copper kettles, tin canisters, candlesticks and the like, all went to wreck."

Still northwards, they sailed into the Arctic Ocean, meeting Eskimos in their little kayaks, but

Cook with natives of the Sandwich Islands

though they searched carefully and Cook made his usual charts, the longed-for passage could not be found. After further discoveries, the ships turned south, and the brave, patient sailors made the long voyage into warmer seas.

Back in the Pacific, among the Sandwich Islands, the ships cruised easily from one island to another and at last dropped anchor off Owhyhee (Hawaii), which they had visited on the voyage out.

At first, the natives were very friendly and feasts were held in honour of Captain Cook, who, once again, was looked on as a god-like person. Unfortunately, the usual thieving became worse than ever, and even the good-tempered sailors grew tired of the natives who swarmed over their decks intent upon stealing anything made of metal. One day, a native was caught taking a pair of tongs, and was given a whipping, but another man snatched the tongs and dived overboard with them. An officer and a party of men who went to catch him were roughly treated by a crowd of excited natives at the water's edge.

That same night, one of the ship's boats, a cutter, was silently stolen from where she was moored. In the morning, Captain Cook himself decided to put an end to this behaviour. He went ashore with a small party of armed marines, and marched to the hut of a friendly old chief. He asked him to come aboard the ship to discuss the theft, meaning probably to hold him there until the boat was returned. The old chief agreed cheerfully and set off with his visitor towards the shore. On the way, however, his wives and relatives set up a loud outcry and ran alongside begging the chief not to leave them. At last, the old fellow became so confused that he sat down on the ground and refused to budge another step.

While Cook was talking to him, crowds of excited natives pressed so closely round them that it would have been impossible to use a weapon. The marines, therefore, backed in a line towards the water, where the boats lay a little way out, waiting to take them off. Excitement grew and stones were thrown ; the party in the boats fired at a canoe and Captain Cook turned and called out to them to stop firing. He still had no fear, but only wanted to prevent bloodshed, and, as long as he faced them, the natives showed him no violence. But as he turned away, he was struck in the back by an iron dagger. He fell into the shallow water and was immediately speared and clubbed to death. In the dense crowd, his men were powerless to help him, and four marines were killed by the maddened savages. The rest, some badly wounded, struggled into the boats, which presently put back to the ships, though the lieutenant in charge was afterwards accused of cowardice.

So, on his third great voyage of discovery, Captain Cook, the real discoverer of Australia and New Zealand, was killed in a petty squabble with the natives whom he had treated with kindness and understanding. Though he was a silent, almost an unfriendly man, his sailors mourned him and would not leave the island until their captain had been given an honourable burial at sea.

After the ships' cannons had been fired and the Englishmen had shown that, if they wished, they could take the most bloodthirsty revenge for the murder, the natives brought back the gun, shoes and body of Captain Cook, with many signs of sorrow at what had been done. In the afternoon, the coffin was lowered gently over the side of the *Resolution* and disappeared from sight into the waters of the Bay of Hawaii.

CLIVE OF INDIA

(1725-1774)

DURING the reign of George II, there were at the same time, but in different parts of the country, three schoolboys, none of whom was particularly good at lessons, but who were all to win undying fame in some distant part of the world. Two of these boys, James Wolfe, the victor at Quebec, and James Cook, the great navigator, left school early —Wolfe to join his father's regiment, and Cook to serve behind a draper's counter. But the third, the naughtiest of the three, was kept at various schools until he was eighteen years old, probably because his parents kept hoping that his schoolwork and behaviour would improve.

His name was Robert Clive, and he lived at Market Drayton, in Shropshire. When he was only seven, he went to stay with an aunt near Manchester, but his uncle had to write home that young Bobby was always fighting the older boys, and, what was worse, he seemed to enjoy it ! Back at home, his parents and schoolmasters soon found that they could do little with him, for he was quarrelsome, reckless and always in some trouble. He became chief of a gang which he led into every kind of daring mischief, until the whole neighbourhood was talking of his wild deeds.

One day, to show off, he climbed to the top of the steeple of Market Drayton church and calmly seated himself astride a stone spout shaped like a dragon's head. Not until the square far below was crowded with townsfolk, gazing upwards in terror for his safety, did he come down as coolly as he had climbed up.

Far worse than this escapade, Clive took his gang to call upon local shopkeepers, and, lightly tossing a stone from hand to hand, suggested to them that it would be cheaper to pay the gang a halfpenny each, with a bag of bullseyes for good measure, than to have their shop windows broken ! It is said that some shopkeepers actually paid pennies for this kind of " protection " until Robert's father, a well-to-do squire, heard of his latest exploit. After young Clive had been well thrashed, his schoolmaster remarked to his father :

" Yet, sir, I do say this, if Bobbie lives to be a man, and can find some way to use his talents, he will make a name for himself, and a great name, too, that few will ever equal."

After this, his father sent him away to boarding-school, where he was as idle as ever ; then to another school, but he did no better. In despair, his parents decided to send him out to India, in the hope that, far from home, he would cease to be a disgrace to the family,—and there was always the chance that he might make a fortune.

So, at eighteen, Robert Clive arrived in Madras, in Southern India, where, since the days of Queen Elizabeth, English merchants had set up a number of trading-posts, each protected by a small fort. Here Clive started work as a " writer " or clerk, which meant that he sat for long hours, in great heat, at a tall desk, writing down in the account books the quantities and prices of the goods which the East India Company bought and sold. The lively boy who wanted adventure was bored with his dull job, and was soon in trouble with the senior officials for his lack of manners and quick temper.

Secretly, he was lonely and miserable, for he wrote home to his mother :

" I have not enjoyed one happy day since I left England. I know only one family here, and I do not like to call on them unless I am invited."

He became more and more downcast, until, one day, alone in his office, he took a loaded pistol from a drawer, put it to his head and pulled the trigger. There was a click, but nothing else happened. He tried a second time to end his unhappy life, but again the pistol refused to fire. At that moment, a fellow clerk entered the room :

" Oblige me, John," said Clive, " by firing this pistol out of the window."

The astonished clerk took it to the window and fired it safely upwards. When the noise of the shot had died away, Clive remarked coolly :

Clive and his friend escaping from Madras

"Thank you, John. I see now that I am meant to make something of my life."

Very soon afterwards, his chance of adventure arrived, for the war which had broken out between France and Britain, spread to India. The French, who also had trading-posts, began to seize the opportunity to push the English out of the country, so that they might enjoy its rich trade without their rivals.

Since the Indian princes were constantly quarrelling among themselves, the French began to help first one and then another. Soon the French became very much more powerful than the British, who were looked on as cowards, too fond of money-making to do any fighting. For several years, both sides had trained natives to be soldiers; they were called sepoys, and fought very well under European officers. The French and their sepoys now went from success to success, until they actually captured Madras itself, with the officers, soldiers and merchants of the East India Company.

Clive was among those who were captured, but the reckless lad from Market Drayton had no mind to be a prisoner-of-war. Darkening his skin, he disguised himself as an Indian and escaped from Madras with a friend. Together they made their way to Fort St David, a place on the coast that was still held by the English, and here Clive offered to join the Company's army. He quickly won a name for himself as a brave and daring junior officer.

Soon afterwards, an Indian prince with a huge army and French support, was besieging the British garrison at a town called Trichinopoly. If it fell, the English would lose the last of their Indian friends, and their trade would be ruined. Back at Fort St David, there was great anxiety, but the governor had too few troops to go to the rescue. At this point Clive suggested a daring plan. He offered to lead a surprise attack on the town of Arcot, the capital of this part of the country, feeling certain that the prince would call off many of his troops from the siege.

The commander could only spare him eight officers (six of these had never fought in a battle) and 500 soldiers, including 300 sepoys. Clive led this little army for fifty miles across country and

Clive at Arcot drives out the attackers

through a tempest of lightning and rain. When they reached Arcot, its garrison were so terrified at the sight of a force appearing in perfect order through the torrential monsoon rain that they flung away their arms and fled.

Clive took possession of the fort and at once ordered his men to start repairing its mud walls which were partly in ruins. He knew that the real attack was about to begin. As he expected, the enemy sent a huge force of 10,000 sepoys and some French troops to retake their capital. The fort was quickly surrounded and attack after attack was launched against its crumbling walls. Clive's men held firm. In two places, great holes were made in the walls, but Clive led desperate charges to drive out the attackers. At night, repairs were made to the mile-long defences, and, by day, every man had to be at his post. Clive was everywhere, switching his troops to meet the enemy, instructing his officers, encouraging the men and tending the wounded. Days and weeks went by, and still the heroic defenders held out: there were only about 200 of them left, with two officers; food stores were running so low that the daily ration was no more than a bowl of rice. Then the sepoys suggested that the Englishmen should have all the rice, while they themselves had the water in which it was boiled. "Englishmen," they said, "need more food than we who are used to famine."

After the siege had lasted for fifty days, the enemy made one last effort to break down the walls, for they brought up elephants, with iron plates on their foreheads as battering-rams. Clive ordered his men to hold their fire until the animals were close, then, mustering every gun, volley after volley was fired at the great creatures, which turned and fled, trumpeting in terror, and trampling down the packed ranks behind. The enemy retreated in despair.

"I never knew the English could fight," said one prince, "but now I have seen they have courage to defend themselves, I shall fight on their side."

After fifty-three days the siege was over. Clive was at once promoted and given command of a strong force. Some of the Company's officers made a loud outcry that they were senior to him, but the sepoys vowed that they would refuse to march under any other officer than Clive.

After Arcot, it seemed as if the tide of fortune turned, for the French plans went from bad to worse and the British gained fresh power and trade in every direction. Even Clive could be spared to go back to England.

The defender of Arcot came home in a blaze of glory to Market Drayton, where his family and the townsfolk gave him a great welcome.

"So the booby of the family has some sense after all!" cried his delighted father when he greeted him.

Clive had made a fortune before he left India, and he was now presented with other gifts, including a sword set in diamonds. He married the sister of the friend with whom he had escaped in disguise

Clive receives gifts from the Indian princes

from Madras, entered Parliament and made up his mind to settle down as an English gentleman. But in two years, he was needed again in India and he returned, not as a "writer," but as Governor of Fort St David.

There was trouble in Bengal, a huge rich province far from Madras, where the English merchants had a trading-post at Calcutta. The new Nawab, or prince, was a young man named Surajah Dowlah, who picked a quarrel with the merchants and captured their trading-post. One hundred and forty-five British men and one woman were taken prisoner. They were driven into a room so small that there was hardly room for them to stand, though they were crushed tightly together ; fresh air could not enter because of the bodies packed closely against the two tiny barred windows. All through the hot Indian night, the prisoners suffered horribly from heat and thirst, many were suffocated, others went mad and died in their furious struggles to reach the windows. In the morning when the door was unlocked, only twenty-three out of the 146 prisoners were found to be alive.

When the news of this disaster, known as the Black Hole of Calcutta, reached Madras, Clive was sent north to restore the position of the British and to recapture Calcutta. He took the town with his usual energy, but he still had a problem to solve. The Seven Years War had broken out between France and England ; if he went back to Southern India, the French, only twenty miles away, would certainly help Surajah Dowlah to attack again. He therefore decided that he must crush Dowlah and put a Nawab friendly to Britain on his throne.

But Clive's army consisted only of about 3000 men, whilst Dowlah faced him with about 60,000. At first he decided that it was madness to risk a battle and he must retreat, as most of his officers advised. By the next morning, however, he had changed his mind and gave the order to advance. The great enemy army broke ranks and fled almost as soon as he attacked, so that the Battle of Plassey,

1757, was one of the most dazzling victories in the history of the world. The British became masters of Bengal, a province larger than the whole of Great Britain.

Clive himself returned to England, loaded with riches and gifts from Indian princes ; he became Lord Clive and again tried to settle down to English life. Later he was a splendid Governor of Bengal, but he made many enemies through his firm rule, and they tried to disgrace him by accusing him of making a fortune dishonestly. Years of hard work and fighting in a hot climate ruined his health, and he died unhappily.

Robert Clive was reckless and quarrelsome as a boy, and he never really lost those faults. But he was a great man and a born general, who, in about ten years, founded an Empire in India. The British ruled that huge continent for nearly 200 years, until 1946, when India gained its freedom but remained a member of the British Commonwealth.

TWO FAMOUS ENGINEERS

(i) James Watt (1736-1819)

AT the time when Bonnie Prince Charlie was leading his Highlanders towards Derby, a pale little boy was playing in his father's workshop at Greenock, on the banks of the River Clyde.

Mr Watt was a carpenter and ship's merchant, supplying sea-captains with stores, compasses and instruments for navigation. His son James was so delicate and timid that his parents kept him away from school and themselves taught him to read and to do arithmetic. James was a lonely little boy who would rather stay indoors reading and drawing than go out to play with other children. His great delight, however, was to run down to his father's workshop where he was allowed to make models of pulleys, pumps and ships that he saw along the wharves of the busy river. Once he made a model of the crane which his father had built to unload the tobacco ships from America, the first crane ever seen at Greenock. When James had finished his model, one of the workmen said to his father:

"Yon wee Jamie's that clever, he's got a fortune in his fingers' ends."

It was not surprising, therefore, that at the age of eighteen, James went to Glasgow to learn how to make the delicate instruments used by scientists and mathematicians. He soon found that there was no one to teach him what he wanted, so he set out for London. There was no railway at that time, nor regular stage-coach, so he rode on horseback all the way, and the journey took him twelve days. In London, he found that he ought to become an apprentice and spend seven years learning the trade. After some while, he persuaded an instrument-maker to take him as a pupil, and he worked so hard that he had learned all he wanted to know in one year !

Hard work and long hours, as well as the need to stay indoors at week-ends because of the Press Gang, made the delicate young man ill. His severe headaches became worse and he put an end to his studies to return to his own Scotland. Here he set up as an instrument-maker for the Glasgow University.

One of the professors found him a workshop under his own lecture-room and gave him permission to use the College library. For the first time in his life, Watt made some friends, and gradually became known as one of the most brilliant young men at the university, as clever in history, science and languages as he was with instruments and engineering. But, although he was clever, Watt did not make much money at his business. He had to take to manufacturing flutes, fiddles and even organs, as well as repairing any instruments or clocks that were brought to his workshop.

The College possessed a model of a steam-engine, made some years earlier by a man named Newcomen. It was a clumsy monster, designed to pump water out of coal and tin mines, and it certainly worked, though it was constantly breaking down. The College model had been sent to London for repair, and when it returned no better than before, someone suggested that James Watt might have a look at it—a suggestion that altered the whole of his life.

Watt examined the model steam-engine, tinkered with it and set it working. "What a capital plaything!" he exclaimed, as it puffed and hissed, while the pumping arm clattered up and down. Then it broke down again. This time he could not see why it should have stopped and he set about finding the cause. He mended it again, and again it broke down. Now the little engine began to fascinate him, filling his thoughts all day; he *would* make it work, he declared. So he went to study one of Newcomen's steam-engines pumping water from a coal mine. The huge grampus snorted steam in all directions, as it devoured coal in huge quantities. It was clearly very expensive to run and it did not carry out its pumping task at all well.

Walking home one evening across Glasgow Green, Watt had a brilliant idea. He suddenly saw how all this waste of power could be avoided. He would design a new machine. Of course,

Watt examines the model steam-engine

he must build an engine to test out his idea. Though short of money, he hired an old cellar near the meat market where he could assemble his own steam-engine. His headaches grew worse, but he would not leave the work alone, though he could hardly sleep at nights for worrying how to feed his wife and children.

"Never despair, Jamie," said his brave wife. "If the steam-engine will not do, I am sure something else will."

He gave up his instrument business and took a job as a surveyor in order to give himself more time to work at night on the engine, but his greatest difficulty was to find workmen with enough skill to make the parts as he wanted them. He had to rely upon blacksmiths and tinsmiths, and, though he wrapped the engine's cylinder in rags, paper and tow, yet steam still hissed and leaked from various cracks. But already the engine worked, and worked better than Newcomen's.

Money was now needed to produce the new machines for sale, and a friend mentioned the brilliant engineer to a Mr John Roebuck of the Carron Ironworks at Stirling. He paid £1000 to clear Watt's debts and gave him a further sum of money in return for a share in the new engine. Poor Mr Roebuck! He never saw his money back again.

Watt went on working, but he still could not get the engine to run well enough to please him. He actually learned German, French and Italian in his spare time, so that he could read what foreign engineers had to say about steam-power. But his health grew worse; then his wife died, leaving him with four motherless children. In despair, he wrote to a friend:

"I am thirty-five today, and I think I have hardly done thirty-five pence worth of good in the world. But I cannot help it. I must go on."

Next, poor Roebuck failed in business and went bankrupt. Among his debts was the sum of £1200 owing to a Mr Mathew Boulton, who said he would forgive the debt if he could have Roebuck's share in the steam-engine.

Mathew Boulton was a lively, cheerful man who had a factory at Birmingham called the Soho Works. Here he made toys, ornaments and various articles of metal, glass and tortoiseshell. He took pride that his goods were well made and that his

Watt's engine at the Soho works

workmen were among the best in the country. In the works he used water-power to drive the machinery, but he had been thinking of using steam if only he could find an engineer clever enough to build a good machine.

So Watt went to Birmingham and was vastly impressed by the skill of Boulton's workmen. Here were men who really understood how to make a cylinder that would not leak. His engine was taken to pieces and brought to Soho Works, where, at last, the vital parts were properly made. When it was reassembled, the engine worked better than ever before. It was the first efficient steam-engine ever made, but we have to remember that it was still a machine which only pumped up and down.

Orders began to come in from Cornwall, where the tin companies urgently needed engines to pump water out of their tin mines. Boulton and Watt had many a battle with these Cornish mine-owners, especially when Boulton demanded a share in the money they saved on coal through using the new machines instead of Newcomen's! Though angry, the owners had to agree, and Watt invented a meter to put on the side of each machine which showed how much it was used, and therefore how much coal was saved.

But there were still struggles before full success arrived. Watt was constantly improving the engine so that it could be used not only to pump water but also to drive air into a blast furnace, and then to *turn* machinery in cotton and wool mills, in iron-works and factories. England was beginning to manufacture goods to sell all over the world and the steam-engine was an enormous improvement upon windmills and water-power.

Of course, money was needed at Soho to build the steam-engines, to train good workmen and to enlarge the workshops. Cheerful Mr Boulton did it all; he borrowed large sums and even sold his wife's property. When the engine works were burnt down one night, he only cried, " Never mind, *now* I shall be able to build it as it *ought* to be built!" and went out and borrowed another

£21,000. He had faith in Watt, but poor James was full of woe; he was constantly ill and always on the verge of despair, fearing that his incessant work would kill him or drive him mad.

"I must drag on a miserable existence the best way I can," he wrote to Boulton, when they were not far from success. But his partner never lost heart or grumbled; he looked after Watt and constantly encouraged him to carry on.

"Whatever you do," he would say to his workmen, "do not worry Mr Watt. Always keep him free from anxiety."

And at last success did arrive. Better and better machines were turned out from Soho Works, more and more orders flowed in from all parts of Britain and Europe. The famous Boulton and Watt engines were needed wherever a new mine or mill or factory was started.

As he grew older, Watt became more contented and his health improved, while Mr Boulton, cheery as ever, took to making coins and medals as a sideline, until he obtained an order to mint all the new coins for England—twopenny, penny, halfpenny and farthing pieces. Four thousand tons of them!

Both partners lived until they were over eighty years of age. Between them, they had brought in the age of steam-power, which changed Britain from a farming and trading country into the greatest manufacturing country in the world. Though he did not invent a steam-engine that moved, Watt lived to see steam-power used for the first steamship and the first railway locomotive.

(ii) George Stephenson (1781–1848)

WATT did not invent the steam-engine, nor did Stephenson invent the railway locomotive, which made him famous. But Stephenson built a far better locomotive than any earlier model, and he did more than any man to give railways to Britain.

George Stephenson was not in the least like Watt, for, though he was a kindly man with a great love of children and a strange knack of taming wild birds, he possessed huge strength and iron determination. When he was young, he was well known for feats of strength and throwing the hammer, and he could take on the toughest opponent in a wrestling match. He was once insulted by a ferocious miner whom everyone feared, and in his first and last serious fight he thrashed the bully, and afterwards made friends with him. Years later, when his men refused to enter a long and dangerous tunnel, he led the way in and remained there helping to repair the roof until all was safe.

"Geordie" was born at Wylam, a mining village not far from Newcastle and no great distance from where Captain Cook grew up. If anything, Stephenson's boyhood was even harder than Cook's. His father, "Old Bob" Stephenson, was fireman of the pumping-engine at the coal mine, or colliery, and he earned twelve shillings a week, on which to keep his wife and six children in their tiny cottage. Young George, the second child, was off to work at eight years of age, looking after Widow Ainslie's cows, for twopence a day, which was more help to his mother than if he had gone to school.

Next, like most of the local boys, George went to work at the mine, picking stones out of the coal as it came from the pit. Then he found himself a better job at eightpence a day, driving the horse that walked round and round winding buckets up the pit-shaft. At fourteen, he was helping his father look after the pumping-engine for a shilling a day, but he had to hide himself when the owner came round, in case he was considered too young for such a big wage!

Alas, the mine closed, and father and son had to find fresh work. The family moved away and went to live in a cottage which only had one room, but George once more found a job that pleased him. He and a young fellow, named Bill Coe, looked after a pumping-engine, each working twelve hours at a time, and when he drew twelve shillings wages at the end of his first week, young Stephenson thought he had almost made his fortune. What was more, the clumsy engine interested him so much that he would take it to pieces at the weekend to see how it worked, oil and clean the parts and have it in order again for Monday morning.

One day, his engine was running so smoothly that the colliery engineer praised him to his father:

"Thy lad's a born engineer," he said.

"Ah, if the lad could read and write, he'd go far," said Old Bob, "but there never was time when he was little, and now 'tis too late."

Too late? Not for Geordie Stephenson. He said to himself that if he could master that pumping-engine, then he could also master this business of reading, by which he would be able to find out more about engines. So, at eighteen, he started to have his first lessons at night school for a penny a week, and it was not long before he rushed home in high excitement to tell his father that he could actually write his name! Presently he moved on to another school, where he paid fourpence a week to learn arithmetic and soon became the best pupil the master ever had. At first, some of the miners jeered when he took his books to work to prop them up by the engine. But he was soon in demand at dinner-times to read out news of the war against Napoleon in the news-sheets that found their way into the district from time to time.

Because he knew as a boy what it was to go bare-foot and hungry, George never wasted a moment or a penny. After his long hours at work and study, he would mend boots and even cut out suits of clothes for the miners. He tried his hand at mending clocks and watches, and became most skilful at the work. One day he mended the shoes of a pretty servant-girl called Fanny Henderson, and, not long afterwards, greatly daring, he asked her to marry him. He was a steady workman and had saved enough to furnish a cottage for her. But their baby was only a year old when Fanny died, leaving him with only two aims in life—to give his son Robert a better education than he had had, and to make himself into a first-class engineer.

He worked harder than ever and had actually saved twenty-eight guineas, when ill-fortune again overtook him. His father was blinded when a boiler exploded and was never able to work again. George paid the old fellow's debts and put his parents into a cottage where he supported them for the rest of their lives. Then his name was called for the army and he had to pay a man to go in his place, which was permitted in those days. He almost made up his mind to sail to America to start again, but, luckily for England, he could not find the passage-money.

Suddenly his luck changed. At Killingworth Colliery, a Newcomen engine had been put in to pump the water from a new shaft. Despite all the experts, the engine could not cope with the job and the owner was in despair. At this point, one of the foremen stepped into the office:

"Mr Dodds," he said, "the men are saying that Stephenson declares he could get the pit dry in a week."

"Stephenson, the brakesman?"

"Aye, sir. He's a clever fellow with machines, a proper engine-doctor they call him."

"Well, bring him in here," said Mr Dodds. "I'll soon see if he's boasting or not."

Stephenson was given the chance to prove his words. Against the advice of the engineers and the instructions of Newcomen, he took the engine to pieces, adjusted it and had it running in three days at twice the power. Two days later, the pit was pumped dry and the miners were at work. Mr Dodds was so delighted that Stephenson was made engine-wright of the colliery at the princely salary of £100 a year.

Now, at last, he could send Robert to school, and the boy started at Dr Bruce's School, Newcastle, wearing a suit which his father had cut out. At night, the two of them went over Robert's home lessons together, the boy teaching his father what he had learned during the day, while the older man passed on his knowledge of machines. Together, they became the greatest railway engineers in the world.

There had been several attempts to build steam-carriages long before Stephenson ever saw one. The wild Cornishman, Trevithick, made a locomotive that actually pulled coal and passengers in Wales, but the wooden rails broke. At the mines, horses had pulled coal wagons along rails for many a long day, but some quicker way of getting coal from the pits to the waiting ships was badly needed. Many people believed that the best solution would be *fixed* Boulton and Watt engines at each end of the rail-track to pull the wagons on a long rope or hawser. The trouble, they said, about a moving steam-engine or locomotive was that it moved no faster than horses and cost far more to keep. In

George and Robert Stephenson doing lessons together

addition, the engineers declared that smooth wheels would not grip on smooth rails. A man named William Hedley proved this idea wrong by running his *Puffing Billy* and *Wylam Dilly* up and down the track at Wylam Colliery.

Stephenson, greatly interested, went across to his old home, Wylam, to study *Puffing Billy*. He was so certain that he could build a better locomotive that he persuaded the owners of Killingworth to swallow their doubts about accidents and expense, and to let him try. In quite a short time, he had completed *Blucher*, his first locomotive, which had a boiler about a yard across and only eight feet long. When it was put on the rails, it pulled a load of thirty tons up a slope at four miles an hour.

Blucher worked, but it did not satisfy Stephenson, for it snorted and hissed, moving forward in jerks, and it cost far too much to run. So, with Robert's help, he quietly set about improving its faults. While others were vainly trying to design steam-carriages to run along the shocking roads of the day, he was learning a great deal about locomotives and the importance of the track they ran on.

So far, a few clumsy locomotives had been used to pull coal-trucks, but in 1823, after much opposition from people who said that the monsters would poison the air and set fire to property, Parliament gave permission for a railway to be built from Stockton to Darlington to carry both goods and passengers. George Stephenson was given the post of chief engineer and his first task was to lay the track.

He himself worked day and night, never seeming to stop for rest or food, urging the men to greater efforts, when they complained about difficulties :

" 'Tis not enough to start from Darlington at dawn," he said. " Save an hour by setting out earlier and be on the spot to start work the minute 'tis light ! Persevere, lads, that's the word, persevere ! "

At Newcastle, he and Robert put all their savings into an engine-works which they set up specially to build the locomotives, and, on 27th September 1825, all was finally ready. First was the engine *Locomotion*, with its high wheels and tall, thin funnel, with Stephenson himself driving. Then came six wagons loaded with coal and flour, next a coach filled with important gentlemen in top hats and tail-coats, then came twenty-one

The opening of the Stockton to Darlington railway

wagons filled with passengers and lastly six more wagons of coal. Huge crowds had gathered " to see the engine blow up," and the passengers and directors sat nervously on the edge of the benches. Stephenson took off the brakes and the engine started slowly but quite smoothly forward ; it gathered speed to a walking pace, rumbled to eight and then to twelve miles an hour !

Bursting into wild cheers, the crowd dashed alongside, waving and hallooing, while many hung on behind or clambered up into the wagons, until, when Stockton was reached, over 600 persons were clinging on somehow !

The world's first passenger train had made its first journey. As the top-hatted gentlemen shook hands with modest, smiling George, he ventured to say that, in his humble opinion, railways would one day carry goods and passengers to all parts of the country—not in his lifetime, mind, but one day.

Stephenson was too modest. Once started, nothing could stop the railways that he had done so much to prove. His greatest triumph was to come at the Rainhill Trials.

Even the opening of the Stockton-Darlington Railway had not convinced everyone that railways had come to stay. When it was decided to build a line from Liverpool to Manchester, there were still many who declared that fixed engines would be far cheaper and safer than locomotives. In fact, Stephenson stood alone in his fight for the locomotive, even after he had laid the track across difficult, marshy country :

" I tell you, gentlemen," he cried to a meeting of the directors, " that locomotive railroads will soon be the highways of the world ! "

" Impossible ! " snapped one gentleman.

"Aye, impossible ! " replied Stephenson. "That's what you said about Chat Moss. You said 'twas 'impossible' to lay a rail-track across the marsh, but I floated the line across. I beg you to give the locomotive a chance—in any case, you've spent too much money not to ! "

In the end, the directors offered a prize of £500

for the locomotive that gave the best performance at a public trial. Four engines entered for the competition which aroused such enormous interest that a grandstand was built at Rainhill and a vast crowd gathered in front of the two-mile stretch of railroad, as if they had come to the greatest race meeting of the century. The *Novelty* and the *Sanspareil* broke down during their runs along the course, while the *Perseverance* could not manage more than a stately crawl at six miles an hour. Stephenson, in his famous *Rocket,* which had been built at Newcastle under Robert's eye, made twenty trips up and down the line, pulling thirteen tons at an average speed of fifteen miles per hour, and reaching the staggering speed of thirty-five miles per hour unloaded.

There was no doubt who had won; even the most stubborn opponents were now convinced that the days of the pack-horse and stage-coach were almost over.

During the next twenty years, hardly a railway was started that Stephenson did not build or plan. His advice and services were asked wherever a new line was being considered in Britain or in several foreign countries. Sensible and modest as ever, Stephenson refused the honours that were offered him and laughed when he was asked if he would enter Parliament:

"Nay, lad," he chuckled, "I'd be out of place among all them fine gentlemen. As for 'George Stephenson, Esquire,' I've been 'Geordie' Stephenson all my life and 'Geordie' I'll stay."

LORD NELSON
(1758-1805)

ON the 14th of September, in the year 1805, there occurred an extraordinary scene in the great naval town of Portsmouth. Dense crowds were gathered outside the George Inn, pushing and pressing forward in their eagerness to catch a glimpse of someone who was clearly expected to come out from the main door. There were retired Navy men and sailors on shore-leave, grizzled old seamen with round hats and tarred pigtails, jostling citizens and shopkeepers in striped aprons, dockyard workers, wives in bonnets and shawls, and barefooted boys by the dozen. A shout went up:

"The Admiral's left by the back way! There he goes, God bless him!"

The crowd moved with him towards the beach, cheering with a fervour that caused even some of the seamen to blink away tears. They were cheering the most popular, the best-loved man in England.

The slight figure in the uniform of an Admiral of the Fleet pressed good-humouredly through the crowd. He was a little, spare man, with light hair and a face that was still boyish, though lined. He wore a green shade over his right eye and the right sleeve of his coat was empty except for the stump that he called his "fin."

Midshipman Nelson going over the side

"If I had two arms, I could shake hands with more of you," he said as he passed through the crowd, pausing to say a word to a group of his old "Mediterranean men" whom he recognised as having served under him in earlier years. The rough seamen doffed their hats and some of the women dropped upon their knees as he passed.

To their cheers, his barge was rowed from the shore to the waiting flagship and the Admiral turned to his friend, Captain Hardy, and remarked:

"I have had their huzzas before, Hardy. I have their hearts now."

The man who carried with him the hearts of the people of England was Horatio, Lord Nelson, adored by the ordinary folk of his country as no man has ever been, not even Drake himself. He seemed to them then, as he still does to-day, to be the very picture of a hero. As a pale, fair boy of thirteen, he had gone to sea from his father's country vicarage in Norfolk to rough it as a midshipman in his uncle's ship. He knew what it was to climb up into the swaying shrouds in half a gale, to struggle with frozen fingers with tangled ropes, to feel sea-sick but still to go over the side with a cutlass against the enemy. He had suffered scurvy, fever and wounds when other lads were still at school, and he never forgot it and never became so great that he could not spare a kindly word for boys as young and wretched as he had been. Once, when Commander-in-Chief of the Mediterranean Fleet, he stopped to ask a round-faced youngster, " You entered the Service at an early age ? " " At eleven years, my Lord," replied the awed boy. " Too young. Much too young," sighed Nelson. Yet as a " middy," he himself had declared after recovering from a bad bout of fever, " Well then, I will be a hero and, trusting in Providence, I will brave every danger."

Thus, to be a hero and to serve his country were the aims of his life. He lost his eye in Corsica, leading a shore party, and he was not even mentioned among the wounded, since he had refused to leave his duty for longer than it took to bandage his head. After the Battle of St Vincent, he was still on deck wounded, with half his hat shot away, his coat in ribbons and his face blackened with gunpowder. In another engagement, " our good Captain," as his men called him, was severely wounded in the arm during an attack on Santa

The wounded Nelson hauls himself aboard

Cruz, and was being rowed back to his ship when an explosion in the darkness announced that another boat was going down. Nelson at once ordered his boat to put back to pick up survivors, and, later, he hauled himself aboard by his one good arm, shouting :

"Tell the surgeon to get his instruments ready. For I know I must lose my arm and the sooner it is off, the better ! "

He had indeed made himself a hero whose

praises were sung by everyone who had ever served with him, from the powder-monkey boys, to the hard-drinking seamen and their strict officers. But, even so, was this enough to make the people cheer him away from Portsmouth with such heart-felt fervour that tough old sailormen choked down their sobs and women fell upon their knees?

The reason was that England stood in great peril. Across the Channel, Napoleon Bonaparte, Emperor of France, had conquered almost every country in Europe by a series of the most dazzling victories in all history. His very name was so feared that mothers hushed their naughty children with " Hush, lest Boney shall have you." Only England stood against him, and if he could get his splendid army across the Channel he would be master of the world. He built a fleet of flat-bottomed barges to ferry his soldiers across the twenty-one miles of water that lay between his vast camp and the Kentish shore. All he needed was a calm sea and a fleet of warships to protect the barges during the crossing.

But the English fleet was still at sea, while the French navy and their Spanish allies were cooped up in four different harbours, not daring to come out to battle. For two years in the Mediterranean, Nelson had watched the great port of Toulon, keeping his ships continually at sea and his men in good heart through the storms and boredom of a long waiting game.

Napoleon gave orders that his ships *must* escape from harbour, so that they could join together in one large fleet. The plan was to sail for the West Indies, join up with the Spanish fleet, and then, in great force, return across the Atlantic, overcome the English fleet and so enable the French army to invade our country and capture London.

While Nelson's squadron was obtaining fresh water and stores, the French admiral, Villeneuve, had slipped out of Toulon and was away through the Straits of Gibraltar with a fortnight's start, before Nelson's frigates could learn which way he had gone. Villeneuve joined the Spanish fleet but missed his other squadrons, then, hearing that Nelson was after him, he sailed back towards Europe and apparently disappeared.

Nelson, who by superb seamanship had almost caught the French, was given leave to England, since he had spent two years, all but ten days, without setting foot on land. He had exactly twenty-five days at home. Then word was brought that the French and Spanish fleets were in Cadiz harbour, making ready to put to sea again.

That was why Nelson had hurried down to Portsmouth by post-chaise to embark on his flag-ship, the *Victory,* which, with her 110 guns and crew of 900 men and boys, seemed to those who sailed in her " a floating city."

Late in September, the look-out of the *Victory* sighted the English fleet, under the command of Collingwood, lying about twenty miles off Cadiz. Even Nelson was surprised at the greeting he received when his flagship joined the fleet—cheer upon cheer floated across the water as the *Victory* moved majestically between the ships. Then, when the Captains and Commodores came aboard to receive his orders, they forgot his rank as their Commander-in-Chief in their pleasure at seeing their hero again. " My band of brothers " he called them.

After three weeks waiting, while the main body of the fleet was kept out of sight and fast frigates watched Cadiz, Nelson was forced to send six of his ships to Gibraltar for fresh water. Knowing this, Villeneuve left harbour and stood out to sea.

Nelson was ready and his plan prepared. At dawn, on the 21st October 1805, an English bluejacket, peering out of one of the gun-ports of the *Victory*, saw the enemy fleet about twelve miles to the east and not far from Cape Trafalgar. There were thirty-three French and Spanish ships to the English twenty-seven.

On the day before, Nelson had done one of those things which so endeared him to the sailors and kept their hearts so high. He had learned that a coxswain, one of the best men on board, had been so busy preparing the mailbags that he had forgotten to put in his own letter to his wife. The despatch ship was bearing away under full sail for England : " Hoist a signal to bring her back," said the admiral. " Who knows but that he may fall in action tomorrow ? His letter shall go with the rest."

As daylight increased, the sailors saw that Nelson was walking on his quarter-deck wearing a uniform coat, bright with gold lace, stars and decorations. Since the French were known to carry expert sharp-shooters, his senior officers thought that he was running a grave risk and they asked Hardy to tell him so :

"Hm," said Nelson briefly, "it is now too late to be shifting a coat."

His first signal ordered the fleet to sail towards the enemy in two columns, the *Victory* leading twelve ships, and Admiral Collingwood in the *Royal Sovereign* heading the other fifteen. The wind had almost dropped, so the English fleet bore on very slowly towards the arc of the French fleet, when the signal officer went to the admiral's cabin and found him on his knees praying for victory. Nelson rose and said :

"Mr Pasco, I wish you to signal to the Fleet— 'England confides that Every Man will do his duty.' You must be quick for I have one more signal to make, which is 'close action.' "

Lieutenant Pasco replied, "I beg leave, my Lord, to suggest that 'expects' would save time over 'confides.' "

"That will do. Make it at once," answered Nelson.

When the famous signal ENGLAND EXPECTS THAT EVERY MAN THIS DAY WILL DO HIS DUTY fluttered from the *Victory,* cheers burst from every ship of the line. It was followed by the flag that ordered them into action.

Then the bands on board struck up "Rule Britannia" and "Britons Strike Home," as the black-and-yellow-painted three-deckers rolled towards the French. "See how that noble fellow Collingwood carries his ship into action," cried Nelson in excitement, as the *Royal Sovereign* opened fire.

Making steadily towards Villeneuve's flagship, the *Victory* was hit several times; her mizzen topmast went overboard, the wheel was smashed and the sails riddled with shot. A great fragment which burst between Hardy and Nelson, as they slowly paced the deck, tore off a buckle from Hardy's shoe. They halted and looked at each other, smiling: "This is too warm work to last long, Hardy," said Nelson.

From close quarters, the *Victory's* terrible broadside thundered out upon the French flagship, utterly crippling her by destroying twenty guns and killing or wounding 400 men. The *Victory* now ran alongside the seventy-four-gun *Redoubtable,* catching in its rigging aloft, until the two ships were hopelessly entangled.

"Never mind," said Nelson. "It does not matter which one we run on board of—take your choice."

A furious battle took place between the two ships; the English guns poured into the French vessel, but her musket men cleared the upper deck, and, from the rigging, sharp-shooters picked off officers and men through the pall of smoke and the roar of the guns.

Hardy, walking the deck, suddenly realised that the Admiral was no longer with him. He turned and saw Nelson on his knees trying to hold

Nelson dying in the cockpit

himself up on his left arm. Then he fell sideways, and as Hardy ran to him, he heard him say:

"They have done for me at last, Hardy."

He was carried below into the cockpit, where three surgeons and their mates, arms and aprons scarlet with blood, were at work by swaying lantern-light, sawing off shattered limbs and binding up dreadful wounds. They laid him in a midshipman's berth, where the sailors might not see him. The musket ball had gone through his chest and spine:

"I felt it break my back," murmured Nelson, but he clung on to life, asking again and again for news of the battle.

Hardy came below again.

"Well, Hardy, how goes the battle? How goes the day with us?"

"Very well, my Lord. We have got twelve or fourteen of the enemy's ships. Five have tacked and are bearing down upon the *Victory*. I have called two or three of our fresh ships round us and have no doubt of giving them a drubbing."

"I hope none of our ships have struck their colours, Hardy?"

"No, my Lord. There is no fear of that."

"That's well. That's well. . . . I am going fast, Hardy; it will be all over with me soon . . . my back is shot through."

Hardy knelt down and took his hand. Above, the guns of the *Victory* ceased firing. The greatest naval victory in our history had been won. Down in the blood-red cockpit, Nelson spoke again.

"Now I am satisfied. Thank God I have done my duty. . . . Thank God I have done my duty."

ELIZABETH FRY

(1780-1845)

AS the Norwich mail coach creaked up a slight rise on its final stage to the city, a band of four or five girls in red cloaks burst from the woods and danced alongside the straining horses and the coach itself, jumping up to look inside, making faces and actually putting out their tongues at the scandalised passengers!

"Go away, you mannerless hussies!" cried a stout lady in a mauve bonnet, who was seated by the window. "I know who you are, and your father shall hear of your behaviour."

With shrieks and giggles, the girls raced off down a woodland path and disappeared.

"And who might these gypsies be, madam?" enquired a red-faced gentleman in the coach.

"Not gypsies, sir—oh dear me, no," replied the stout lady. "They are the Gurney girls, left motherless these two years and running as wild as you please."

"I do *not* please, madam," observed Red-face severely, " but did I understand you to say Gurney ? I do business with John Gurney, the Norwich banker, member of a leading Quaker family. Cannot be the same."

"It is indeed the same," sighed Mauve-bonnet. "Quaker or no, those girls are wild, spoiled creatures."

While this conversation was taking place in the coach, the "wild spoiled creatures" had reached their home at Earlham Hall. Still laughing, they ran across the wide trim lawns and tumbled upstairs to the schoolroom for an important part of the business of the day—writing up their diaries.

Diary-writing was all the rage. Everyone set down their opinions and thoughts and, from time to time, diaries were read aloud to the other members of the family. Rachel, writing about their naughtiness on the highroad, put down " I do think being rude is most pleasant sometimes," which was an honest confession, in days when young ladies were expected to behave like prim little angels.

Louisa, the liveliest and naughtiest of the sisters, wrote : " I am eleven years old. I will write about Earlham. My father is master, Kitty is mistress. Governess, disliked by most of us, sits in the drawing-room almost all day. . . . The first maid is Judd, a convinced Friend, Nurse coming next ; her greatest happiness is to see us neat. She often tires me by scoldings about keeping our clothes neat."

Kitty, or Catherine, the eldest, was indeed mistress of Earlham. She was seventeen when her mother died, and it was taken for granted that she should assume the task of bringing up her ten brothers and sisters, as well as being head of a large house. She did it wonderfully well and they adored her; even Louisa wrote: " I love my father better than anybody except Kitty, she is everything to me."

Poor Kitty had her hands full and she felt that she never again knew the glee and happiness of the others. There was Rachel, the family beauty, whose heart was to be broken one day; Betsy, the quiet one, who was slow at her lessons; Priscilla, called " Cilla " in the diaries, pretty but delicate; naughty Louisa; Richenda; Sam, whom Betsy loved; Hannah; John; Joseph; and little Daniel the youngest.

Their father, John Gurney of Earlham, was a generous parent and, after his beloved wife died, he did his best to carry out her wishes that every one of the eleven children should be free and happy. He filled his fine house with troops of friends and relations, allowed his girls to run wild while they were young, and bought them bright clothes to wear and ponies to ride. How they enjoyed themselves! There were dances and parties—even a prince of the Royal Family came to visit them and was highly delighted with the company of these lively girls. There were visits to London and the seaside, and rides into Norwich.

" We went into Norwich," wrote Louisa in

her diary when a Gurney cousin stood for Parliament. "We had blue cockades (rosettes) and I bawled out of the window at a fine rate, 'Gurney for ever!'"

And when nothing else offered, they would have the blind fiddler up to the house to play them merry dances.

If well-bred neighbours frowned upon these gay doings, it was nothing compared with the disapproval of the Quaker relatives. The Gurneys belonged to the leading Quaker family of the county. Uncle Joseph was an Elder at the Meeting House in Goats Lane, Norwich, to which the girls were taken every Sunday by their father.

The Quakers were a religious sect of earnest people, who were supposed to have gained their strange name from their founder, George Fox, crying out, "Tremble at the Word of the Lord!" Others said that, as they sat in silence in their solemn Meeting Houses, a trembling or "quaking" would come over those who were moved by the Holy Ghost to pray aloud.

The Meetings were unlike Church services, since the Quakers, or "Friends" as they are still called, did not believe that "steeple-houses," priests or music were needed by Christian people. So they sat in silence, waiting until one of their number was moved to speak. Certain Friends, who had the power to preach, were made ministers, and one of them might choose to speak for two hours at a time, to the dismay of Louisa and her sisters.

The Gurney girls at the Meeting House

For the Gurney girls, the Sunday Meetings at Goats Lane were torture. They hated sitting still, and they knew that their gay cloaks and pretty clothes were strongly disapproved by Uncle Joseph and the other " plain " Quakers, who wore the " plain " dress and called everyone " thee " and " thou."

Louisa's favourite word was " disgusting," which she shortened to " dis " ; Goats Lane she always referred to as " Goats," and " Goats was dis " became a frequent entry in her diary. Once she added, in her amusing way, that the day was spoilt, for they all felt " rather goatified and cross. Oh, how I long to get a broom and bang all the old Quakers who look so triumphant and disagreeable! "

Betsy, the third daughter, was a little quieter than the others. Louisa wrote, " dearest Betsy, she seems to have no one for a friend," for she often missed " Goats " owing to illness, and she was already a thoughtful girl, with a streak of obstinacy, so that no one could move her once she had made up her mind. She loved the wild games and dancing as much as the others, but there were things which they did not understand ; she was terrified of the dark, yet would force herself to go up to the great dim attics which were supposed to be haunted. She dreaded the sea and the bathing-machine, and for years she suffered from nightmares about drowning and death. But, though she often worried about being good, she found religion boring and the Quakers rather absurd.

One Sunday morning, Betsy could have escaped " Goats " because she had woken with stomach-ache, but she decided to go in the carriage because a well-known Quaker from America was going to speak.

The Meeting House was crowded and the Gurney girls in their red cloaks sat in the front row. Betsy herself was also wearing purple boots with scarlet laces. The American Friend, William Savery, felt grieved to see such gay dress in Norwich. Presently he rose to speak. Almost at once, Betsy stopped fidgeting and began to listen ; the gentle, penetrating voice seemed to be speaking to her alone, until, as she wrote afterwards, " a faint light spread over my mind and I felt that there is a God."

After the Meeting, she drove home alone in the carriage with the speaker and he continued to talk to her. Next day, he called at Earlham and Betsy spent most of the day in his company; then he departed to London, leaving Betsy " in a whirl." She fought against the thoughts that Savery had planted in her mind, for she did not want to become a plain Quaker and give up all the gaiety that her sisters loved so well.

Her affectionate father, seeing his daughter troubled, took her to London for a holiday with cousins. They visited the theatre and the opera, there were parties and dances. It was all very gay and delightful, but she also met William Savery again and heard him preach. When she got back to Earlham, her sisters could see that she was changing and they were sorry. " We all feel about it alike," wrote Richenda, " and are truly sorry that one of us seven should separate herself from the rest." But it was clear that Betsy would soon become a " plain " Quaker.

Perhaps another holiday might put things right, so John Gurney took his daughters to Weymouth and to Wales, where they visited Aunt Priscilla, whose house was a centre of " plain " Quakerism. To a Meeting in the house came Deborah Derby, a noted preacher who was said to have strange powers of prophecy, and, when she rose and began to preach to the assembled Friends, she gazed steadily at Betsy. In a ringing voice, she told her that she was chosen to be " a light to the blind, speech to the dumb and feet to the lame," that she would spend her life giving service to others. Poor Betsy, thrilled and scared by this revelation of God's special purpose, was only eighteen, and she wrote in her diary, " I know now what the mountain is I have to climb. I am to be a Quaker." She meant, of course, a " plain " Quaker.

But it was a long time before she understood what God's purpose was to be. Back at Earlham, she looked for some way to serve others, and she found Billy. He was a little boy of six, one of the ragged, dirty cottage-children, one of many who had little care and certainly no schooling. Would he like to come up to the big house and hear a story? Billy's eyes shone and he came on Sunday to be carried up to the attic where Betsy told him the first Bible story he had ever heard, in that clear, marvellous voice which was later to fascinate people wherever she went. Next Sunday, Billy brought a friend, and then more friends of various sizes and ages, until a whole troop of them gathered in the attic to listen to the stories.

The children were certainly wonderfully well-behaved with Betsy, but they were also dirty and smelly, and the family refused to have all these urchins inside the house. Betsy was never defeated by difficulties, and she demanded the use of a large brick outhouse, the laundry in fact, and there she held her Sunday School for sixty or seventy

Betsy with her " Imps " in the attic

ragged children—" Betsy's Imps," her sisters called them.

At this time Joseph Fry began to appear at Earlham. Joe was young and reasonably handsome, but so shy and awkward that the Gurney girls called him " young fry," and thought little of his manners and loud guffaw. Joe, however, had set his heart upon fair-haired Betsy, and though she turned him down again and again, he continued to visit Earlham. His family were rich Quakers in the City of London, and Mr Gurney began to look in a kindly way upon the persistent young man, but he said that he would not compel any daughter to wed against her will.

At last, Joe brought the matter to a head. He gave Betsy a gold watch one evening with the solemn promise that if she gave it back by nine o'clock next morning, he would go away and never trouble her again. Betsy passed a sleepless night, but next morning she kept the watch, and Joe had his answer. They were married at " Goats " next August with all the Gurneys in the Meeting House to see their first sister married.

She was Betsy Gurney no longer, but Mistress Elizabeth Fry, who must move to London to her husband's home and business. She said good-bye to her beloved Earlham, to her father and sisters, and to her " Imps," eighty-six of them, and they wept to see her go.

In London, Elizabeth was now a " plain " Quaker, and she took, with some heart-burnings, to wearing the " plain " dress with its old-fashioned cap and quiet colours. Yet it was far from easy to please her husband's family. At Earlham she had been the odd one out, and now she found herself in the same position, for she was still looked upon as a " gay " Gurney, not yet plain enough for the strict Frys.

Gradually, she won them over by her gentle ways and her refusal ever to change what she believed to be right. She often entertained sixty or more Quakers in her big house, and was much in demand as a nurse in times of illness. Her sisters were regular visitors, especially when a new baby arrived. She named most of her children after her own family. There was Katherine, then Rachel, John, William, Richenda, Joseph. Altogether she had ten children, and she planned their upbringing and education, though they were the only people whom she ever found difficult to manage !

But what of Deborah Derby's prophecy that she was to be " a light to the blind, speech to the dumb, and feet to the lame " ? How could the mother of a large family and mistress of a great household, with family and Quaker duties in many parts of the kingdom find time for her great mission in life ?

Despite all her duties, she began to visit the poor. She discovered Irish Row near her own home, where, down filthy alleys ankle-deep in mud, people lived in tumbledown hovels, their windows stuffed with rags, the floors rotten with damp, and where fever stalked every year because there were no drains or sewers. To these most wretched people, Elizabeth talked and smiled, bringing them clothing and food when they were in want. Best of all, she made friends with them, for she never preached or lectured, but sympathised and comforted them. A child fell ill, and she nursed her back to life ; that gave her the opportunity to start a school for them. She was one of the first to believe in vaccination and she herself learned how to vaccinate children against the dreaded small-pox.

During one hard winter, a boy was found frozen to death on a doorstep. At once Elizabeth opened a soup-kitchen for the homeless in a barn, and a clothes-store with the aid of money and garments given by kind Quaker ladies. She was a born nurse and provided bandages and medicines for those who could never afford a doctor. And all this time she was travelling about the country preaching at Quaker Meeting Houses, for she had discovered the most marvellous power to speak of what she believed Christianity to mean.

One day, a gentleman from America, a Friend who knew both William Savery and Deborah Derby, called to see Mrs Fry. He had visited the prison at Newgate and he had found conditions there so dreadful that he had come to the one person who, he had heard, would dare to try to put them right.

So Elizabeth Fry went to Newgate Prison. There were eighteen prisons in and around London at this time, and Newgate was known to be the worst of them all. Eight hundred prisoners of every kind were crowded in a building so foul and fever-ridden that a windmill had been put upon the roof " to draw off the evil air." In its gloomy rooms, the prisoners were herded together, murderers and lunatics, innocent persons awaiting trial, debtors, pickpockets and thieves. A boy arrested on suspicion of poaching might be chained to a cut-throat thief only too ready to teach his trade to a young lad. Except that the women and children were in a separate part of the prison, everyone ate, slept, cooked their food and washed, if possible, in the same stinking room. There was no sanitation.

It was to try to help women prisoners in these conditions that Elizabeth went to Newgate. There were 300 of them with many children in four rooms. They were filthy and desperate, many were half-naked because they had bartered their clothes for food. These women were so ferocious that the prison officials begged Mrs Fry not to enter the wards. The Governor himself confessed that he seldom went near; the turnkeys were horrified, they themselves only went in by twos, but a lady in her fine clothes would be torn to pieces!

"I thank thee, but I am not afraid," said Mrs Fry. "I pray thee to let me in."

She went through the gate, which was locked behind her, and disappeared into a mob of screaming, fighting women. No one knows exactly what her first words were, but the women fell silent.

In her lovely, compelling voice, she said, "I am come here to help you. If you will assist me, I may be of service to you."

Not a sign of fear or disgust showed in her face as she looked around her and as she bent down to a child who was looking up at the strange lady.

"This little one has need of clothes," she said, tenderly picking up the child as if he were one of her own. "See, I have something here."

She distributed a bundle of clothes as far as possible, then she talked to the women, listening to their fears and wants, showing a special interest in the children and promising help as soon as possible. Before she left, she knelt down on the filthy floor and prayed.

Elizabeth Fry had seen what was needed and no Governor or boards of authorities could stop her from finding remedies for the evils of Newgate. First, the women needed clothes, but her husband's business was hard-pressed owing to the war, so she formed a Committee of Ladies to gather materials and to sew garments, especially for the children. Because she herself was a mother, she knew that even the most hardened wretch must have some feeling for her little ones. Very well, she would feed and clothe them. Then she asked the prisoners if they wished their children to have a better chance in life than they themselves had had.

Surely, said Elizabeth, a school would help them to learn useful ways of earning an honest living. Then they would start a school, but the prisoners themselves must make the rules and find their own schoolmistress. The women chose Mary Connor, a quiet good girl who had been arrested for stealing a watch that even the judge believed she had not taken.

But now the Governor and the authorities said this sort of thing was impossible. Quite a good idea, of course—but nothing would succeed with these ferocious women. They knew them—and, in any case, there was no room.

" No room ? " said Mrs Fry. " Is that the sole objection to my plan ? "

She went back to the prisoners and asked them to find a room. A small cell was scrubbed clean and the first school in a prison started, with Mary Connor as schoolmistress and pupils up to the age of twenty-five. It is good to know that Mary was

Women prisoners making quilts, while Elizabeth reads the Bible

so successful that she eventually obtained a free pardon.

The next thing was to find the women some work to do, so that they would not spend their time quarrelling and idling. They must sew, and sell the goods that they made. Authority pointed out that there was much unemployment of honest folk, and it would be difficult to find a market. Mrs Fry discovered that there was a steady demand for patchwork quilts among the prisoners in Australia who had been released, and she arranged for a firm of exporters to ship the women's work to Botany Bay. Wives of Quaker merchants secured oddments of cloth and the prisoners set to work.

Mrs Fry divided the women into small groups, each in charge of a monitor. Marks were awarded for good behaviour and arrangements were made to save some of the money earned by needlework, so that they would have a nest-egg when they were released or sent to Australia.

Visitors, officials and Aldermen of the City were dumbfounded when they came to Newgate to see the results of the work of troublesome Mrs Fry and her Ladies' Committee. Instead of a mob of screaming, ragged creatures, they saw the women respectably dressed, sewing quietly in groups, and the whole place cleaner and more decent than it had ever been in its long, shameful history. Mrs Fry was reading to them from the Bible, and the important visitors were kept waiting until she had finished, for, she said, " I never allow any trifling circumstance to interrupt the reading of the Holy Scriptures."

Quite suddenly, she was famous. The papers were full of her remarkable work for prisoners. She was the talk of the day in Court and Society circles ; everyone wished to meet this woman who had stepped quietly into territory that normally belonged to men. The House of Commons asked her to report upon prisons, and she was presented to the Queen, though her Quaker beliefs did not permit her to curtsey. From all over Europe came letters, invitations and requests for advice. Fame troubled and distressed Elizabeth Fry, but she realised that it might help forward the work that was needed in so many directions.

Due to her example and pleadings, many reforms were made in the prison system and in the treatment of convicts transported to Australia. Gradually the worst features of the system were changed and the public came to realise that crime cannot be checked by savage punishment and inhuman treatment.

She died in 1845, at the age of sixty-five, worn out by her ceaseless work, but surrounded by the love of her family and of her country.

What was her secret? How did she succeed where so many had failed, or had been blind to the misery which existed on every side in nineteenth-century England? She was loving and kind, but she was also hard-headed; she saw what was wanted and she set about winning her way with a gentle obstinacy that no one could overcome. Many of her ideas were far ahead of her time, when women were supposed to have no place in society except the home. But the real secret of her life was her steadfast belief that she was sent into the world by God to be " a light to the blind, speech to the dumb, and feet to the lame."

THE STORY OF DAVID LIVINGSTONE
(1813–1873)

(i) The Missionary

IT was barely light as a small sturdy boy trotted down the street towards the cotton factory; he was only ten years old, and he had to be at work by six o'clock, but this morning he was filled with excitement. It was the end of his first week at work, and in the evening he would proudly take home his first wages. He would hand it to his mother, but she had promised that he might keep back the price of a Latin grammar-book that he had seen in the window of a second-hand shop.

The boy was David Livingstone, second son of a poor family living near Glasgow. He bought his book and learned Latin as he stood at the spinning-machine. As he grew older, he worked at his lessons far into the night until he was able to go to college to study to be a doctor. His great desire was to go to China as a missionary and he knew that the work of spreading the Gospel would be greatly helped if he could also heal the sick.

Livingstone's canoes on the Zambesi

Alas for his hopes ! War in China meant that it was impossible to send out missionaries for the time being. Greatly disappointed, he turned into a meeting hall one evening to listen to the famous missionary, Doctor Moffat, who was to speak about his work in South Africa. Sitting there, David heard Moffat say :

" On a clear morning, I can see from the hills near Kuruman, the smoke of a thousand villages where no missionary has ever been."

Livingstone's heart leapt when he heard these words, and at the end of the meeting, he stayed behind hoping to have a word with the doctor.

" Do you think, sir," he asked, " that there is work for me in Africa ? "

Looking the shy young man up and down, Doctor Moffat saw at once that he was immensely strong and determined.

" Yes," he answered, " if you would be willing to push northward into the unknown country, there's great work for you in Africa. But first, go to my mission station at Kuruman, learn the language, and, when I come out, I will advise you."

Livingstone did not hesitate. He finished his medical examinations to become a doctor and then went to the London Missionary Society to ask if they would send him out to Africa.

It was in the year 1840, when Queen Victoria had been on the throne for only three years, that he said good-bye to his mother and father and his four brothers and sisters and took ship to Cape Town.

From the Cape, he journeyed by slow, jolting

ox-wagon the 700 miles to Kuruman, the most northerly point in South Africa that Christianity had reached. Beyond, stretched a vast country of plain, forest and desert unknown to white men, where the black people lived in fear of magic, of witch-doctors and of Arab slave-traders.

At first, Livingstone threw himself with heart and soul into the work of the mission station, preaching, treating the sick, learning the African languages and making friends with the Bechuana people. Always in his mind were those thousand villages, and more, where no Englishman had ever been.

Presently, he decided to push northwards to start a new missionary settlement at Mabotsa, in the land of the People of the Monkey, with whom he was friendly because he had cured their chief's daughter of an illness. Unfortunately, Mabotsa was in a valley infested by lions which boldly attacked the cattle, and even children.

Livingstone decided to show the terrified tribesmen that if he killed one or two lions, the rest would take themselves off. Leading a party to where it was known that lions were attacking the herds, he fired and wounded one of the great beasts. As he was re-loading his gun, it sprang upon him, seized him by the shoulder and, as he himself wrote, " growling horribly, close to my ear, he shook me as a terrier does a rat." Three Africans bravely went to his rescue and the lion dropped Livingstone to spring at them; all were badly mauled before the lion fell dead from his wounds. Livingstone's left shoulder was so badly injured

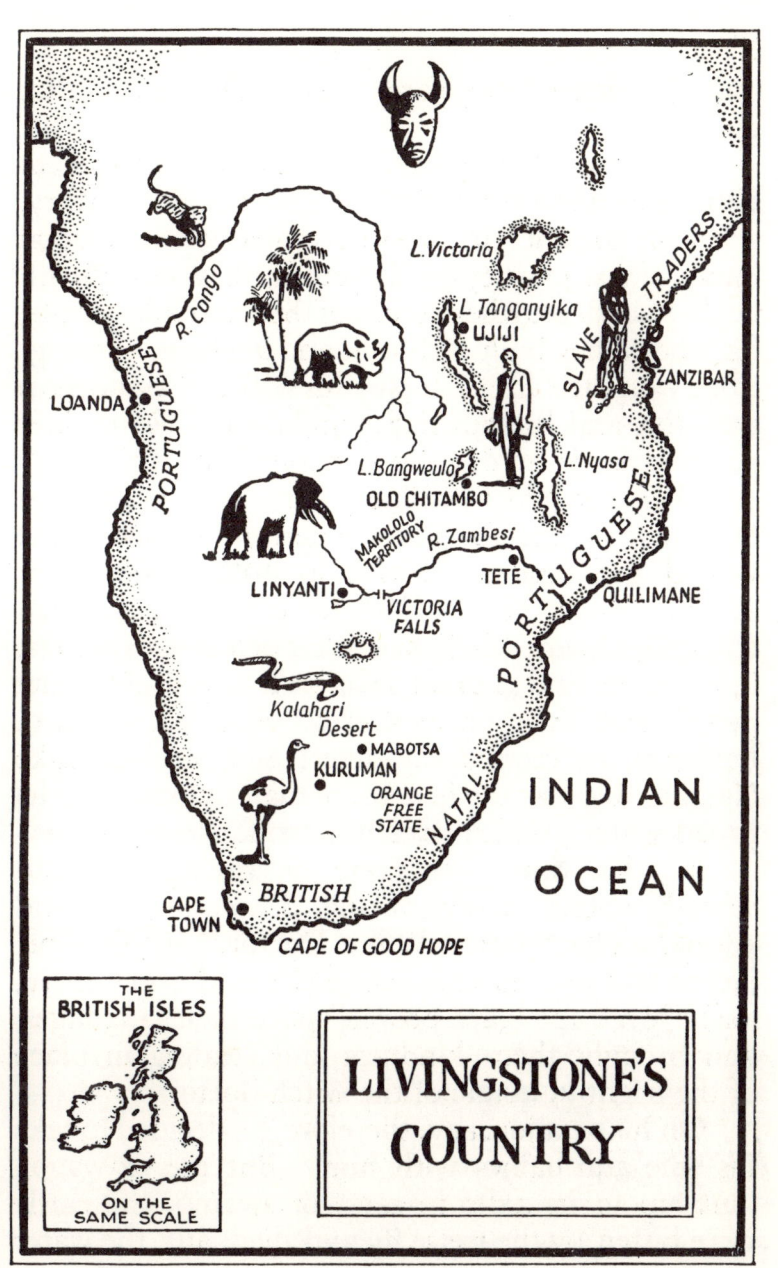

LIVINGSTONE'S COUNTRY

that he never afterwards had full use of that arm.

Next year, Doctor Moffat and his wife returned to Kuruman, and David married their daughter, Mary, a brave, patient girl who accompanied him upon many of his journeys. Together, they moved still farther north into the country of the Makololo people, for whom they built a church and a school. Livingstone won their friendship by his skill and kindness as a doctor, and by showing them how to irrigate their parched fields by digging trenches from the river.

Then the chief willingly lent him guides for his journeys into the bush, where he preached the Gospel and tended the sick in distant villages or kraals. Soon he decided to cross the dreaded Kalahari Desert, which had so far defeated explorers, in order to find a great lake and to preach to the people who lived on its shores. After six weeks of hardship, he crossed the desert and reached Lake Ngami. He was the first white man to look upon its broad waters, which stretched too far to see across.

By this time, the fame of Livingstone had spread among many of the peoples of Central Africa. The "Great White Doctor," in his short jacket and peaked cap, was welcomed everywhere, for he loved the black people, spoke their languages, and brought them kindness and healing in place of the frightful magic of the witch-doctors.

On his next journey, therefore, he decided to take his wife and babies with him. But the ox-wagon sank up to its axles in sand or swamp, the cattle were bitten by the tsetse fly and died, and the water tank ran dry. The family struggled on, the children crying from thirst and insect bites, until they reached the village of a friendly chief who gave them goat's milk and the tender meat of a young antelope. He cried out in wonder when he learnt that they had crossed the great " thirst-land."

Leaving his family in the care of the chief, Livingstone went on northwards because he had heard talk of a great river. A few days later, he came to the banks of the Zambesi, one of the mightiest rivers in Africa, and, as he watched its broad waters flowing by, he realised that this unknown river might well be what he was seeking—a highroad into the heart of Africa, up which Christian missionaries, trade and civilisation might travel.

On his return, however, he also realised that the climate was too unhealthy for his young children. With their mother, they had shared the dangers, fever and mosquito bites, but he knew that he must carry on his work alone. Gradually he made his way south to Cape Town, and, with a heavy heart, saw his family sail away on the first ship leaving for England.

(ii) *Across Africa*

By ox-cart, canoe, and on foot, Livingstone journeyed back to the country of the Makololo. He passed along rivers lined with tall reeds where flamingoes fished and hippopotami swam and grunted, through forests where elephants crashed away trumpeting, past ant-hills as tall as houses and across rolling grasslands, until he reached Linyanti, the capital village of the Makololo.

At Linyanti, he asked the chief for volunteers to accompany him on a great journey to " the white man's sea " on the west coast of Africa. Twenty-seven black tribesmen said that they would go with him ; they took their spears but left their shields in their huts, so that strangers would know that they were travelling peaceably. Livingstone's stores consisted of a few biscuits, a little tea and sugar, twenty pounds of coffee and three books, with a horse-rug and a sheepskin for bedding, a little tent and a tin box into which were crammed a spare shirt, trousers, shoes and some scientific instruments, including his Magic Lantern to show Bible pictures in the villages !

Paddling by canoe up the Zambesi, they travelled westward. It was extremely hot and unhealthy, and Livingstone began to suffer from fever. His black friends looked after him carefully, cutting grass for his bed at night, pitching the tent and sleeping outside it to guard him. Presently, they left the river and penetrated the thick forests, swarming with birds and insects. The way became both difficult and dangerous ; then they came into country where some of the chiefs were women, one of whom gave Livingstone an ox to ride on, which he named Sinbad. Food became very scarce and they were obliged to eat zebra meat and the bitter flesh of elephants. An unfriendly tribe demanded payment to allow them to pass, and when all the coloured beads had been given away, the Makololo

Livingstone showing Bible pictures with his Magic Lantern

men had to part with their own ornaments. Unceasing rain, hunger and fever reduced Livingstone almost to a skeleton; he was so weak that he had to be supported by his companions as he tottered along.

At last, they came to the crest of a high ridge up which they had toiled for days; before them lay a pleasant, green land, and, with new heart, they made their way down. The Makololo were amazed at the sight of " the white man's sea," believing that they had come to the end of the world, which seemed to say to them " I am finished, there is no more of me."

As they neared the coast, a friendly Portuguese sergeant saved them from being sold into slavery and led them into the town of Loanda, where the Portuguese settlers treated them kindly. The only Englishman in the place gave up his bed for Livingstone.

"Never shall I forget," he said, "the luxury I enjoyed in feeling myself again on a good English bed after six months of sleeping on the ground."

An English warship at anchor off Loanda offered Livingstone a passage home, but he would not leave his black friends. Had he not promised their chief that he would bring them safely back? So, although still weak from the fever, he began the return journey. Since he could not travel more than ten miles a day, it took a whole year to reach Linyanti, but they were welcomed with tremendous joy by the Makololo, and word spread through the forests and plains that the White Doctor had kept his word of honour.

Livingstone's great strength enabled him to make a speedy recovery and he was soon off on his travels again, this time in the opposite direction, eastwards to the Indian Ocean, paddling with the stream, down the Zambesi.

One day, he noticed ahead what seemed to be columns of smoke rising into the sky, and, as they drew nearer, the air was filled with a dull roaring sound which grew louder and louder. The Makololo said that it must be "Mosi-oa-tunya," which meant the "smoke-sounder." Puzzled, he pushed on and came near to where the great river plunged over a gigantic cliff, and the force of the water sent up columns of fine spray and vapour that rose high into the air like smoke. In honour of his Queen, Livingstone named this waterfall "Victoria Falls."

Leaving the river, they came into a country that was strangely deserted and wretchedly poor.

The native peoples were nervous and suspicious of the travellers; sometimes they fled from their villages, at others they would have attacked but for Livingstone's fair dealing with the chiefs. Often he noticed bones and skulls at the side of the path.

He had reached the territory of the Arab slave-traders, who for years had raided the villages to capture or buy slaves, which they drove to the coast—men, women and children chained together and yoked to poles. Livingstone was filled with angry grief at the wicked cruelty of this trade and he made up his mind that he would devote the rest of his life to destroying it. If he could open up Africa to Christian trade and religion, the slave markets would be broken.

He suffered again from fever, but the last part of his great journey was through beautiful country. This time he left his faithful Makololo friends at a place called Tete, telling them to wait until he came for them. They waited for three years, knowing full well that he would return. Finally, he reached Quilimane on the shores of the Indian Ocean. In four years he had explored 11,000 miles of unknown country and was the first white man to cross Africa from west to east.

With one faithful black servant who begged to stay with his master, but who died, alas, on the voyage, Livingstone returned to England to rejoin his dear family. The gaunt, lined missionary found himself a public hero and his book about his travels was so popular that he could have retired comfortably. But the black friends who were waiting for him, and the cruelties of the slave-trade, never left his mind. He knew that he was needed in Africa.

(iii) The Last Journey

There were six more years of exploring in Central Africa, before Livingstone set out on his last journey. His wife had come out to join him but she soon died of fever, and the lonely man was unable to settle in England. He went back to Africa to continue his fight against the slave-trade and his task of mapping the vast country that was now his home.

He left Zanzibar on the east coast with a party of thirty-six followers, well equipped with stores, camels, mules and donkey. They reached Lake Nyasa safely, but rumours of savage attacks by the Zulus caused most of his party to desert back to the coast where they spread stories that Livingstone had been killed.

The faithful Susi, with Chusa and four or five black boys, stayed with him and, together, they trudged on towards the great Lake Tanganyika. Once again, food became scarce, and the animals died, but worst of all, his medicine chest was stolen and so he had no means of checking the fever that constantly attacked him. The difficulties increased, but he never ceased his observations and careful notes of the country through which they passed : " I am ill with fever," he wrote in his diary. " Every step I take jars my chest. I am very weak ; I can scarcely keep up the march."

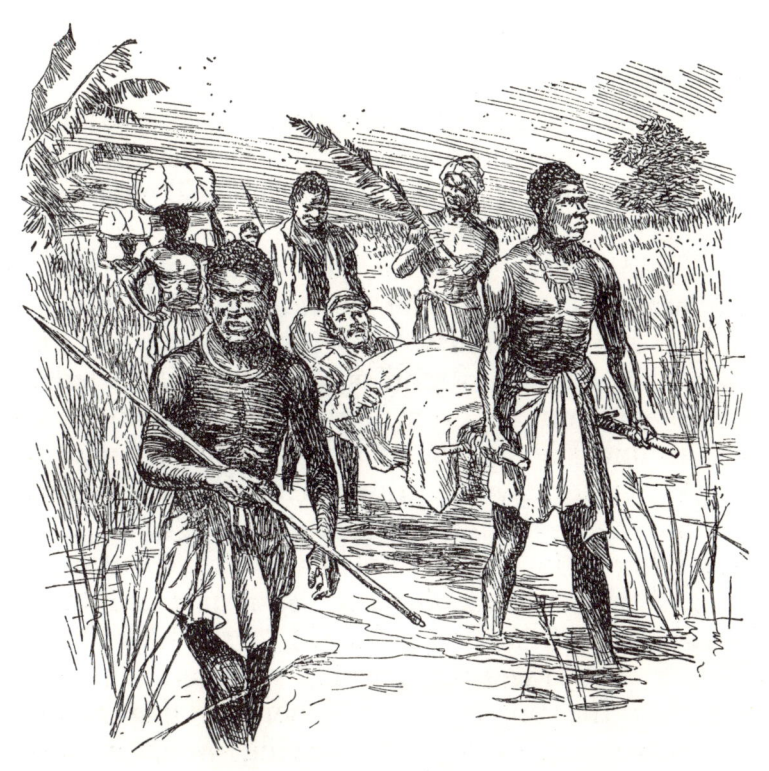

Livingstone's boys carry him on a litter

When swamps made walking too difficult for him, his boys carried him on a litter made from branches. At last they reached Ujiji on the shores of Lake Tanganyika, a centre of the slave-trade to which the Arab slavers brought people for sale. Livingstone's strength returned and he did all he could to prevent the horrible trade. "The sights I have seen make my blood run cold," he said. Often he risked death from hidden spearmen as he travelled the surrounding country, helping the people of remote villages and encouraging them to resist the slavers. The rest of his stores were stolen; letters from England never reached him and his own letters were stolen from runners on their way to the coast. The Arab traders did not want interference from white men.

Thus it was that for four years no news of Livingstone reached the outside world. At last, public alarm caused an American newspaper, the *New York Herald*, to send out an expedition led by an adventurous reporter named H. M. Stanley. He was to find Livingstone or bring home his bones.

As Stanley's well-equipped expedition was tracking him through the forests and plains, Livingstone was lying ill in Ujiji; he was very weak but full of courage. One day, his boy Susi darted into his hut, crying, " An Englishman! I see him! " and rushed off to meet the arriving strangers who were entering the village. An American flag headed the procession of porters carrying on their heads bales of goods, kettles, pots and stores of every kind.

Pushing his way through a crowd of natives, Stanley came forward to where a white man with a long grey beard was standing outside a hut.

" As I advanced slowly towards him," said Stanley afterwards, " I noticed he was pale, looked worried, wore a bluish cap with a faded gold band round it, had a red-sleeved waistcoat and a pair of grey tweed trousers. I walked to him, took off my hat, and said, ' Dr Livingstone, I presume? '

" 'Yes,' said he, with a kind smile, lifting his cap slightly.

" Then we both grasped hands and I said aloud,

' I thank God, Doctor, I have been permitted to see you.'

" ' You have brought me new life—new life,' murmured the tired explorer."

The two men liked each other and Stanley remained with the doctor for some time, helping him to get well with his company and good food, but nothing that he could say would persuade Livingstone to go home to rebuild his ruined health. " I must finish my task," he said simply.

Soon afterwards, with new stores, donkeys and cows, Livingstone set out again with all his old eagerness for exploration, but it soon became clear to his faithful Susi that his master's strength had gone for ever, and he became too weak to walk.

In April 1873, through the torrential rains that turned all the land into a swamp, his boys carried him into Chitambo's village by Lake Bangweolo, where they tenderly made him a bed in a little hut. At night, his boy, looking in to see how his master was, noticed that he was kneeling in prayer by the side of his rough bed. Next morning, Susi found him still kneeling there, his body stretched forward and his face in his hands upon the pillow. The Great White Doctor was dead.

With loving care, his servants buried Livingstone's heart under a great tree by the lake ; then they wrapped his body in bark and carefully carried it a thousand miles to the coast. There they gave him to his own countrymen who took him home and buried him in Westminster Abbey. But his heart lies in Africa.

FLORENCE NIGHTINGALE

(1820–1910)

EARLY in the reign of Queen Victoria, two anxious parents were taking tea together in the well-furnished drawing-room of a large country house.

" I beg you, my dear, not to distress yourself so," said Mr. Nightingale, as his wife dabbed her eyes with an embroidered handkerchief.

" But I was never so angry and ashamed in my life," declared Mrs Nightingale. " To think that my own daughter should wish to enter a hospital ! Everyone knows them to be places which are both disgusting and unhealthy, and the nurses no better than drunken old creatures ! I declare that Florence is making me quite ill."

The Nightingale family had been very upset that day by a most shocking request from their daughter Florence. She had actually asked if she might go for three months to Salisbury Hospital to learn nursing. " It was," she said afterwards, " as if I had wanted to be a kitchenmaid. Mama was terrified." Her sister had hysterics and her father was deeply offended.

Mr Nightingale was a rich man who passed a pleasant existence reading and travelling about Europe. Both his daughters, who were now young ladies, had been born in Italy, and when the family was in England they stayed at one or other of their two country houses, with servants, footmen, cooks and maids to look after them. As the girls grew up, they entered London Society and were presented to the young Queen at Court. Naturally, like other fashionable young ladies, they went to dances, theatres and parties, and their Mama expected that each would presently marry some rich and suitable young man.

Unfortunately, Florence had brains as well as beauty. Though the young men admired her greatly, she had taken an obstinate notion to have a career instead of a husband. What was worse, it became clear that she wanted, above everything else, to become a nurse !

No wonder Mama was upset. At this time, as she kept saying, hospitals were evil-smelling, dismal places in which only the poorest and lowest people were " nursed " by ignorant women. It was unheard of for a young lady with a rich Papa even to enter such places.

Yet, though the Nightingales went abroad to Switzerland, Paris and Rome, though they entertained in London and met young men who fell in love with their daughters, Florence continued to dream of nursing as her career. Secretly she got up at dawn to study medical reports; she filled notebooks with facts and figures about diseases and hospitals, and studied medicine by candlelight, sitting wrapped in a shawl when the rest of the household was asleep.

Whenever she could, she slipped away to visit hospitals and the homes of poor people in London and in foreign cities. At last, while abroad with her parents, she managed to spend three months in a German hospital. To her it was a wonderful experience, but her mother and sister were furious.

"They would hardly speak to me," she wrote. "I was treated as if I had come from committing a crime."

Back in London, Florence Nightingale gained what she had been seeking for sixteen long unhappy years. Friends helped her to become Lady-Superintendent of a Hospital for Sick Gentlewomen. Even Mama was defeated and said, through her tears, "We are ducks who have hatched a wild swan."

Less than a year later, bewhiskered Victorian gentlemen opened their morning papers and read with surprise that England was at war with Russia. "Never mind, it will be over in six months," they remarked comfortably to their wives.

The war was fought in the Crimea, a part of Russia bordering on the Black Sea, and the aim of the British and French Armies was to destroy the great naval port of Sebastopol. It was found to be so strongly fortified that 50,000 soldiers battered away at it in vain. Near the town, three furious battles were fought, in which both sides suffered heavily in the hand-to-hand fighting. As the Russian winter closed in, our soldiers found themselves in trenches and camps around the town, and their suffering from illness, wounds and the bitter weather rapidly became desperate.

"January and February are my two best generals," said the Russian Tsar, "for they have killed far more of the enemy than all my armies."

Though no one had suspected it, the British Army had fallen into a state of gigantic muddle. Stores, tents, cooking equipment, hospital supplies and clothing were lost or had never arrived, and the soldiers in their scarlet and black uniforms lacked overcoats, blankets and even boots. Brave enough and well used to the hard conditions of army life, the poor fellows became ragged, shoeless scarecrows, half-starved and dying in hundreds from dirt and disease.

News of this dreadful state of affairs reached England and a furious outcry arose. What was to be done for the soldiers?

There were two people who knew exactly what to do, and they first sat down and wrote to each other. One was the Secretary of State for War, Sidney Herbert, an old friend of Florence Nightingale. He knew that she was the only expert on hospitals in England, so he wrote to ask her if she would go out to take charge of nursing the wounded. On that same day, Miss Nightingale had already written to him stating that she was going to Constantinople.

Within a week she left London with thirty-eight stout, middle-aged nurses, who were to be paid from twelve to twenty shillings a week—so long as they behaved themselves and obeyed Miss Nightingale in everything.

When she arrived, Florence found that the army hospital was at Scutari, on the Turkish side of the Black Sea, across which the wounded were brought by boat in batches of 200. Many died on the crossing, and those who survived had to crawl up a steep hill to the hospital, dragging their comrades who were too ill to move.

As for the hospital, it was a vast barracks, more like a decaying town than a place for sick and wounded men. Four miles of dark, airless corridors were jammed so tightly with wounded that there was scarcely room to pass between where they lay in their bloodstained rags. The walls oozed with damp, the rotting floors were filthy and the air was poisoned by the foul stench that rose from vast sewers under the building. No wonder more than forty men out of every 100 died, not from their wounds but from hospital fever !

As she looked around, Miss Nightingale found that the men had neither blankets nor clean shirts, and that the only persons to tend them were a few overworked army doctors and a handful of soldiers less badly wounded than the rest. There were no bandages, sheets, bowls or drugs ; no spoons, knives, dishes or tables. Hunks of raw meat were flung into iron pots of warm water to provide food for those strong enough to eat it ! The dead and

The wounded arriving at Scutari, watched by Florence Nightingale

the dying lay side by side in hopeless confusion, and no one in the army seemed able to supply any of the simplest equipment for a hospital.

Yet Miss Nightingale was not at all welcome. " Who is this woman ? " complained the doctors and officers. " Female nurses are not wanted by the army." So they took absolutely no notice of her or of her thirty-eight nurses. For days she bit her lips in silent anger and kept her nurses rolling bandages, while she waited to be invited to help.

In that vast, filthy barracks, conditions went from bad to worse. More and more shiploads of wounded, starving men arrived from the Crimea and there were still no stores of any kind. Then someone remembered that Miss Nightingale had not only brought nurses but large sums of money which the people of England had collected for their soldiers. They were forced to turn to her for help.

"I am a kind of General Dealer," she wrote, "in socks, shirts, knives and forks, wooden spoons, tin baths, tables and forms, cabbages and carrots, operating tables, towels and soap." As if by magic, she produced the stores that were so desperately needed, and, once she had done that, she gradually took charge. First, she provided two hundred scrubbing brushes and yards of sacking to wash the walls and floors; piles of filth were wheeled away in barrows, and a proper kitchen was set up to cook invalid food. Until she came, the army had managed to wash exactly seven shirts at Scutari; now she started a laundry. When hundreds more wounded arrived, she hired 200 workmen out of her own money to clean and repair a wing of the building that had been damaged by fire.

Gradually the common sense of an obstinate woman overcame the dirt and stupidity of Scutari. Better food, clean bedding, fresh air and careful nursing worked wonders.

To the men, it seemed indeed as though a miracle had happened. "We felt we were in Heaven," said one. "Before she came, there was

MAP SHOWING THE CRIMEA

cussing and swearing, but after that, it was as holy as a church." The Lady-in-Chief, as she was called, a slight figure in a black dress with white cuffs, collar and apron, and a white cap under a black silk square, moved ceaselessly along the miles of corridors. Sometimes she spent hours on her knees dressing ghastly wounds; always she stayed beside a man who was dying, comforting him to the end.

One of the nurses afterwards described how she went round the wards at night:

"It seemed an endless walk," she said. "As we slowly passed along, very seldom did a moan or cry fall upon our ears. A dim light burned here and there. Miss Nightingale carried her lantern which she would set down before she bent over any of the patients. I much admired her manner with the men—it was so tender and kind."

They were rough fellows, the private soldiers of this time, whose officers looked upon them as drunken brutes, but they adored the Lady-in-Chief. "She was wonderful," said an old soldier. "What a comfort it was to see her pass even. She would speak to one, and nod and smile to as many more. We lay there by hundreds, but we could kiss her shadow as it fell."

And when the long rows of beds had been visited and the wounds dressed, Miss Nightingale would sit for hours through the night, writing tender letters to wives and mothers, long reports to Sidney Herbert, and angry letters about the stupid officers who hindered her work. It was bitterly cold, and she always hated cold, but she wrote on and on.

Next she tackled the needs of the men who were getting better. She started reading-rooms, classes and games, while the officers looked on with horror. She would only "spoil the brutes" they declared. But, for her sake, the rough fellows not only stopped "cussing and swearing," they actually started to save their pay when she arranged to send money home for their wives.

Still not satisfied, she crossed the Black Sea to

Queen Victoria receives Florence Nightingale

visit the camps and hospitals of the Crimea, travelling in a cart over bleak, rocky tracks in the depths of winter. She became ill with fever and almost died. When at last it was known that her life was no longer in danger, many of the soldiers who had stood silently waiting for news wept openly.

At last the war ended and when the hospital at Scutari was empty, Miss Nightingale came home. Her friends scarcely recognised the thin, white-faced figure with her hair cut short under her cap, but her eyes still glinted with determination. Queen Victoria gave her a jewelled brooch bearing the words, " Blessed are the Merciful," and the people of England, who welcomed her like a heroine, collected a great sum of money—the Nightingale Fund—to enable her to train more nurses.

But first, she must go on with her work for the

private soldier. The suffering and courage of the troops had filled her with admiration—and how she admired courage! She said that she had become "mother to 50,000 soldiers" and she fought hard and long against the old-fashioned War Office to get better pay and better hospitals for the men.

She refused to give up her work because her health was ruined and she had become an invalid. From her couch in her London home, she received important visitors and sent out a never-ending stream of letters, reports and advice about barracks, hospitals and training schools for nurses. For fifty years after the Crimean War she worked ceaselessly for the sick and wounded. She had reached the great age of ninety when she died.

At her funeral, in 1910, a newspaper reporter noticed in the porch of the church a little old man in black, wearing the Sebastopol medal. He had once been Private Keller of the 23rd Foot Regiment, wounded in the eye at Sebastopol and taken into Scutari Hospital. He couldn't remember much after all these years, he told the reporter, but he knew that, as he lay there in the great dark ward, a tall lady went softly along the beds, carrying in her hand a lantern—"It was one of them old-fashioned lanterns," said Private Keller.

CAPTAIN SCOTT
(1868-1912)

AS everyone knows, the two coldest parts of the world are the North and South Polar Regions; it is only just possible for men to keep alive in these desolate expanses of ice and snow, which seem unlikely ever to be of much use to the rest of the world. Yet brave men from America, Norway and Britain have suffered unspeakable hardship and danger to explore these frozen deserts. Why have they done so?

Someone once asked a mountaineer why men tried to climb Mount Everest. He answered simply, " Because it is there." He meant that there are always men who want to *know*, just for the joy of knowing; that, through the ages, they have been the restless men who set out upon voyages towards the unknown, not for riches or fame, but because they wanted to find out what lay beyond the horizon. The difficulties and dangers were a challenge to be fought and overcome.

A man who grew up with this inner feeling

that it is better to suffer hardship in search of adventure than to stay tamely at home, was Robert Falcon Scott. As a boy in Devonshire, riding his pony Beppo to school, he set his heart upon entering the Royal Navy, though the doctor said he was too delicate and his father called him " Old Mooney," because he was something of a day-dreamer.

" Con," as his brothers and sisters called him, proved the doctor and his father wrong, for, at thirteen, he was strong enough to become a cadet on the training-ship *Britannia*. As a midshipman and, later, as a sub-lieutenant, he steadily showed that he was to become a brilliant naval officer.

He was thirty-one years old when he heard rumours that an expedition to the Antarctic was being planned. Though at this time he knew little or nothing of Polar exploration, it seemed to him that this was a chance to explore one of the almost completely unknown parts of the world, for the pure adventure of finding out.

He therefore called upon Sir Clements Markham, who was in charge of the preparations for the expedition, and who quickly realised that he had found the born leader whom he needed to take command.

At this time, no one had reached the South Pole. Captain Cook had been the first man to cross the Antarctic Circle, and then, in 1841, an English explorer, Ross, had sailed farther south to a point he called Victoria Land, from which he sighted Mount Erebus and Mount Terror, named after his two ships. Shortly before Scott's first expedition, some Norwegians had made several sledging journeys and had spent a winter in this frozen land. These explorations showed that the South Polar region was surrounded by a vast expanse of sea, dotted with frost-bound islands which were stepping-stones to the mountainous, ice-covered continent in which lay the point known as the South Pole.

In 1901, " Con " Scott, promoted to the rank of Commander, left the Thames in his famous ship *Discovery*, and, after a six-months voyage, reached McMurdo Sound, a stretch of water separating Victoria Land from the islands on which stand Mounts Erebus and Terror. *Discovery* steamed for hundreds of miles along the side of the mysterious Great Ice Barrier, which had baffled Ross. It is a massive wall of ice, 150 feet high, and quite smooth and level at the top. After several days a point was reached where the Ice Barrier became much lower until it was only a few feet above the water.

Here Scott went up 800 feet in a balloon to survey the surrounding country. He could see distant land, which he named King Edward VII Land, rising high above the sea, and looking south, an endless glacier and high mountain ridges stretching away beyond his sight. This was the Antarctic continent which he would have to cross to reach the South Pole.

Winter was coming on, when the cold would become more intense and the sea channels would be entirely frozen for many months. The wooden

Discovery dropped anchor in McMurdo Sound, stores were landed and a hut set up for winter quarters. Here the explorers spent the long winter, making sledging journeys, gathering much information and preparing themselves for the next task.

In November, which is Spring in the southern hemisphere, Scott chose as his two companions, Dr Wilson, surgeon, scientist and explorer, and Ernest Shackleton, of equal Polar fame. Together they set off south with a team of nineteen dogs pulling four loaded sledges.

A splendid start was soon slowed down by soft snow, and the dogs began to weaken far sooner than anyone had expected. The heavy loads and intense cold proved too much for their strength, and, one by one, they died or had to be mercifully killed. Then the three men themselves pulled the sledges; it was bitter, slogging work, for they dragged part of their precious stores ahead and then returned for the remainder. Thus, for a month, they were forced to cover every mile three times over. Slow progress meant that food rations had to be cut, so that the three men were hungry during every march. But they trudged on, and by the end of December, they had reached a point farther south than any man had ever been.

Then Shackleton fell ill from scurvy, and Scott knew they must turn back. Soon the sick man was too weak to walk, so the others dragged him along on the sledge. Frost-bitten and utterly worn out, they reached the ship in February. They had covered 960 miles in ninety-three days, but it had

Scott and Wilson drag Shackleton back to the " Discovery "

been a desperately close thing and they had only just escaped with their lives.

That winter, the *Discovery* could not get free from the ice, and the relief ship, which had been sent out to help her, was unable to approach through the frozen seas, so the expedition was forced to settle in for another winter. It was not until the spring of 1904 that the *Discovery* was able to break out into clear water and sail for home. In those three years, Scott's expedition had learned a great deal about the frozen, mountainous land of the Antarctic. They had discovered new seas and islands, had made the first long journey overland, and had proved that a company of men could remain for long periods in that terrible climate, if they had the right food and fuel. They had also discovered, among many interesting facts of nature and science, eggs and nests of the Emperor Penguin, a great bird, standing four feet high and weighing upwards of a hundred pounds. But they had not reached the South Pole.

After his return, Scott was engaged for several years upon his duties in the Royal Navy, but in 1909, he was able to make plans for a new expedition, on which he would take his friend Dr Wilson, and a number of scientists, botanists, and surveyors, all eager to add to man's knowledge of the world.

His ship this time was the *Terra Nova*, and, besides its company of fifty-nine carefully chosen officers and men, it carried three motor-sledges, nineteen Siberian ponies and thirty-four sledge dogs. When Australia was reached, Scott received the startling news that a Norwegian explorer, Amundsen, was also on his way south, and he, too, was anxious to become the first man to reach the South Pole. Scott refused to be hurried, since he knew the importance of careful preparations.

Anchored again in McMurdo Sound, the expedition made for Hut Point and tried out the motor-sledges on the icy plains. They proved to be far more trouble than they were worth and it was agreed that the hardy little ponies and the dogs would give a better chance of success. News now arrived that Amundsen had landed in the Bay of Whales and was about to try for the Pole by a route some sixty miles shorter, using dogs and skis, on which the Norwegians were expert travellers.

By November 1st, 1911, Scott's plans were complete. Several parties had gone ahead to make

MAP OF THE ANTARCTIC

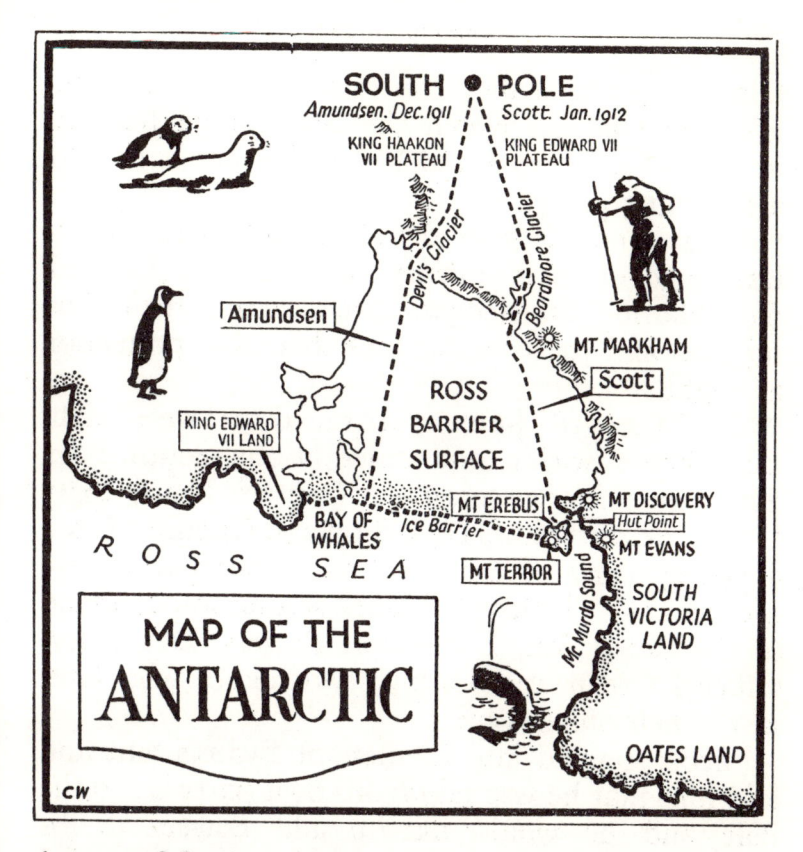

depots of food and oil at points along the route to the Pole. Their task was to lay a trail of stores and then return, allowing the final party to travel lighter and to be less weary for the last march to the Pole, and, on the way back, to travel from one store depot to the next.

Right from the start, Scott's luck was out. The weather was unusually bad, even for these parts, and the ponies, unable to stand up to the bitter conditions, either died or had to be shot. When the explorers came to the fearsome Beardmore

Glacier up which they had to struggle to reach the great plateau on which the South Pole lies, the dogs were exhausted and had to be sent back with a returning party.

Scott and his men therefore had to tackle the last stage of their journey on foot, marching all day, hauling the sledges which carried their food supplies and the precious tent that gave protection at night.

On the 3rd January 1912, there were eight Englishmen within 200 miles of the South Pole. They were in two parties: Captain Scott, Petty Officer Edgar Evans, Dr Wilson and Captain Oates, a young army officer. In the other party were Lieutenant "Teddy" Evans, second-in-command of the expedition, Lieutenant Bowers, and Petty-Officers Crean and Lashly, two heroes who later saved their officer's life.

Scott stepped into Lieutenant Evans's tent and told him that he was taking his own party on to the Pole and he would like to add Bowers to his team. The other three must go back. Lieutenant Evans agreed at once, although he was deeply disappointed at having to return, but he knew that he, Lashly and Crean were already desperately weary from having set off earlier than the others on the task of preparing the route.

Next morning, tents packed, sledges loaded, the eight men shook hands all round; three tremendous cheers were given for the party of five as they stepped out towards the Pole. The other three turned their faces north and started their long, almost disastrous, journey back to the ship. From time to time, they looked back over their shoulders

> " until we saw the last of Captain Scott and his four companions—a tiny speck on the horizon, and little did we think that we would be the last to see them alive."

For the next twelve days, Scott and his party trudged on across the wastes of snow, at a speed of just over one mile an hour. Though the sun shone brilliantly by day, the temperature was always many degrees below zero. But the men were well clad to withstand the conditions, although it was dangerous to remove a mitten for a minute to fasten an obstinate strap or adjust the tiny screws of a measuring instrument.

They liked and admired each other. Besides Scott himself, there was Petty Officer Evans, an experienced Polar man of giant strength, their expert at putting up the tent and packing the sledge so that it ran smoothly; there was little Bowers, the life and soul of the party, always enjoying himself and keeping the records of weather, heights, as well as photographs. " Soldier " Oates, who had earlier looked after the ponies, was a splendid worker; and Dr Wilson, tough as steel, was cook, doctor and general adviser to them all. They made a perfect team.

At the back of every man's mind was the question, " Will the Norwegians get there first ? " And, at the thought, they pressed on a little harder. Scott kept a diary which he wrote up when lying in his sleeping-bag each night. Very near the Pole he wrote :

"Tuesday, January 16. (Camp 68. Height 9760 feet. Temperature minus 23.5 degrees.) About the second hour of the march, Bowers's sharp eyes detected what he thought was a cairn. Half an hour later he detected a black speck ahead. We marched on, found it was a black flag tied to a sledge bearer ; nearby the remains of a camp ; sledge tracks and ski tracks going and coming and the clear trace of dogs' paws—many dogs. This told us the whole story. The Norwegians have forestalled us and are first at the Pole."

It was a terrible disappointment. They found a tent still flying a Norwegian flag and a letter from Amundsen to Scott. They planted the Union Jack and took a photograph of themselves, with Bowers sitting in the front, pulling a string to work the camera. Then they turned back. It was 950 miles to the ship.

The way was painfully slow, and the joy and excitement had gone out of them. The sun hardly appeared, but the snow was soft, with whirling blizzards that often made it impossible to sight the cairns that marked their track home. Then, to everyone's dismay, Petty Officer Evans, their "iron man," began to show signs of failing. His nose and face were frostbitten and his hands badly blistered. He fell heavily into a crevasse, injuring his head. The pace became slower, as they halted to wait for the sick man to drag himself up to them ; he kept

Whirling blizzards made it impossible to see the cairns

saying that he was all right, but, after struggling along for several days, he suddenly collapsed and died.

The four survivors pushed on at the best speed they could manage; they knew that their strength was going and food was running short. The gales exhausted them, so that each march became shorter than the previous day's. Warm food and dry sleeping-bags might have saved them, but the supplies of oil for cooking and heat in each depot were found to be far lower than they should have been. In some mysterious way, oil " creeps " from tins in very low temperatures.

Captain Oates had been suffering for some time from cold feet, even when on the march. He was badly frostbitten and grew more lame with every mile; at night his feet swelled alarmingly and it was slow agony in the morning to put on his boots. Wilson, himself suffering, tended Oates's feet at every stop, encouraging him with, " Slog on, 'Soldier,' just slog on."

Oates was very brave. He did not complain, but he knew he was a burden to the others, slowing them up and risking their lives. He begged them to leave him in his sleeping-bag, but they refused, and helped him on a few miles until it was time to pitch the tent for another night. Scott wrote in his journal :

" Oates's last thoughts were for his mother, but he took pride in thinking that his regiment would be pleased with the bold way in which he met his death. . . . He slept through the night hoping not to wake; but he woke in the morning. It was blowing a blizzard. He said, ' I am just going outside and may be some time.' "

He went out and walked away into the whirling snow, knowing that he was going to his death, wanting to go, in the hope of giving his companions a chance to save themselves. Scott said :

" We knew it was the act of a brave man and an English gentleman."

The three began to realise that their own end

was not far off unless the luck changed. It was colder than ever and the blizzards hardly ceased, but they fought on, covering twenty miles in four days. By now they were very weak, but One Ton Depot was only twenty-one miles away, and if they could reach it, there was food and fuel-oil in plenty to give them back their strength. So they threw away all the gear they could spare, though Wilson insisted on keeping the diaries and records, as well as some stones of scientific interest. All were cheerful, and at night in the tent they talked of what they would do when they were back home in England.

On March 21st, they were only eleven miles from the depot and safety, but a blizzard worse than any before kept them in the tent all day. There was no fuel left and food for only one more day. Next morning, and the morning after, they made ready to start, but it was impossible to step outside into that blinding, whirling drift of snow. Somehow, they lasted for eight days without food. The blizzard never ceased. Quietly, bravely, they died from hunger, cold and utter weariness.

They neither grumbled nor bemoaned their fate, for it seemed better to have come so near success than to have stayed idle and comfortable at home:

"We are in a desperate state, feet frozen, etc.," wrote Scott, " but it would do your heart good to be in our tent, to hear our songs and the cheery conversation. . . . We are very near the end, but have not, and will not, lose our good cheer."

Then he added :

"The real thing that has stopped us is the awful weather and the unexpected cold towards the end of the journey . . . but for my own sake I do not regret this journey, which has shown that Englishmen can endure hardships, help one another and meet death with as great a fortitude as ever in the past—it seems a pity but I do not think I can write any more.

R. Scott."

Eight months later, a rescue party from the ship found Scott, Wilson and Bowers in their tent, lying in their sleeping-bags as they had died. A cairn, with a cross made from two skis, was built above their bodies, and they lie there still, in that vast silent waste.

Before the *Terra Nova* left the Antarctic a great cross was carved out of Australian jarrah wood and set up in full view of the *Discovery's* old anchorage and the Great Ice Barrier. On it are written the names of the five who died—Scott, Wilson, Oates, Bowers and Evans—and underneath are these splendid words :

To Strive, To Seek,
To Find,
And Not To Yield.

LAWRENCE OF ARABIA

(1888-1935)

ABOUT forty years ago, a young Englishman sometimes wandered into the market-place of Damascus. Merchants, travellers, cut-throats and beggars lingered in its ancient streets, arguing in shrill anger with traders whose goods were set out on the pavements. Here, a bare-legged boy drove a couple of goats through the crowd; there strode a hook-nosed tribesman with his long-barrelled gun on his shoulder; veiled women carrying oil-jars chatted under the shelter of an archway, and Turkish merchants, deep in conversation, fingered the little strings of amber beads that they carried for amusement. On every side rose the babble and din of Arabs, Jews, Turks and Syrians, talking and arguing at the top of their voices.

No one paid any attention to the little Englishman with an unusually long face, for he was dressed in a loose, faded robe and wore a headcloth with its rope head-band, like any Arab on a visit to the city. Like any other visitor, he lingered by the fountain to hear the gossip of the day, and dark mutterings against the Turks who ruled the land which belonged to the Arabs.

The Englishman was Thomas Edward Lawrence, member of an expedition which had come to the Middle East to study castles which the Crusaders had built long ago, and to dig for ancient, buried cities. Whenever his work permitted, he liked to go off alone, in Arab dress, to study the people and languages of these dusty lands.

Languages had never been difficult for Lawrence, since the time when, a little boy in Wales, he had surprised his brothers by learning to read at the age of four and starting Latin at six. He became so interested in the Arabs that he learned to speak Arabic almost perfectly, and he came to feel more comfortable in a loose robe and sandals than in the dress of a European. Later, he learnt the difficult art of riding a camel and was able to go for long periods without food or water, like the Arab tribesmen among whom he made many friends.

Then, in 1914, the Great War broke out between Germany on one side, and England and France, with their allies, on the other. Turkey, at this time, ruled over several countries in the Middle East, including Palestine and Arabia, although the tribesmen living in the desert were not easy to govern. Turkey was friendly with Germany, so, when the war began, Britain wanted to break Turkish power in the Middle East by helping the Arabs to revolt against their rulers.

With his great knowledge of Arab customs and languages, it is not surprising that Lawrence was sent to Egypt to help in this plan to defeat Turkey by driving her soldiers out of Palestine and Arabia.

It was by no means an easy task, because Arabia is a vast, little-known land, with huge stretches of waterless, stony desert, crossed by camel tracks known only to the wandering tribesmen.

The men of the desert were robbers and herdsmen, moving about with their tents, camels and goats from one oasis to another, and, from time to time, raiding other tribes or the " soft " people who lived in towns and villages on the plains.

Lawrence said of them : " They would ride immense distances day after day, run through sand and over rocks bare-foot in the heat for hours without pain, and climb their hills like goats. Their clothing was mainly a loose shirt, with sometimes cotton drawers, and a head-shawl, usually of red cloth, which acted as towel or handkerchief or sack." But it was clear to him that, though the Arabs hated the Turks, it would be impossible to turn them into ordinary, well-disciplined soldiers.

Fortunately, the geography of the country gave him a straightforward plan. Most of the people of Arabia live in the small towns and villages of a long, narrow plain. There are the holy cities of Mecca and Medina, from which a single railway ran for hundreds of miles across country to Damascus. This railway, guarded by forts and strong-places, was the only means by which the Turks could move their soldiers, stores and food. Beyond the plain lay the desert, into which the Turks dare not go.

First and foremost, Lawrence must find a leader to unite the quarrelsome warriors, and he found one in Feisal, the handsome son of a great chief, named Hussein. He also made friends with powerful chiefs Abdullah, Auda and Talal. With their friendship, some British help, and a few bags of gold sovereigns, Lawrence began his work of raising a revolt against the Turks. He needed the gold, because the Arabs were too poor to fight for long without plunder. Unless they had some reward, they would constantly drift away to look after their families and flocks.

Riding across the deserts, from oasis to oasis, the little Englishman in silk robes made hundreds of journeys, collecting camels, horses, and fighting-men. He suffered from heat, thirst and fever, as he tried to persuade the tribesmen to join Feisal in a crusade against the Turks.

" Al Urens, destroyer of engines "

As his forces increased, Lawrence realised that he must let the Arabs use their own brand of fighting. Sometimes with a small party on racing camels, sometimes with many tribesmen, he led surprise attacks on the enemy's strong-points, and especially upon their vital railway, blowing up its trains, rails and bridges. After a sudden attack, when they had snatched up as much loot as the camels could carry, he and his men would vanish into the desert, where the enemy could not follow.

The Turks never knew where or when the

next attack would come and they were forced to keep large numbers of soldiers in the area to guard and repair the railway and towns. In this way, the Arabs greatly helped General Allenby and his British army to advance in Palestine.

The Arabs called Lawrence "Urens," which was how they said his foreign name, and the Turks offered a reward of £20,000 for the capture of "Al Urens, destroyer of engines." But no Arab ever betrayed him.

Although they did not realise it, the Turks actually captured Lawrence. He sometimes went into towns disguised as a peasant or a woman, to talk to the Turkish soldiers and find out useful information. One day, in Deraa, the Turks seized him when he was looking at their defences and aerodrome. Because he spoke Arabic perfectly, they failed to recognise their great enemy, and though he was beaten with a whip until he was unconscious, no word of English escaped his lips. Early next morning, in great pain from his injuries, he managed to escape and rejoin his friends.

On another occasion, he and a small party buried some explosive under the railway track and, as usual, led wires from it to the exploder by a bush some distance away. Presently, one of the tribesmen hidden behind rocks 200 yards away crept forward to warn him that a train was coming very slowly. Crouched by the tiny bush, Lawrence saw the long train come level with him, its first ten trucks filled with Turkish soldiers. He slammed down the handle of the exploder, expecting to see the train blown skywards. Nothing happened! Frantically, he banged the handle up and down, until he realised that the exploder was out of order. Meanwhile, the train rolled very slowly by, only fifty yards away, with Lawrence now in full view of the soldiers! He pretended to be a Bedouin shepherd and waved to them with one hand, while his other hand tried to conceal the exploder. He dared not make a dash to his hidden friends but had to sit smiling foolishly at the soldiers until the train had rumbled away. Undoubtedly they thought that he was a half-witted shepherd who enjoyed watching the trains go by.

Though the desert was burning hot by day, it could be bitterly cold at night, especially in the bare hills towards the north of Arabia. Lawrence suffered so much from wounds and from exposure through sleeping out in rocky hollows, that he had to force himself along. He wrote:

"For a year and a half, I had been riding a thousand miles each month on camels. In my last five actions, I had been hit, and my body so dreaded further pain that now I had to force myself under fire. Generally I had been hungry: lately always cold: and frost and dirt had poisoned my hurts into a festering mass of sores."

But, at last, the Arabs reached Damascus, having driven the Turks before them in a series of desperate battles. Lawrence sent the Arab chiefs ahead of him into the city, but a horseman galloped back to tell him that Damascus awaited him. As he entered, the whole city went mad with joy, men capered with glee and the women tore the veils from their faces while flowers and silks were thrown on the ground before him. Above the din rose a steady chant, repeated again and again, like waves rolling around the city of spires and towers. The men were chanting "Feisal, Urens, Feisal, Urens." His work was done. The Arabs had freed their country from Turkish rule.

After the war ended in 1918, Lawrence, who had refused all medals and decorations for his work, wanted to live quietly in England. He wrote a magnificent book called *The Seven Pillars of Wisdom*, which describes his years with the Arabs, but he did not wish to be famous, so he changed his name to " Shaw " and joined the Royal Air Force as a mechanic. One day in 1935, riding his powerful motor-bicycle through country lanes, he swerved to avoid a couple of boys and was killed.

Lawrence was only forty-seven when he died. He was a brilliant man, proud, brave but unhappy, for he felt that many of the promises which he had made to his beloved Arabs had never been kept. He left us a great story and one of the finest books ever written.

SIR ALEXANDER FLEMING
(1881-1955)

HISTORY books contain many stories of ordinary boys who grew up to become famous men. People who knew Captain Cook or Stephenson or Livingstone when they were poor lads earning their first few shillings must have been surprised when they afterwards heard of their great discoveries. It is sometimes difficult to believe that stories of this kind are still happening—that boys and girls from quite ordinary homes, who may not even have been brilliant at school, can still become as famous as any of the great figures in history. There is, for example, the story of the man who discovered penicillin.

Everyone nowadays has heard of penicillin. It is so commonly used in hospitals and sickrooms that it is no longer called the "miracle drug." But, apart from a handful of doctors, no one knew anything at all about it when the Second World War started in 1939. It seemed to arrive like a miracle, in the middle of a war, to save the lives of thousands of soldiers and, afterwards, of sick people all over the world, just when it was needed most. Penicillin was the greatest discovery in medicine for many years ; the papers were full of its marvellous powers and everyone wanted to know about the man who had discovered it. He was a little man with twinkling eyes and a Scots accent, who seemed amused at the fame which had suddenly fallen upon him. His name was Alexander Fleming.

He was a farmer's son, youngest of eight brothers and sisters, who lived at Lochfield Farm, in Ayrshire, in south-west Scotland. Hugh, the eldest, was clearly going to be a farmer like his father; then came Thomas, who was away at college when Alexander was little; then his big sisters, Jean and Mary. Nearer to his own age were Grace, John and Robert with whom he trudged downhill to school.

Lochfield Farm stood on an upland plateau, from which the valleys slope down towards the wide estuary of the River Clyde, but inland, the moors stretch away to the east, open sheep-country, crossed by many a stream or burn. Here a boy might wander all day in the summer and meet only a shepherd with his dogs.

When he was five, Alexander joined John and Robert at school, with their sister Grace to keep them in order. There was a mile or so to walk, across the fields and down the glen to the village school, which had only fifteen pupils—the four Flemings, four children from another family and a few others from moorland farms. Alexander liked school.

"That wee school up on the hill, that's where they really taught you something," he said many years later. "There were fourteen or fifteen of us. We had many teachers there; they never stayed long, but . . . they taught us how to read, write, spell and count, so that when we came down to the big school at Darvel, we weren't disgraced."

His brother, Robert, said that Alexander never seemed to work very hard at school, but he learnt his lessons easily, without seeming to bother about them. What he really cared for was to be outdoors, usually by himself, tramping over the moors, searching for birds' nests and wild flowers, observing with quick eyes the habits and changes of Nature. He would lie for patient hours on the bank of a stream, watching the water for the opportunity to catch speckled trout by tickling or " guddling " them with his fingers, until at the exact moment, the fascinated fish was deftly flicked on to the bank.

Alexander was only seven when his father died, and his mother was left to run the farm and bring up her family. Fortunately, Hugh was soon ready to carry on his father's work and, with her advice, he made such a success of it, that he settled there for life. So, if Hugh was to be the farmer, then Thomas, the second boy, must make his way in the outside world, and he went to Glasgow University to study medicine and, especially, the diseases of the eye.

But for Alexander, it was still school. Now he was old enough to move to the big school at Darvel, four miles walk down the glen, and four miles home in the evening. By this time, he was a sandy-haired, sturdy boy, who felt himself a bit above the mere town boys who missed the fun of a long tramp to school and the delights of rock-climbing and rabbit-trapping on the way home.

Next came the move to Kilmarnock Academy, sixteen miles away and too far for a day-boy to walk. On Mondays, he was off at dawn, striding the six miles to the railway station; during the week, he was boarded out, and on Fridays, he himself said:

"I had to walk from Newmilns Station to Lochfield, except sometimes when I took the old horse-bus to Darvel. It would be regarded as a crime now to allow a schoolboy to walk six miles. . . . Well, it certainly kept me fit anyway."

After a year or two at Kilmarnock, a great decision was taken. Alexander was to go to London. His brother Thomas was doing very well there as an oculist, or eye-doctor, and John and Robert had already joined him. Now he offered to have his youngest brother as well. So Alexander, who might have been a farmer like his father, went south to see what London was like.

It was 1895, and London was a vastly different place from the heather-covered moors beyond Lochfield. It was a world of jostling, gas-lit streets, of hansom-cabs and penny-farthing bicycles, of great houses and miserable slums, with a thousand sights, sounds and smells never dreamed of in Darvel.

But the sturdy boy with the Scots accent took to London as easily as he had taken to lessons; indeed, at Regent Street Polytechnic he found the school work was no harder than what he had been doing two years earlier. Presently, one of his sisters came down to look after the brothers, and then, to their joy, their mother arrived to keep house and the family was together again. Alexander was sixteen and must start work, for money was none too plentiful. So he found a job in a shipping

Fleming playing water-polo

office in the City of London, within sight of St Paul's. The wages were small and the work rather uninteresting, so, for a bit of excitement, he joined the London Scottish Volunteers as a private soldier.

This meant that he spent his spare time at weekends and holidays as a volunteer soldier. He enjoyed drilling and marching and the company of fellow Scots. They soon discovered that the keen-eyed lad from the moors was a fine shot with a rifle, so he was chosen to shoot in competitions for the regiment. He was also an excellent swimmer and, one day, he was picked for the water-polo team in a match against the doctors and students of St Mary's Hospital.

Just afterwards, something important happened. A relative died and left Alexander a small but useful sum of money. His brother Thomas advised him to leave the shipping office and to spend the money on being trained for a doctor. Well, thought Alexander to himself, a doctor's life would be more interesting than being a clerk, but how to go about it ? Which hospital or college did one write to ?

" My brother Thomas," he said, " pushed me into medicine. Then I had to choose a medical school. There are twelve such schools in London. I did not know any of them, but I had played water-polo against St Mary's, so to St Mary's I went."

And at St Mary's, for several years, Alexander followed the usual road of a medical student. He went to lectures, watched operations, visited the hospital wards, tended his first patients waiting in the draughty corridors of the shabby old hospital, and also enjoyed himself. He swam, shot and acted in plays, and at the end of every year, without seeming to trouble himself very much, he was always top student in the examinations. He won scholarships and prizes so regularly that a friend said that Fleming's memory allowed him to remember the whole of a book after reading it once !

As his final examination drew near, it seemed likely that Fleming would become a brilliant surgeon or a wealthy doctor in Harley Street—except for one thing. He had attended many lectures by Sir Almroth Wright, and he so admired him that, on the day after he qualified as a doctor, Fleming joined Wright in what was called his " back-room."

Almroth Wright was a bacteriologist, which means that he had made a special study of *bacteria* or microbes, which are often called germs. Microbes are little " creatures " that attack our bodies and cause illness in various ways ; they are so tiny that they can only be seen with the help of a powerful microscope. Fifty years ago, very little was known about the behaviour of these tiny " creatures," or why they cause illness and death, but Wright had gathered about him a team of young doctors to study microbes (or bacteria). In their "backroom," with microscopes, glass-tubes, bunsenburners, bottles, jars and rubber tubing, they carried out experiments to see if they could discover how various diseases behaved, how blood changed when people were ill, why one kind of microbe killed another. There was a good deal of scoffing at Wright and his " wizards," as they pored over samples of blood on little dishes and tested various antiseptics to see how they worked.

It was important work, but the chances of money or fame were very small. There were failures and disappointments, and results were very, very slow, for any new discovery had to be tested over and over again before Wright would agree that a tiny piece of knowledge had been added to what was known about illness and disease. Yet Fleming was exactly the right man for this work ; he was patient and silent, with wonderfully clever hands and keen eyes, and, most important of all, he had the heart to work on and on, perhaps for years, in this difficult, almost unknown field of medicine.

When the Great War of 1914-1918 came, Fleming became an army doctor and carried on his work in France, where the sufferings of thousands of soldiers made him even more determined to help to conquer pain and disease.

When a soldier is wounded in battle, it usually happens that a piece of his clothing, dirty and muddy, is carried deep into the wound by the bullet or shell-splinter. The wound becomes bad or " septic," and disease spreads through the body. Sometimes an arm or a leg has to be amputated, or the man dies—not of the wound, but from the poison in his body. This happened in thousands of cases in the Great War. Fleming knew that disease of this kind was caused by microbes which increased very rapidly. It might be possible to kill them by washing the wound in an acid, called an antiseptic; this was always done as soon as possible, but the soldiers still died in huge numbers.

In our blood there are red and white cells, which can only be seen under a microscope. The white cells constantly fight the microbes which cause disease; if the white cells are defeated, a person becomes very ill or may die. Unfortunately, the antiseptics which killed the microbes, often killed the white cells too, and this prevented the wounded soldier from getting better.

Thus, after the war, Fleming went on working for years, trying to find an antiseptic that would not only check microbes from growing, but which would not harm the blood-cells, so that the body could carry on its own fight against disease.

He made several discoveries and added a good deal to the knowledge of doctors, but the perfect antiseptic seemed as far off as ever.

Fleming notices a greenish mould

One day, in his shabby little room at St Mary's, he paused to examine the shallow glass dishes on which he had grown some microbes in a special liquid. Usually these little dishes were covered by glass lids, which had to be lifted when the microbes were examined under the microscope. In one dish, he was surprised to notice a greenish mould, rather like the fungus that collects on " mouldy " pieces of old bread, cheese or meat. That meant that a tiny, invisible spore (or seed) must have floated on to the dish when the lid was off, a day or two earlier.

Most people, even scientists, would have thought the plate was spoiled and would have washed it clean, but the good bacteriologist is always curious. Fleming took a closer look and then made a careful examination. He saw that a strange thing had happened. Where the greenish mould was growing, the disease microbes had vanished. Did that mean that this kind of mould killed a certain type of microbe or germ? Could he find out exactly what the mould was? Then could he make a quantity of the mould and test it against other germs?

" Hm, this is very interesting," he said. " I like this sort of thing; it might turn out to be important."

So he began to work slowly, steadily, to find out the secrets of the mysterious mould. There were failures, but presently he grew enough of the mould to make from it a clear liquid, which he called penicillin. Various tests showed that the liquid could kill microbes or stop them growing; it was much stronger than most antiseptics, yet, when injected into mice and rabbits, it did not harm their white blood-cells. He proved that it could also be used for human beings, and that it killed the germs which cause pneumonia, diphtheria, sore throats and boils.

But penicillin was very difficult to make and it quickly lost its power; it also seemed impossible to change the liquid into solid crystals or powder. So, for nearly ten years, no one, apart from a few medical scientists, had heard of penicillin. It stayed at St Mary's Hospital and was used only for small experiments in the laboratory.

Then, by chance, Ernst Chain, a young biochemist, came across a paper in which Fleming had described his work on penicillin. Chain showed this to Professor Florey and together they made a close examination of the substance. After two years, with the help of scientists at Oxford, they managed to make a little penicillin in the form of a brown powder.

Eight mice were given doses of disease microbes and four of them were also injected with penicillin ; the first four died within twenty-four hours, but the others lived. More experiments followed, and it began to look as if Fleming's hopes were not in vain. Soon afterwards he used it upon a human being.

An old friend of his was desperately ill in St Mary's Hospital. Various drugs were tried but he grew worse and seemed certain to die. Fleming wondered if penicillin might save him. He asked Professor Florey for some of the brown powder. As he himself said, " I had no concentrated penicillin ; in fact, there was none in the world then, except the little which Florey had at Oxford."

Florey gave him his whole stock, which was injected into the dying man, " and, instead of killing him, in a week this man was practically well."

That decided them that, at all costs, penicillin must be produced in large quantities. But how ? It was 1942 ; German bombs were falling on Britain and every man and woman was needed to fight or work ; our scientists, chemists and factories were far too busy to start making a new drug. Yet, the British and American Armies were training for the great battles which would take place when they crossed the Channel to fight the armies of Hitler. Thousands of men, women and children would be wounded, hungry and ill. Could not penicillin save them if only there was enough of it?

Several British firms, taught by Fleming and Florey, began to make the drug, but there was not enough. Our friends and allies in America were asked to help, and, at once, they turned over some of their great laboratories to the task of making the " miracle drug." By the time the armies needed it, penicillin was ready. It saved the lives of countless soldiers and, later, there was enough for the diseased and suffering people of Europe.

Fame now burst upon Fleming. All his life as a doctor, he had gone to and from St Mary's, loving his work in the old laboratory and enjoying a game of billiards in the evening and the company of his friends at Chelsea. Suddenly the newspapers were full of his praise; he received prizes and invitations from all over the world; he was knighted at Buckingham Palace by King George VI and honoured in his own Scotland; he travelled to Spain, Holland, Italy, India, Brazil and America, where the President announced that the whole world owed him a debt of gratitude.

And in the centre of this hubbub of praise, Fleming himself remained as modest as ever, not saying much, but chuckling to himself at all the fuss that was being made, and his eyes twinkled like a schoolboy's as the universities of the world showered their honours upon him. He always said that the discovery of penicillin was due to luck.

"In 1928," he said, "I hit on penicillin. The very first stage . . . was due to a stroke of fortune."

But people who knew him understood that it was his years of hard work and keen observation that trained him to see what the green mould in the glass dish might mean. Even Fleming said:

"Before you can notice anything strange happening, you have got to be a good workman, a master of your craft."

Of all the honours that he received, perhaps the dearest to his heart was when, in 1946, the town of Darvel made him its first freeman. As the world-famous man looked at the crowd of his own people who had come to greet him, his mind went back to the days when he trudged downhill to Darvel School and tickled trout on the way home. He wished he could remember all the faces of those in the crowd who knew him then, but still it was fine to be back in his own countryside again.

"The country is just the same," he said. "The same pools are in the burn, the same stones are there; and I have no doubt that the same trout we guddled as boys are under the same stones."

BACKGROUND TO THE STORIES IN PART FOUR

Dates	Stories	Other People
Geo. I, 1714–27	Lady Nithsdale	Robert Walpole
Geo. II, 1727–60	Bonnie Prince Charlie	Robert Bakewell
		1750. Hargreave's Spinning Jenny
	James Wolfe	Pitt the Elder
Geo. III, 1760–1820		Brindley's Canals Wedgwood's Pottery Robert Adam Arkwright
	Captain Cook	Crompton's Mule
	Robert Clive	
		John Wesley
	Watt and Stephenson	Cartwright's Power Loom
		John Howard, "the prisoner's friend"
		Mungo Park in Africa Trevithick
	Lord Nelson	Pitt the Younger William Murdock Wellington Telford John Macadam

Background

1715. "The Fifteen"—James II's son, the "Old Pretender," failed to win back his father's throne.

The "Forty-Five" rebellion ended at Culloden Moor. "Butcher" Cumberland savagely punished the Highlanders. Charles Edward escaped to France and ended his life as a pathetic drunkard.

The Seven Years War (1756–63) against France began badly, but in 1759 occurred the "Year of Victories." In Canada, *Quebec* was captured. In India, Clive won the Battle of *Plassey* (actually 1757), and at sea, Admiral Hawke won the Battle of *Quiberon Bay* and Boscawen defeated the French at *Lagos*. British infantry fought splendidly at *Minden*.

Cook was murdered at Hawaii on his third great voyage, 1779.

Clive spent three periods in India, first making his name at Arcot (1751). After the *Black Hole of Calcutta*, he defeated Surajah Dowlah at *Plassey*. Lastly, as Governor of Bengal, he established British rule. It must be remembered that Clive was a servant of the *East India Company*.

In 1763 Watt started to improve Newcomen's engine. He perfected it in 1781, with Boulton. Steam-power quickly changed the face of England, bringing the factories (and slums).

Stephenson's work followed that of Watt by applying steam-power *successfully* to locomotives running along rails.

Following the French Revolution, *Napoleon Bonaparte* rose to become the greatest general in history, and master of Europe. Nelson's victory at *Trafalgar* in 1805 saved us from invasion and defeat. Wellington's long campaign in Spain weakened Napoleon, who was finally defeated at *Waterloo* (1815).

Dates	Stories	Other People
Geo. IV, 1820–30	Elizabeth Fry	
William IV, 1830–37		Faraday Wm. Wilberforce
Victoria, 1837–1901	David Livingstone	Lord Shaftesbury
	Florence Nightingale	Dr Lister Louis Pasteur
Edward VII, 1901–10		Cecil Rhodes Marconi
George V, 1910–36	Captain Scott T. E. Lawrence	Shackleton Lloyd George Haig Allenby Alcock and Brown J. L. Baird
George VI, 1936–52	Alexander Fleming	Winston Churchill
Elizabeth II, 1952–		

BACKGROUND

At this time Mrs. Fry was carrying out her work at *Newgate Prison*.
1829. *Stephenson's* " Rocket " won the Rainhill Trials.

The first hansom cab and the first bicycle appeared in London.

1840. The Penny Post.
Livingstone's travels inspired *Stanley, Speke, Burton* and others to continue the exploration of Africa, which was divided between a few European powers.
Britain and France supported Turkey against Russia in the Crimean War (1854–56). The chief battles were Alma, Inkerman and Balaclava. Nothing was gained by the war, except Florence Nightingale's opportunity to reform hospitals and nursing.
1857. The Indian Mutiny.
1899–1902. The South African War.

Motor cars appeared on the roads.
Blériot flew across the Channel.
The first films were shown.

The Great War 1914–18 was fought by Britain, France, Russia and, later, the U.S.A. against Germany. Most of the fighting was trench warfare in Northern France and Belgium, but there were other smaller campaigns, including the Middle East campaign.

Broadcasting started in 1922.
BBC Television started in 1936.

1939–45. The Second World War.
1947. India became independent.
1951. The Festival of Britain.
1957. Ghana became independent.
1958. Fuchs crossed Antarctica.

INDEX

(The principal figure in each story is shown in capitals, thus—ALFRED. Other important people in the stories are shown in small type, thus—Shackleton, 474.)

AGRICOLA, 25-31
AIDAN, 67-73
ALBAN, 32-39
Alden, John, 293-296, 300-302
ALFRED, 83-102
Amphibalus, 34-36
Amundsen, 476, 480
Anne Boleyn, 231-232, 245
Anne, Queen, 330, 332-337
Argyll, 304, 308-314
Asser, 100
AUGUSTINE, 58-66

Ball, John, 177, 184
BECKET, 127-136, 219
Bertha, Queen, 63-66
BOADICEA, 19-24
Bohun, Henry de, 164
Boulton, Mathew, 404-407

BRUCE, Robert, 157-166, 220
Buda, 54
Burbage, 275-278

CAEDMON, 78-82
CARACTACUS, 12-18
CAXTON, William, 207-218, 222
CHANCELLOR, Richard, 235-243, 348
Charles I, 303, 312
Charles II, 318, 321, 329
CHAUCER, 185-194, 221
CHURCHILL, John and Sarah, 329-338, 350
Claudius, 14, 17
CLIVE, Robert, 390-399, 507
COLUMBA, 50-57

510

INDEX

Comyn, 157, 159
COOK, James, 376–389, 507
Cumberland, 358, 360, 507
Cuthbert, 72

DRAKE, Francis, 255–268, 348

Edgar, Atheling, 117
Edward I, 151–162
Edward II, 162
Edward III, 167–176, 191, 221
Edward IV, 214–217
Edward VI, 235, 247–250

ELIZABETH I, 244–254, 282–286, 348
Erasmus, 230

FLEMING, Alexander, 493–505
FRY, Elizabeth, 429–445, 509

George I, 339, 342
George II, 356, 358, 364
Gilbert, Sir H., 281, 283
GREGORY, Pope, 58–66
Gurney, John, 429–437
Guthrum, 94–95

Hardy, Captain, 419, 426–428
Harold, 109, 111–115, 219
Hawkins, John, 257–259
HENRY II, 127–136, 219
Henry III, 148
Henry IV, 193

HENRY V, 195–206, 222
Henry VIII, 245–248
HILDA, Abbess, 74–82

Ivan the Terrible, 241

James I, 286–288
James II, 330–332, 355
John, 137–146

LAWRENCE, T. E., 485–492
Leopold of Austria, 138–139, 145
LIVINGSTONE, David, 446–459, 509
LLEWELYN, 147–156, 220
Louis XIV, 333, 334

Malcolm Canmore, 118–126, 219
Manny, Sir Walter, 171
Margaret of Burgundy, 212
MARGARET of Scotland, 117–126, 219
MARLBOROUGH, 329–338, 350
Mary, Queen, 246, 250–254
Montcalm, 367, 375
MONTROSE, 303–316, 349
MORE, Sir Thomas, 227–234, 348
MULLINS, Priscilla, 290–302, 349

Napoleon, 422, 507
NELSON, 418–428, 507

INDEX

NIGHTINGALE, Florence, 460–470, 509
NITHSDALE, Lady, 339–347, 350

Oates, Captain, 479, 482
Oswald, 67–71

PATRICK, 40–49
Paulinus (Roman general), 21–22
Paulinus (monk), 74
Penda, 67, 71
PEPYS, Samuel, 317–328, 350
PHILIPPA, Queen, 167–175

RALEIGH, Sir W., 281–289, 349
Ranulf de Broc, 134
RICHARD I, 137–146, 220
Richard II, 176–184, 221

Saladin, 137, 142

SCOTT, Captain, 471–484
Seymour, Lord, 249
Shackleton, 474
SHAKESPEARE, 269–280, 349
Stanley, H. M., 458
STEPHENSON, George, 408–417, 507, 509
STUART, Charles Edward, 354–362, 507

Tacitus, 31
TYLER, Wat, 176–184, 221

Victoria, Queen, 460, 469
Villeneuve, 423

WATT, James, 400–407, 507
WILLIAM I, 108–116, 219
William III, 331–333
Willoughby, 235–238
WOLFE, James, 363–375
Wyatt, Sir Thomas, 252

10/71